EMPOWER
your students
• • • • •

Tools to Inspire a Meaningful School Experience

Grades 6–12

lauren **porosoff** • jonathan **weinstein**

Solution Tree | Press

a division of
Solution Tree

555 North Morton Street
Bloomington, IN 47404
800.733.6786 (toll free) / 812.336.7700
FAX: 812.336.7790

email: info@SolutionTree.com
SolutionTree.com

Visit **go.SolutionTree.com/instruction** to download the free reproducibles in this book.

Printed in the United States of America

Library of Congress Cataloging-in-Publication Data

Names: Porosoff, Lauren, 1975- author. | Weinstein, Jonathan, author.
Title: Empower your students : tools to inspire a meaningful school
    experience, grades 6-12 / Lauren Porosoff and Jonathan Weinstein.
Description: Bloomington, IN : Solution Tree Press, [2017] | Includes
    bibliographical references and index.
Identifiers: LCCN 2017011523 | ISBN 9781945349249 (perfect bound)
Subjects: LCSH: Motivation in education. | Classroom environment. | High
    school teaching. | Middle school teaching.
Classification: LCC LB1065 .P585 2017 | DDC 370.15/4--dc23 LC record available at https://lccn.loc.gov/2017011523

Solution Tree
Jeffrey C. Jones, CEO
Edmund M. Ackerman, President

Solution Tree Press
President and Publisher: Douglas M. Rife
Editorial Director: Sarah Payne-Mills
Managing Production Editor: Caroline Cascio
Senior Production Editor: Tonya Maddox Cupp
Senior Editor: Amy Rubenstein
Copy Editor: Miranda Addonizio
Proofreader: Kendra Slayton
Text and Cover Designer: Abigail Bowen
Editorial Assistants: Jessi Finn and Kendra Slayton

Acknowledgments

● ● ● ● ●

We want to start by thanking all of the teachers who empowered us by showing us that our learning mattered and that we mattered, especially Hadassah Bar-El, Billy Barrios, Janis Birt, Edward Black, Robert Clancy, Judy Dorros, Joan Freedman, Kent Johnson, Gregg Quilty, Paul Sheehey, Roy Sparrow, and Barbara Silber.

We also want to thank our professional and academic mentors: Melanie Greenup, Laura Johnson, Kate Kellum, Arlene Molovinsky, Cindy Nash, Claire Pettengill, Kelly Wilson, and the faculty at the University of Mississippi's Department of Psychology.

Many thanks are due to our friends and colleagues at the Mississippi Center for Contextual Psychology and in the Association for Contextual Behavioral Science, who gave us the fundamentals of mentorship while teaching us some cool stuff about behavioral analysis, relational frame theory, and acceptance and commitment therapy.

Matthieu Villatte's course on relational frame theory, and his book *Mastering the Clinical Conversation* that he wrote with Jennifer L. Villatte and Steven C. Hayes (2015), shifted our thinking about how teachers can master the classroom conversation to help students act in accordance with their values.

We also want to thank the teachers currently and formerly at the Ethical Culture Fieldston School whose work inspired the examples in this book, especially Tony Marro, Njeri Semaj, Kyle Silver, and Dina Weinberg, who helped us understand what it can look like to empower students in athletics, language, mathematics, and art classes.

We greatly appreciate the teachers and clinicians who participated in our workshops through the Progressive Education Network (PEN) Conference, the Association for Contextual Behavioral Science (ACBS) World Conference, and the New York State Association of Independent Schools (NYSAIS) professional development programming. Their insights helped us refine this work. The teachers at the Ethical Culture Fieldston School have also supported this work by trying out the activities and discussing their implications.

This book is significantly better than it would have been because of our colleagues and friends who read and gave us feedback on our chapters: Yash Bhambhani, Kathleen Brigham, Chad Drake, Liz Fernández, Jason Ford, Judy Hagemann, Meg Hanson, Laurie Hornik, Kate Kellum, Tinia Merriweather,

Amy Murrell, Claire Pettengill, Stuart Quart, Kelly Sigro, Tom Szabo, Noni Thomas López, and Jessica Wolinsky.

Amy Rubenstein is an absolute godsend of an editor. Watching her edit our work was sort of like watching Sherlock Holmes solve a mystery: we never would have noticed the things she noticed, but once she pointed them out it was so obvious that she was exactly right every time. She's generous with her time, thought, and kindness, and this book is so much better because of her. We also want to thank Tonya Cupp for helping our writing make actual sense, answering our bajillion questions, and handing us the metaphorical water bottle as we were on our final sprint. We also want to thank Douglas Rife, Kendra Slayton, Kelly Rockhill, and everyone else at Solution Tree.

Our dear friend Laurie Hornik, in addition to reading even the bad early drafts and giving helpful feedback, is a constant supporter of this work and holds us accountable to our values in the most compassionate ways possible.

We thank our parents, Leslie and Harold Porosoff and Eve and Lou Weinstein, and our two magical children, Allison Porosoff and Jason Weinstein.

And most of all, we thank our students, especially those who found school boring, pointless, exhausting, embarrassing, or painful. They're the ones who inspire us to do this work. The best we can do is to keep becoming the teachers we want to be, so we can empower our students to become the people they want to be.

Solution Tree Press would like to thank the following reviewers:

Kimberly Church
Spanish Teacher
Languages Other Than English
  Instructional Coach
Lebanon Trail High School
Frisco, Texas

Patrick Hill
Principal
Portal Middle High School
Portal, Georgia

Luke Spielman
Assistant Principal
Riverside Middle School
Watertown, Wisconsin

Corey St. John
Director of Teaching and
  Learning
Winterset Community School
  District
Winterset, Iowa

Table of Contents

● ● ● ● ●

Reproducible pages are in italics.

CHAPTER 2
Motivation: Empower Students to Make Their Values the Reason for Doing Schoolwork

CHAPTER 3
Participation: Empower Students to Create Opportunities to Enact Their Values

CHAPTER 4
Openness: Empower Students to Share Their Values 63

CHAPTER 7
Resilience: Empower Students to Treat Themselves According to Their Values . . . 113

Part II: Strategies That Empower Students 127

CHAPTER 8
Empowering Dialogue: How to Activate Student Values Through One-on-One Conversations 129

CHAPTER 13
Empowering Yourself: How to Bring Your Own Values to Your Work

CONCLUSION
Paths to Empowerment

APPENDIX
Examples of Values

About the Authors

• • • • •

Lauren Porosoff teaches middle school English at the Ethical Culture Fieldston School in the Bronx, New York. At Fieldston, she's served as a grade-level team leader and a diversity coordinator, and she's led curriculum mapping and professional development initiatives. An educator since 2000, she has also taught middle school history at the Maret School in Washington, DC; and second-, fifth-, and sixth-grade general studies at the Charles E. Smith Jewish Day School in Rockville, Maryland.

Helping students make their work meaningful has been a constant in Lauren's teaching practice, and that interest led her to learn about methods of values-guided behavior change in acceptance and commitment therapy, relational frame theory, applied behavior analysis, motivational interviewing, and other applications of contextual behavioral science. Informed by these methods of values-guided behavior change, Lauren developed applications for the classroom, such as the processes for curriculum design she describes in her book *Curriculum at Your Core: Meaningful Teaching in the Age of Standards*.

Lauren has written for *AMLE Magazine, Independent School, Phi Delta Kappan*, the PBS NewsHour blog, *Rethinking Schools*, and *Teaching Tolerance* about how students and teachers can clarify and commit to their values at school. She's presented on these topics at regional and national conferences of various professional organizations, including the Association for Contextual Behavioral Science, Learning and the Brain, the National Council of Teachers of English, the New York State Association of Independent Schools, and the Progressive Education Network.

To learn more about Lauren's work, visit EMPOWER Forwards (http://empowerforwards.com).

Lauren received a bachelor's degree in English from Wesleyan University and a law degree from George Washington University.

 **Jonathan Weinstein** is a clinical psychologist with the U.S. Department of Veterans Affairs. He serves as the Suicide Prevention Coordinator at the Veterans Affairs Hudson Valley Health Care System and holds an appointment as assistant professor of psychiatry and behavioral sciences at New York Medical College. Prior to serving in suicide prevention, Jonathan served as the post-traumatic stress disorder and substance use disorders coordinator at the James J. Peters Veterans Affairs Medical Center in the Bronx, New York. Before working for Veterans Affairs, Jonathan served in a variety of mental health and education roles in New York, Baltimore, and Mississippi stretching back to 2000.

Jonathan has long been interested in diverse applications of contextual behavioral science, particularly in underserved settings. As an early contributor to the development of relational frame theory and acceptance and commitment therapy at the University of Mississippi Center for Contextual Psychology, Jonathan studied behavioral analysis and its applications for behavior therapy, social categorization, and education. Jonathan's publications appear in *Behavior and Social Issues*, *The Psychological Record*, and *Salud y Drogas*. He has presented on these and related topics at national and international conferences including those of the Association for Contextual Behavioral Science, the Association for Behavior Analysis International, the Association for Behavioral and Cognitive Therapies, Learning and the Brain, and the Progressive Education Network.

Jonathan received a bachelor's degree in history from Vassar College, a master's degree in public administration from New York University, and a doctoral degree in clinical psychology from the University of Mississippi.

To learn more about Jonathan's work, visit EMPOWER Forwards (http://empowerforwards.com).

To book Lauren Porosoff or Jonathan Weinstein for professional development, contact pd@SolutionTree.com.

Introduction

• • • • •

EMPOWERING STUDENTS TO TRANSFORM WHAT SCHOOL MEANS

When our daughter Allison gets to high school, what will her experience be like? Will it be like her mother's? Will she be mostly invisible in her classes, well-behaved enough that her teachers don't notice that she isn't doing homework or paying attention? Will she read none of the books in her English class but use her preexisting writing skills to get As anyway? Will she be so silent in the rest of her classes that her teachers won't miss her on the days when she skips? What will happen on the days she does come to class? Will she sometimes pretend to take notes but actually write stories and poems in her notebooks? Will she sometimes have no writing ideas and instead draw little caterpillars with the same number of segments as minutes left in the period, filling in a segment for every minute that goes by, using the caterpillar as a measure of hope that eventually she'll be set free?

When our son Jason gets to middle school, what will his experience be like? Will it be like his father's? Will he be too much of a behavior problem to place into the "smart class," even though he's bright? Will he be condemned to sink to the low expectations of teachers who have given up on him? Will he read ahead in his history book but find no one with whom he can share his discoveries? And if he makes his way into regular education, or even an advanced class, will he talk too much in an effort to prove he belongs? Maybe he'll turn out to be good at cello, and music will be the one period in his schedule that lets him interact with the bright students. Or maybe he'll get into so many fights that his principal will invite him to come to school early for extra recess to get his energy out. Maybe at morning recess he'll bond with a deviant peer group who will comprise the heart and soul of his high school's wrestling team. And even if he goes on to succeed in high school and get into a great college, what will become of those friends he left behind?

These are only partial stories of what school was like for us. The other side is that when we were in school, we both read books that made us think and wonder. We learned about issues that held our attention long after the unit was over and did work we felt personally invested in. We both had teachers who made us feel like we mattered. Our school experiences were mostly good. They must have been, because we both chose to continue attending school far beyond when it was mandatory. By the time we were getting advanced degrees, we'd stopped seeing school as something *done to us*—as if it were an assembly line and we were the products—and started seeing school as something *we were actively doing*, as if it were a workshop and we were artisans crafting our own lives, guided by our own values. Do our students have to wait until after graduation to see school that way, or is it possible for us to empower them to actively participate in school right now?

Our students might not feel particularly empowered. They don't design the curriculum. They don't decide which teachers they get; how they're taught and assessed; which peers are in their classes; how much homework they have; how many hours, days, and years school lasts; or what graduation entails. But while students can't determine *what* happens at school, they can choose *how* they want to approach school. What if they could learn to approach school as a set of opportunities to serve their values?

This book shows middle and high school teachers how to help students do just that. All tools are for grades 6–12 and teachers can adapt them based on their students' characteristics. Part I suggests a variety of activities that help students discover and develop their own values, imagine assignments and interactions as opportunities to serve their values, and overcome barriers to enacting their values at school. Part II offers strategies teachers can use to turn each part of their own work into a context for empowering students. The ultimate goal in both parts is for students to transform what school means—from a set of demands placed upon them into opportunities to make their lives meaningful. But first, let's see how students respond when school means complying with someone else's demands, how they might instead decide for themselves what school means, the role values play in transforming what school means, and how transforming school's meaning is empowering.

Reframing School

We give our students a wide variety of tasks to perform. *Have a seat. Read chapter 17 and take notes. Build the highest possible tower out of toothpicks and marshmallows. Calculate the molarity of this solution. Draw this vase. Circle all the direct objects. Fill in the bubble next to the best answer.* How many tasks are students given in a school day? A year? A K–12 career?

Let's look at how students respond to such demands. Imagine that in a seventh-grade history class, students have been given a physical map of North America and are asked to write a two-page analysis of how physical geography impacts a region's economy. Riley cares about thinking deeply, but she also has trouble expressing her thoughts in writing, and she quickly gets stuck. She looks around the room and notices all of her classmates typing away. "I hate essays," she thinks. She starts coloring in the lakes and rivers on her map, wears down the point of her pencil, and gets up to sharpen it. The noise gets the attention of her teacher, who chin-points her back to her seat. Riley says she isn't feeling well and needs to go to the nurse.

Riley is avoiding the task. Putting heads on desks, looking at the clock, texting, whispering, skipping assignments, skipping class, sighing, groaning, complaining, doing the minimum amount of work, staring out the window, doodling—the list of behaviors that students use to avoid doing their schoolwork is depressingly long.

But even when students look engaged, they might be avoiding learning. Sitting next to Riley is Andre. Andre is very bright and cares about expressing his ideas. In fact, he writes lyrically complex songs in his spare time (and sometimes during class), and he's a fairly regular contributor to the school newspaper. But when he gets the history essay assignment, he doesn't feel inspired like when he's working on a song or opinion piece. He decides to write about the Appalachian region because his teacher talked about it a lot. He types up what he remembers her saying, knowing his teachers usually like his writing and that he'll probably get an acceptable grade.

As far as his teacher can see, Andre is deeply involved in his work. That's because he isn't avoiding the *task* (like Riley), but he is avoiding the *challenge*. Perhaps you've seen students choose topics or classes they think are easy; they know they can do a good job and get a good grade, but they're avoiding the effort that might lead to better learning.

Next to Andre is Jake. Jake loves big ideas, often imagines alternative explanations, and shares his creative thinking during class discussions. But this isn't a class discussion. It's a graded assignment, and Jake feels anxious. He goes to his teacher's desk and says he thinks he's going to write about mining and recreation along the Western Cordillera. His teacher asks what his question is, and Jake says, "I just wanted to see if that was OK." A few minutes later, Jake returns with his laptop. His word processing program is suggesting that the word *Cordillera* should be corrected to *Cordially*. The teacher says to leave it. After a few more minutes, Jake is back, asking, "Is it OK if I switch my topic? I want to write about the fishing and oil industries in the Gulf Coast region." The teacher asks if this is because of the Cordillera thing, and Jake insists that he just wants to write about the Gulf Coast. "I made a new outline; do you want to see it?" The teacher says she's sure it's fine and sends Jake back to his desk to write. As class ends and most students turn in their essays, Jake is still working. "Can I finish at home?" he asks. When the teacher says no, he asks, "Is it OK if it's *almost* two pages?" Yes, says the teacher, it's fine. Jake prints and hands in the essay, and on his way out of the classroom he asks the teacher, "When do you think you'll grade these?"

Jake most certainly isn't avoiding the task, and neither is he avoiding the challenge. He might end up with a great essay, and he might learn a little bit about how to improve his writing. He might even bump up his grade, especially if his teacher rewards frequency of class participation or effort. But by asking for so much guidance, he's avoiding the critical and creative process of choosing what and how to write, so he's not growing much as a writer. When students ask for a lot of approval, or when they politely and obediently do as they're told, undoubtedly they're getting *something* out of following instructions. But they might also be avoiding the questioning, doubting, debating, and decision-making behaviors that involve more risk but that lead to deeper learning.

Whether students are avoiding the task itself, the challenges it might present, or the risk-taking and decision-making aspects of doing it, they're all ultimately avoiding learning. When something elicits avoidance, behavior scientists call that something an *aversive* (Chance, 1998). We usually think of aversives as unpleasant situations like a bitter taste, loud noise, or rabid dog. What do people do when they encounter such situations? They spit out the bitter food, cover their ears to blot out the noise, run away from the dog—whatever it takes to escape. Eventually they learn to avoid it in the first place. Again, if students are avoiding school tasks, or at least some aspect of doing them, there must be something aversive about them.

When students act like their schoolwork is aversive, how do we respond? Sometimes we reward students for their avoidance behaviors by giving them the attention and good grades they're after. Sometimes we don't notice when students avoid learning or we accept the behaviors because they don't hurt anyone. We can't possibly call out every student for staring into space. If we ignore avoidance behaviors, the students get to escape engaging with difficult work and the learning that comes along with it. That consequence—escape—feels good for the students, so they continue the behavior (Geiger, Carr, & LeBlanc, 2010).

Sometimes we do respond to acts of avoidance—by altering the consequences. We give low grades, detentions, suspensions, and lectures. But punishing avoidance behaviors can easily backfire (Sidman, 1989). Let's say you have a student who constantly talks to her classmate instead of doing her work. If you ask her to stop talking and threaten to call her mother, you might successfully decrease the talking, but now your class is more aversive for this student. She'll find a new way to avoid engaging in class (or find a way to avoid getting caught talking), and she'll probably keep talking in other classes. Punishing avoidance behaviors might reduce future instances in a specific context, but it also makes school more aversive and ultimately leads to more avoidance. Because there are so many different avoidance behaviors, students have no trouble finding new ones (Friman, Hayes, & Wilson, 1998).

The other way we try to limit avoidance behaviors is to make the learning environment appealing so these behaviors are less likely. We design active lessons, play learning games, give stretch breaks, create fun projects, use cool technology, smile, tell jokes, give inspirational speeches, and use any other tricks we've discovered. Of course we have the responsibility of engaging our students in class, but teachers aren't always equipped to deliver engaging lessons. Some schools pressure us to drill for standardized tests. Some schools offer no funds for professional development, so those of us who lack know-how never learn. Some schools have no budget for the supplies we need to create more dynamic learning environments. And even a brilliant teacher in a well-funded school won't be able to engage all students at all times, as different lesson formats appeal to different students; some skills are less fun to practice; and factors like time of day, social dynamics, and life stressors affect students. We can minimize the effects of these factors, but like any externality, they're almost impossible to control completely.

However we respond to student avoidance behaviors—whether we reward them in students like Jake, ignore them in students like Andre, punish them in students like Riley, or try to make school less aversive in the first place—our responses don't consistently work for everyone and sometimes make matters worse. What all of our unworkable solutions have in common is that they're *ours*. Any time we do something to reduce student avoidance, *we* are doing something. The student him- or herself is not.

Avoidance is a natural response to an aversive. Instead of trying to change students' avoidance behaviors, we could help them think of school as something else. We can empower them to transform what school *means*, from a series of demands they find aversive and do their best to avoid, into a series of opportunities to serve their values. If they can learn to see school as a context for serving their values, they'll approach it differently.

Making Something Meaningful

How is it possible to transform something aversive into something meaningful? Say a student borrows your pen and discovers it's out of ink. She returns it and says, "It doesn't work." You scribble to try to get ink to come out, but it's no use. "This pen is garbage," you say, and throw it out. If your goal is to write, a dry pen has no worth at all. But you might imagine situations where a pen with no ink has *more* worth than a pen with ink. A sculptor might think the dry pen is better because he can scrape clay out from under his fingernails without turning them blue. You can imagine times when it doesn't matter if the pen has ink or not, like if you want to poke holes in the ground for planting seeds or use the cap as a whistle. *We* define the pen's function and therefore give it worth. Decide something has a different function, and we change what it means to us—even though we haven't changed the pen. When we change what something *means*, we relate to it differently. Students can change what school means and relate to it differently, too.

Let's look at a different example. Tina Marie Clayton (2005, as cited in Blackledge, 2003) studied employees who thought of their workplace as chaotic—a feeling teachers likely relate to. Employees who were told the workplace wasn't really all that chaotic didn't develop better attitudes toward it. But employees who learned that chaotic places are conducive to creativity did develop better attitudes toward their workplace. The place itself didn't change, and their assessment of the place didn't change either—but what a chaotic workplace *means* did change.

Now let's look at an example related to school. Say Teddy is doing poorly in mathematics. He tends to give up quickly on his homework because it's so frustrating and exhausting and it makes him feel stupid. Sometimes he does it, especially if his parents are there to nag him. Sometimes he does only the easy problems and then gives up. Sometimes he rushes through the work and suspects most of his answers are wrong. And sometimes, he just doesn't do the work at all.

Asking his mathematics teacher for different homework might help, but she could say no or assign different but equally difficult homework. If he receives an easier assignment, Teddy could get the message that he's too dumb to do the "real" work. But imagine if, instead of changing the homework itself, Teddy learned to connect the homework to goals that matter to him: "This homework will help me learn math, and that will help me when I become a sports agent" or "Persisting in math will help me learn how to keep going when something gets tough, and that will help me during baseball practice." Armed with these understandings, he has a better chance of confronting the struggle rather than avoiding it. Students can learn how to reframe their schoolwork to make it serve their values.

Meaning is not inherent in a thing, whether it's a pen, a work environment, or a school assignment. Meaning comes from our history of relating to the thing. We might have a history of seeing dry pens as garbage, chaotic workplaces as stressful, and mathematics assignments as torture—aversives we'd understandably avoid. But at any moment, we can notice that dry pens, chaotic workplaces, and mathematics assignments might have *other* meanings, and we can choose meanings that reflect our values. Things we'd ordinarily avoid become things we readily approach when we connect them to our values. Since values are central to transforming meaning, the next section explains what values are.

Defining Values

When people and institutions name their values, they often use abstract ideas like *courage, creativity*, and *excellence*. Abstract ideas, by definition, don't exist in the physical world, and it's not particularly empowering to look for something that doesn't physically exist. People also say they value their relationships with certain people, their time spent in certain places, and their achievement of certain things. But people, places, and things often aren't in our control. We can lose them, they can change, or they can become less important to us over time. Of course, it's wonderful to have important people, places, things, and ideas in our lives. But it's not all that empowering to *rely* on these things outside ourselves to make our lives meaningful.

What if we decide to think of our values as how we act? One technical definition of *values* is "freely chosen, verbally constructed consequences of ongoing, dynamic, evolving patterns of activity, which establish predominant reinforcers for that activity that are intrinsic in engagement in the valued behavioral pattern itself" (Wilson, 2009, p. 64). When we refer to values in this book, we'll use a simpler version: values are qualities of action that make life meaningful.

As qualities of action, our values answer questions like, How will I approach my life? or How will I choose to do this? In a student's case, his or her values answer questions like, How will I approach school? How will I choose to do this assignment? How will I choose to relate to my peers? The words that answer these kinds of questions are adverbs: approach school *courageously*, do this assignment *imaginatively*, relate to my peers *responsibly*. The appendix has lots more examples of adverbs students might use to answer questions about how they want to live. We will refer to the appendix frequently throughout the book.

Every time we mention values, we mean the values people choose for themselves. At no point do we advocate telling students what their values should be. Rather, the activities and strategies in this book help students transform school into a context for enacting values *they* choose. We refer to these activities and strategies as *EMPOWER work* to keep the focus on its purpose (exploration, motivation, participation, openness, willingness, empathy, and resilience) and to distinguish it from work designed to promote particular values at school. Parents in particular might need help understanding this difference, because they're the ones who do teach their children what to value. Visit **go.SolutionTree.com/instruction** for a free, downloadable letter to parents that you can use or adapt.

Values are positive qualities of action, so they sometimes get confused with other positives in life: preferences and goals. Let's see how values are different.

Values Versus Preferences

Finding a behavior fun, enjoyable, or comforting doesn't necessarily mean it serves values. Living in accordance with values often brings deep satisfaction and vitality, but the day-to-day effort of committing to values doesn't necessarily feel pleasant, and sometimes it feels like a burden (Hayes, Strosahl, & Wilson, 2012).

Imagine that Teddy values relating to people authentically. He's feeling lost in mathematics class, and he doesn't like the teacher, but he decides to see her during office hours to improve his skills and build a more positive relationship with her. Asking for extra help might feel embarrassing and meeting with this teacher might feel stressful, but Teddy is acting on his values. Conversely, if he enjoys being the center of attention and making people laugh, he might tell jokes in mathematics class. If this behavior alienates some classmates and his teacher, then his pursuit of his own good feelings actually moves him away from his values, since he really wants to relate to people in an authentic way.

Values Versus Goals

Psychologists who write about values often distinguish them from goals (Harris, 2009; Hayes et al., 2012; Wilson, 2009; Wilson & Murrell, 2004). Values describe the function of the behavior, while goals describe the form. Unlike goals, which you can check off a to-do list, values are ongoing. For example, getting a B in mathematics is a goal. Once Teddy gets his B, he's done working toward his goal. He could set a new goal of maintaining his B or even getting a B+, but that's another goal. But working persistently is a value—an ongoing process he can engage in every day, in mathematics and other classes, and when playing baseball and fishing, and after he graduates and becomes a sports agent, and in marriage and parenting, and in any and all aspects of his life that he chooses.

Goals aren't as empowering as values because achieving goals isn't entirely in the student's control. Focusing totally on the goal of getting into a good college means that if the student isn't admitted, can't afford tuition, or can't make passing grades once enrolled, then he or she might feel lost and even worthless. But students who have clarified their values and don't get into the colleges of their dreams can find other meaningful ways to, say, work persistently and relate to people authentically. They can also make their school experiences serve those values *today* instead of only preparing for a specific tomorrow.

Acting Upon Values

If values are *qualities* of action that make our lives meaningful, what exactly are the actions? Without concrete, specific behaviors through which we can make our values manifest—what contextual psychologists call *committed action* (Hayes et al., 2012)—the articulation of values is just talk. Or worse, if students identify qualities of action that make life meaningful but don't find ways to enact their values at school, then school just gets in the way of a meaningful life and becomes even more aversive.

Committed actions are positive behaviors—*dos* as opposed to *don'ts*. For example, a student who values treating people respectfully might decide she wants to stop interrupting in class. But it's hard to stop engaging in a behavior when the behavior serves a purpose. Perhaps the interruptions make her feel less anxious or solicit immediate attention. Stopping her interruptions will take away these benefits without replacing the function they serve. What could this student do in class that would actively show respect? She could look at the person whose turn it is to speak. She could listen for dismissive comments and make a more validating comment. She could express appreciation for a classmate's interesting idea. Maybe she'll stop interrupting others and maybe not, but if she values treating people respectfully, then these positive behaviors would probably give her a sense of vitality and contribute to a more meaningful experience at school.

Commitments to values-consistent actions "are not the same as promises, predictions, or historical descriptions. Although they extend into the future, they occur in the here and now" (Hayes et al., 2012, p. 329). The activities in this book focus on today, this week, a current assignment: *What will I do now?* A present-focused committed action, followed by another and another, can develop into a pattern of actions that makes school more meaningful. Students might find new ways to live by their values in the future, but they don't need to wait until they're older or until someone gives them permission. They can do it right now.

The *I* in *What will I do now?* is important too. Only the students themselves can make and keep these commitments. But teachers can help them imagine possibilities: what to do, when, and how. We can also strive to create a safe environment in which students can discuss their values and what changes they want to make in their lives. If behaving in a particular way is truly important to them, they're vulnerable. They might fall short of achieving their own expectations, and then they have to confront their failure to be who they most want to be. They might believe that they can't, shouldn't, or don't want to change, or they might worry about embarrassing themselves, getting in trouble, or disappointing those who care about them. Sharing values invokes many difficult thoughts and feelings, which is why trust is crucial. How can we build that trust in our classrooms?

Establishing Trust

Having our students' trust begins with making sure they can trust *us*. In class, we make sure they learn essential content and skills, and we give them assignments that are worth the time we expect them to put in. We prepare, focus, listen, and use every minute productively. These might sound like basic teaching principles, but planning meaningful lessons and assignments sends the message that our students' time matters, and by extension, that they matter. When they see that they matter to us, they're more likely to do hard work—including the work of clarifying and committing to their values. When everyone in the room—the students and the teacher—is doing hard work, we build a sense of solidarity: we're in this together.

Like any learning experience, learning about their own values will involve attempts, mistakes, questions, and doubts. You can affirm these moments of risk with statements such as, "I'm not sure you quite got the idea, but I really appreciate that you're trying to understand what I'm saying." Or, "You seem hesitant, and I think it makes a lot of sense to take your time working out an idea like this." If taking a risk becomes a source of affirmation instead of embarrassment, students are more likely to do it. Affirming responses also make you a source of compassion and reassurance, which helps students feel safer as they explore and share their values (Gilbert, 2014).

Beyond treating your students like they matter, you can also help them treat each other like they matter. One way is to give them opportunities to respond to each other's work in an interested, nonjudgmental way. For example, on a writing assignment, you can ask students to summarize what a peer is saying, indicate lines that stand out without saying why they stand out, or ask questions to show curiosity (Elbow & Belanoff, 2000). This type of responding is different from typical peer review, where the point is to critique. Even critique, when offered in the spirit of improving work, can build trust. Again, these are fairly basic practices you can use while teaching regular old academic content, but they help students become the kind of supportive community required for them to talk about their values.

Whatever you do to build community among middle or high school students, you'll get moments when they're disrespectful or outright mean to each other. In these moments, you can simply say, "We're not doing that." Saying *we* holds not only the offending student but the entire classroom accountable for treating each other with respect and kindness. Of course, you can follow up later with a particular student if a longer conversation is warranted. Chances are that student is feeling vulnerable, and his or her behavior is an effort to avoid that feeling.

Yet another way to make space for vulnerability is by being vulnerable yourself. You can notice and name *your* attempts, mistakes, questions, and doubts. For example, you might say, "That made no sense. Now I'm embarrassed." Or, "I feel like this isn't working and I don't know why. What do you all think is going on?" or even, "I have this thing I want us to try but I have no idea if it'll work. How would you all feel about trying something weird?" Just as your students' behaviors will sometimes cause problems, yours will too. You can notice and name those behaviors: "That came out sounding really critical. I'm really sorry."

Finally, you can invite students to be vulnerable with each other. Understand, though, that they don't, won't, and shouldn't trust each other. Distrust is a safer bet in ambiguous circumstances (Wilson, 2009). If we trust someone who's untrustworthy, we face consequences from social humiliation to financial ruin to death, but if we don't trust someone who turns out to be trustworthy, we just miss an opportunity to build a relationship. Middle schools and high schools aren't famous for being havens where no one hurts anyone. If students avoid making themselves vulnerable, that just means they have normal responses to realistic fears; they are not doing something wrong.

The very students who find school highly aversive and would benefit most from connecting it to their values will often be the most avoidant. You might notice an urge in yourself to convince them to participate, to argue with them if they say they don't care, or to use your power to coerce them into the work. These urges come from our passionate desire to make our students' lives better. But if we try to convince, argue with, or coerce students, will that make school more or less aversive? Will that get them closer to discovering their values? Will that help them be vulnerable the next time? We recommend simply inviting students to participate. Whether they take you up on that invitation is, as always, up to them. But even if they *don't* take you up on it—even if they make sarcastic jokes or roll their eyes or refuse to talk—they will also understand that you respect them enough to give them an authentic choice. That builds trust, too.

Despite all these suggestions, there is no rule book you can follow to create trust in your classroom. In fact, if you start focusing on doing the "right" thing to encourage trust, you're no longer focusing on the actual human beings who need you to be your authentic, lumpy, vulnerable self if they have any hope of being theirs. Your best shot is to be as present, attentive, compassionate, and flexible as your beautifully imperfect self can muster.

Moving Toward a Science of Empowerment

Again, values are qualities of action. Contextual behavioral science is a modern version of behavior analysis that proceeds from the assumption that actions—behavior—can only be understood in relation to their context (Villatte et al., 2015). In your classroom, for example, student behaviors are influenced by contextual factors such as the furniture arrangement, the time of day, their moods, your mood, the words you use, current events at school and in the world, their relationships with each other, race and gender dynamics, and their various physical needs. Altering elements of a person's context, whether that means moving the furniture or changing the way he or she thinks about school, can profoundly affect that person's behavior (Hayes & Brownstein, 1986).

Contextual behavioral science's ultimate goal is to help people notice the various elements of their context and then do what's consistent with their values—not what's easiest or most fun, not what makes them look cool or sound smart, and not what relieves them from unpleasant feelings like sadness, anger, fear, shame, and boredom. Accepting unpleasant thoughts and feelings is a normal part of living in accordance with our values. That ability to choose, in any context, a life guided by values is what we mean by empowerment.

Using This Book in an Empowering Way

Part I of this book (chapters 1 through 7) offers activities that help students transform school into a context for values-consistent behavior. These activities help students discover the elements of empowerment: exploration, motivation, participation, openness, willingness, empathy, and resilience. Chapter 1 covers exploration, which begins with curiosity; chapter 2 covers motivation and helping students find reasons for doing their schoolwork; chapter 3 addresses participation and helping students create opportunities to enact their values; chapter 4 is about openness to sharing one's values; willingness to serve one's values when it's difficult to do so is addressed in chapter 5; empathy, which allows us to treat others according to our values, is explained in chapter 6; and chapter 7 covers resilience and helps students treat themselves according to their own values. The activities in part I help students increase the influence of their values and reduce the influence of unhelpful judgments about themselves, others, and school itself. By accepting difficult thoughts and feelings as a normal part of living in accordance with their values, students are empowered to find meaning and purpose at school.

While part I is about what students themselves can do to connect school to their values, part II (chapters 8 through 13) is about what teachers can do to empower students through various aspects of their work. Those aspects include dialogue with students, partnerships with parents, collaboration with colleagues, curriculum development, and self-directed inquiry, as well as practicing the values that are important to you.

In contextual behavioral science, something is good when it *works* in a particular context—not because it fits a predefined image of what's good (Biglan & Hayes, 1996; Fox, 2006; Hayes, Hayes, & Reese, 1988). We encourage you to approach this book's strategies and activities flexibly so they work for your students and school. We hope the freedom to do what works for your classroom empowers you to empower your students.

PART I

Activities That Empower Students

The activities in this part of the book empower students to transform school into a context for values-consistent behavior. The chapters are:

- **Chapter 1**—"Exploration: Empower Students to Become Curious About Their Values"

- **Chapter 2**—"Motivation: Empower Students to Make Their Values the Reason for Doing Schoolwork"

- **Chapter 3**—"Participation: Empower Students to Create Opportunities to Enact Their Values"

- **Chapter 4**—"Openness: Empower Students to Share Their Values"

- **Chapter 5**—"Willingness: Empower Students to Serve Their Values Even When It's Hard"

- **Chapter 6**—"Empathy: Empower Students to Treat Each Other According to Their Values"

- **Chapter 7**—"Resilience: Empower Students to Treat Themselves According to Their Values"

We wrote the activities as scripts to give you a sense of what they might sound like, but we hope you *won't* memorize and follow them. Instead, adapt them so they work for you and your students. Convert handouts into slides, have students use tablets instead of paper and pencil, or use digital sharing tools. Extend parts that seem important and cut parts that don't. Decide which activities to use and in what order. We don't intend these activities to be a curriculum; we mean for you to incorporate them into *your* curriculum.

Each activity includes ideas for how to follow up and create variations. Most are ways to account for students' needs and interests, overcome obstacles, or use the activity in particular situations that commonly arise in schools. Sometimes there are ideas for content-specific variations, but all activities are intended for any middle or high school class in any subject. Again, we hope you'll come up with your own creative variations that work for you and your students.

Each activity also includes a discussion of challenges that might come up. In general, students might seek approval from each other or from you, stay attached to their beliefs about themselves, or avoid unwanted feelings like fear, embarrassment, or hurt. These behaviors are all forms of psychological rigidity that can easily prevent students from clarifying their values and acting on them (Hayes et al., 2012). If these activities are to empower students to transform school into a meaningful and vital place, we don't want students to subvert that process by creating more rigid rules for themselves or finding new reasons to avoid school. Just notice those reactions and move on.

We have not experienced high school students, who are older, being generally less willing to participate in the activities presented in this book. The teacher's psychological flexibility, the relationships among the students and with the teacher, and the teacher's ability to adapt the activity to the students' needs rather than rigidly follow the directions make the difference.

We wish we could indicate how many minutes each activity will take so you could plan accordingly, but the time required depends on whether you choose to do all of the activity or just some parts, how much time you devote to discussion and reflection, your previous experience with this sort of work, and many other elements of the context. Instead of trying to figure out how long an activity will take and then setting aside that much time (or deciding not to do the activity because it takes too long), we recommend deciding first how much time you're willing to allocate to an activity and then adjusting and adapting it so it fits that time. We also hope that empowering your students to enact their values at school will be worth the time you make to do it.

Many of the activities are intentionally playful. Students might fly paper planes, make stickers, sing, draw on paper plates, or roam around the school. Or they might use goofy metaphors: time becomes beans, failures become soggy clothes, hiding their prejudicial thoughts becomes sitting on their hands. If you think your students will find these activities too goofy—and then feel insulted and shut down— you can try acknowledging the weirdness or making up a different version that feels a little less weird. (We include suggestions for how to do this.) But the playfulness serves a purpose. It helps students relate differently to their experiences at school and creates room for discovery and behavior change. You might be surprised by how much your students, even the older ones, enjoy and benefit from play.

As playful as the activities are, they also represent serious encounters with values and vulnerabilities. Teachers who use these as cute activities to fill time can actually do more harm than good. You can establish an atmosphere of safety, trust, and compassion before attempting these activities *and* through doing them. You can serve as what some psychologists call a *secure base* for your students—that is, a "nurturing place to return to when things become overwhelming" (Kolts, 2016, p. 40). Listening, affirming risks, normalizing hesitation, and interrupting moments of disrespectful behavior can help students trust you and the environment you're creating.

Finally, most activities assume the teacher's active participation. You, too, will fly a paper plane, make stickers, sing, draw on a plate, and roam around the school. You'll also do a fair amount of sharing—even when the students are keeping their experiences private. That's hard when you're the authority figure or when you're used to putting students at the center. But the only way they'll know it's okay for them to be vulnerable is if you are. We address your vulnerability at the end of every chapter.

Chapter 1

• • • • •

EXPLORATION

Empower Students to Become Curious About Their Values

If students don't decide how they want to focus their energy, someone or something will decide for them. For example, we as their teachers give them messages about what's most important all the time. Have you spoken to your students as if your class or a particular assignment were the most important thing ever? Or given a suggestion—to practice trumpet more often, proofread their essays more slowly, take fifteen minutes a day to review Spanish conjugations—as if they have absolutely nothing else going on in their lives? Multiply those messages by all the different teachers who give them. Then add messages from family, friends, work, local and world events, music, television, social media, their own bodies, and everything else that vies for their attention. Don't forget to add all the thoughts buzzing around in their developing brains: hopes, fears, plans, memories, worries, and desires. It's a lot.

The activities in this chapter help students explore what matters to them so they can make values-informed decisions about what they do with their time. And since they can't always choose what they do with their time, these activities also prompt them to consider how every part of their lives can become a potential arena for enacting their values. Each activity includes sections with a list of required materials for each student, a sample script so you can envision how the activity might work in your classroom, a follow-up section so you can help your students enact the values work initiated by the activity, variations for additional approaches, and challenges so you get a heads-up about struggles you might encounter.

Flight Plan

Great pt.

Although students aren't always in control of what happens to them or how they spend their time, they're always in control of how they approach situations and relationships. How will they choose to treat the student who has no friends? How will they choose to treat the student with a million friends? How will they choose to approach the mathematics test? How will they choose to approach the mathematics teacher?

This activity helps students distinguish between what is meaningful to them and how they want to make their lives meaningful at school. It works well at the beginning of the year as a way for students to get to know each other (Porosoff, 2016).

Materials for Each Student

For this activity, each student will need a pen, sheet of 8½ × 11–inch paper, and the "Examples of Values" handout (page 214).

Sample Script

→ I do this stuff often w/ my 11th & 12th

The following sample script gives an idea of how this activity might work in your classroom.

> Today we're going to think about what makes our lives meaningful.
>
> On your paper, I'm going to ask you to list some of the people and things that are important to you. I'm going to make a list too. Try thinking about: (*Pauses between prompts to give students time to write.*)
>
> - Family members you have a particularly strong connection to
> - Close friends
> - Teachers or coaches who have made a difference
> - Groups that matter to you, like a dance troupe or sports team
> - Significant activities, such as athletics or arts
> - Places that matter to you, whether they're in your neighborhood or places you've traveled to
> - Areas of knowledge you're curious about
> - Issues you're passionate about
> - Important skills or processes you've learned
> - Objects you cherish, maybe because of who gave them to you or how you got them
> - Things you've made
> - Books that had an impact
> - Memories you want to hold on to
>
> Take a few more moments to write.
>
> Now we're going to do something a little weird. We're going to take the papers we wrote our lists on and fold them into airplanes. Fold them with the words on the inside so they can be private. If you already know how to make a paper airplane, go ahead and make it the way

you know. If you don't know how, you can either get help from a classmate, or let me show you the way I learned. There are so many kinds of paper airplanes! (*See figure 1.1.*)

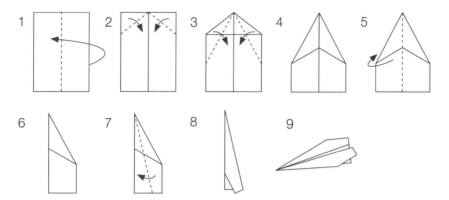

Source: Ushakaron, 2011.

Figure 1.1: Make a paper airplane.

*Visit **go.SolutionTree.com/instruction** for a free reproducible version of this figure.*

Imagine that this plane represents your life. Write your name on the plane's tail, to represent that it's *your* life. On board are the important experiences you've had so far. Take a moment to hold the plane of your life and think about your cargo: the people, places, things, ideas, and experiences that are important to you right now. What's it like to think about all that cargo on board the plane of your life?

Notice that the cargo you have now might not be there your whole life. Some topics will become less important to you in the future. Memories might fade. Things can get lost, stolen, or ruined, or they can feel less important over time. Places can change, or we can lose access to them or outgrow them in some way. And people who matter to us can leave or we can leave them, or our relationships can change.

I want to acknowledge that for some of you, just thinking about the possibility of loss can hurt or feel weird. If I wrote about people and things I really care about, I might not want to think about losing them or even be able to imagine them becoming less important. But if you're feeling upset or weird, that's a sign that what you wrote about genuinely matters to you. (*Pauses if students want to share reactions.*)

Notice, too, that you'll take on new cargo throughout your life. You will learn new things, make new friends, and develop new interests and ideas. What might that be like?

We're going to fly our planes soon. What might happen when we all fly them at the same time? (*Elicits lots of responses and points out how each flight can represent an outcome in life:* We might crash into each other *[have conflict]*, crash-land *[fail despite our best efforts]*, get stuck and need help, fly where we want to go *[achieve exactly what we want]*, or try to fly straight and end up making a stunt loop *[succeed in an unexpected way]*.)

On my count, let's fly these things. One . . . two . . . three!

Now, I'm going to ask you to take someone else's plane back to your seat. Don't unfold it or peek inside.

How does it feel to have another person's plane?

In a few moments, you're going to fly your classmate's plane. What are some of the situations, here at school, where someone else's plane will be in your hands, so to speak? (*Pauses if students want to share reactions.*)

On my count again, we'll fly each other's planes. One . . . two . . . three!

Now find your own plane again. Think about *how* you want to pilot the plane of your life—not *where* you want to fly but *how*. How do you want to approach your classes? Your friends? Your classmates who aren't your friends? How do you want to treat your teachers? How do you want to treat yourself? How do you want to behave toward your families and communities?

For some people, it's hard to think of words that describe how they want to live, so I'm going to give you a handout that you can use. You can also make up your own words. (*Gives out "Examples of Values" handout [page 214] and reviews it with students.*)

On the wings of your plane, write words that describe how you want to pilot your life. How can you enact these qualities right here at school? How would you like to enact your values more fully?

So we might lose some of our cargo, and we might take on new cargo. What we get in life isn't always in our control. We might have a really well-thought-out flight plan, but where our lives go isn't always in our control either. But how we pilot our planes is always in our control.

So let's each decide how we want to pilot our planes and fly them again. Ready? One . . . two . . . three!

Follow-Up

If your students save their airplanes (or if you collect and save them), you can return the planes to your students at a later date and ask if the values they wrote on the outside still feel salient. How have their values changed? How have they lived their values since they made their planes? How can they live their values today? For example, if a student said she values behaving responsibly, how did she behave responsibly since she made the airplane, and how can she behave responsibly today? Students can share responses with partners or the full group. Questions like these can help them see that values, as qualities of action, are always available to them in a variety of contexts—including school. If they didn't live their values in the last few days, weeks, or months, can they start now?

Variations

Symbolic activity - college essay unit? existentialism unit. Transcendentalism

The paper plane works well because of its metaphors. Keeping, losing, and taking on cargo represent how our possessions, relationships, achievements, and interests can be transient. Our flight paths aren't always in our control, but our piloting is. If folding paper won't work for your students, or if they wouldn't be able to handle the mayhem of flying paper planes in class, they can draw planes on paper or with an app, or you can draw a plane to use as a graphic organizer.

You can use this activity to help students think about their cargo and piloting with respect to your specific subject. For example, if you're a science teacher, you might ask your students what has been meaningful in their previous years of studying science in and out of school: "What topics interested you? What seemed important?" Then you could ask how they want to approach science now: "How do you want to approach this class? How do you want to use scientific skills and knowledge? How do you want to treat your fellow student-scientists? How do you want to treat the science lab?"

Challenges

Certainly

Students might find making paper planes a little hokey. (We prefer to think of it as playful.) They might have trouble with the idea of giving up valued possessions, relationships, and activities—particularly if they've worked hard to gain or maintain them—or with the concept that they're not in control of outcomes. Those who have experienced loss, such as in a recent move or a death in the family, might find this activity upsetting—but being upset isn't bad. Feeling sad about a loss indicates that something important is missing, and the point of this exercise is for students to discover what's important to them. Noticing, appreciating, and mourning what was important in the past helps them recognize opportunities for meaningful connection in the present and future.

Those who haven't experienced loss might get upset about the mere idea of loss. The point isn't that students *will* mess up, get stuck, have conflict, or lose people and things they love. The point is that other people, things, and even the outcomes of their plans might not be in their control, but the qualities of their actions always are. You can tell your students that in every moment, even in the face of pain and defeat, they always have the choice to live by their values. The very act of appreciating the good qualities of an experience or mourning a loss is an exercise of that choice.

Hills of Beans

In this activity, students think about how different people in their lives send messages about how they should spend their time and how they can still serve their values in the context of these messages.

Materials for Each Student

For this activity, each student will need a pen, notebook, cup with 168 dried beans, about twenty sticky notes, and the "Where I Put My Time" handout (figure 1.2, pages 20–21).

	Sunday	Monday	Tuesday	Wednesday	Thursday	Friday	Saturday
12:00–1:00 a.m.							
1:00–2:00 a.m.							
2:00–3:00 a.m.							
3:00–4:00 a.m.							
4:00–5:00 a.m.							
5:00–6:00 a.m.							
6:00–7:00 a.m.							
7:00–8:00 a.m.							
8:00–9:00 a.m.							
9:00–10:00 a.m.							
10:00–11:00 a.m.							
11:00 a.m.–12:00 p.m.							

12:00–1:00 p.m.											
1:00–2:00 p.m.											
2:00–3:00 p.m.											
3:00–4:00 p.m.											
4:00–5:00 p.m.											
5:00–6:00 p.m.											
6:00–7:00 p.m.											
7:00–8:00 p.m.											
8:00–9:00 p.m.											
9:00–10:00 p.m.											
10:00–11:00 p.m.											
11:00 p.m. –12:00 a.m.											

Figure 1.2: "Where I Put My Time" handout.

Visit go.SolutionTree.com/instruction for a free reproducible version of this figure.

Sample Script

The following sample script gives an idea of how this activity might work in your classroom.

> It seems like everyone gives us messages about how we should spend our time, whether it's on schoolwork, athletic practice, music practice, a job, family, friends, a romantic interest, or the million other things we do. Today we're going to think about how we can spend our time.
>
> Each of you is getting a small cup of beans and a bunch of sticky notes. (*Distributes the materials.*)
>
> Imagine that the cup represents a week of your life. Just like you have only so many beans in your cup, you have only so much time in a week. The sticky notes are going to represent different ways of spending your time that are important to you, like maybe going to school, being with family, hanging out with friends, taking care of a pet, playing a sport, practicing your violin, exercising, and even basics like sleeping and eating. You're going to write one important way you spend your time at the top of each sticky note. Begin whatever you write with an *-ing* verb: *going* to school, *being* with family, *taking* care of your dog, *dancing* ballet. As you write your notes, spread them out.
>
> Now you'll put beans on each note to represent how much time your parents or guardians would want you to spend doing each of these things if it were totally up to them. Use up all of your beans, because you're always doing *something*, even if it's staring into space. You might need to add more notes if you think of more things your parents or guardians would want you to do. Some notes might end up with no beans. (*See figure 1.3.*)

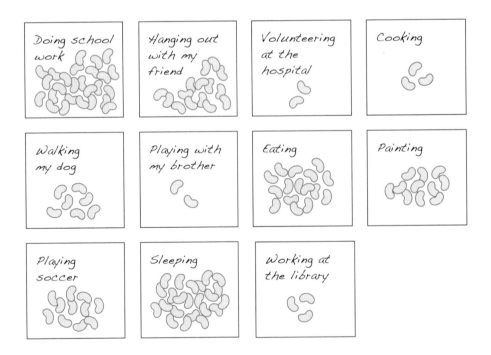

Figure 1.3: Sample hills of beans.

Take a moment to write about this arrangement, labeling it *Family*. It represents how your parents or guardians would want you to spend your time. What do you notice? Where are there a lot of beans? Where are there none?

Now, if you were going to spend your time exactly the way you think your *teachers* would want you to, where would your time go? Please rearrange the beans as much as you need to, and add any notes you need.

Take a moment to write about this new arrangement, which represents how your teachers would want you to distribute your time. You can label this one *Teachers*. Again, what do you notice? What about this configuration is similar to the last one? What's different?

Next, if you were going to spend your time the way you think your *closest friends* would want you to, where would your time go? Again, add any notes you need and rearrange the beans so they represent how you imagine your closest friends would want you to spend your time.

And again, write what you notice. You can label this writing *Friends*. What's similar to the other two? What's different?

Up until now, you've thought about how other people want you to spend your time—or at least, how you think these other people want you to spend your time. Now, think about how *you* want to spend your time. It is, after all, your time!

Please rearrange the beans as much as you need to, and add any necessary notes. You're going to leave the beans in this configuration for now, and—last time—write what you notice.

Does anyone want to share any of their observations? Were there any interesting similarities and differences? How does it feel when you start noticing that different people who care about you are giving you different messages about your time?

Do you ever feel like you have to spend your time a certain way because of what you're trying to achieve? Do you ever feel like you have to spend your time a certain way to make someone else happy? How can you take care of yourself when you're faced with these different messages?

Now I'm going to ask you to count the number of beans on each note. Write the number on the note itself. Once you've counted the beans in each pile, you can put them back in the cup.

Here's the part I didn't tell you yet. I didn't give you a random number of beans; I gave you 168 beans. Why 168? Because that's the number of hours in a week. So now, I'm going to give out a weekly schedule. (*Distributes the "Where I Put My Time" handout [figure 1.2, pages 20–21].*) Write in how you *will* spend your time. For example, if you said you want to devote thirteen hours a week to your family, *which* thirteen hours can you devote to your family? Or, if you'd like to devote forty-six hours a week to playing tennis but can't fit that into your schedule, are there any small changes you *can* make to get a little closer? (*Supports students as they fill out their schedules, such as by pointing out that a particular activity can do double or triple duty. For example, a yoga class might be part of athletic training, self-care, socializing, and connecting to a higher power.*)

Who found this activity difficult? Are any of us alone in wanting to arrange our time a little differently? Do you think your family members arrange their time exactly the way they want to? Your teachers? Your friends? How might some of them spend their time if they could? How can you help them? If that's what you could do to be kind to them, what could you do to be kind to yourself?

Follow-Up

In future weeks, you can ask students to revisit their schedules and discuss, as a class or in writing, the extent to which they're allocating their time according to their values. They might have obligations that limit them, but they might be able to tweak their schedules so they can serve their values more fully (such as, "I'll spend an hour playing with my little brother every Saturday" or, "When wrestling season ends, I'll see my friends after school on Thursdays"). Whether they change their schedules or not, you can continually help your students gain greater awareness of the demands on their time, make informed decisions about how they use time, and take care of themselves in the face of mixed messages and conflicting interests.

Since the schedules will show you what your students do outside school, you can also help them think about school in the same way they think about their interests. Say a student loves baseball and spends hours practicing. If he struggles with writing, you can talk to him about how it feels to practice his batting stance and how it feels when he finally masters it. From there, you can ask whether he'd be willing to spend a little more time practicing writing, which might feel frustrating and tiring while he's doing it but might lead to feelings of satisfaction. Students' areas of interest will be the arenas in which they enact their values.

Variations

Nice to provide these ideas.

In a history or English class, students could imagine how a character or key figure would want them to arrange their beans: "If you were going to spend your time how Gandhi would want you to, where would your time go?" In a geography or language class, students could assess how their cultures inform the ways people spend time: "How is my bean arrangement a product of my culture? If I lived in the place I'm studying, how would I arrange my beans?"

Instead of beans, you could use any small manipulative of uniform size, such as paper clips or beads. If your school food policy allows it, you could use edibles like cereal or raisins and have the students eat them at the end of the activity.

Instead of writing their observations after arranging the beans, the students could share their observations in pairs or as a class, or they could simply observe without recording. They could also walk around and look at each other's final bean layouts and notice similarities and differences among them all.

Challenges

Any time students use phrases like *I should, I have to,* and *I can't* to describe the ways they spend time, you can gently ask, "Whose voice is telling you that? A parent's? A friend's?" Feeling a sense of obligation isn't bad; it can indicate a healthy sense of respect for other people and for their own commitments. But a lot of *shoulds* can also indicate rigidity and missed opportunities to serve values in other areas of life. Dilemmas like these have no right answers, so a good discussion will consist of more questions: How does the time you spend on homework affect you in the long term? What would happen if you spent more time making art? How would your life be different if you spent more time with your sister? What do you miss when you choose to spend three hours a day watching videos?

Also, focusing on different areas of life in which students can enact their values is a little misleading: a human can survive spending absolutely no time studying, but if we don't take care of our physical bodies, we die. It's possible to pursue values in any domain even if basic needs for food, water, and shelter go unmet. Slaves held religious ceremonies, concentration camp inmates made art, and prisoners write poetry. But just because individuals in a state of deprivation can enact their values does not mean someone with access to nutritious food, comfortable sleeping accommodations, leisure time, and medical care should ignore them all in the name of achievement.

Do you know any students who have at some point ignored their physical needs in pursuit of some academic, social, or other goal? For example, are students sleeping enough? If lack of sleep comes up, you could make it part of the discussion: "What are you gaining and losing when you don't sleep? If you don't sleep enough, what parts of your life suffer?" This activity can be an opportunity to start conversations about self-care routines and a way to encourage your students to not ignore their bodies when they set goals and make commitments in other domains.

Typical Tuesdays

Students consider how their day-to-day lives have already changed and will continue to change. They think about the ways they spend their time at different points in their lives, and how they can serve their values even if they don't have control over where they have to go or what they have to do.

Materials for Each Student

For this activity, each student will need a pen, paper, and the "Typical Tuesdays Throughout My Life" handout (figure 1.4, page 26).

These activities get students to be more self-reflective focus on emotional intelligence.

	Kindergarten Me	Me Today	Adult Me	Middle-Aged Me	Elderly Me
Early Morning					
Late Morning					
Early Afternoon					
Late Afternoon					
Evening					
Night					

Figure 1.4: "Typical Tuesdays Throughout My Life" handout.

*Visit **go.SolutionTree.com/instruction** for a free reproducible version of this figure.*

Sample Script

The following sample script gives an idea of how this activity might work in your classroom.

Today we're going to think about how we used to spend our time when we were little, how we spend time now, and how we might spend it in the future. I'm going to ask you to think back to when you were in kindergarten. Let's say it was a regular Tuesday in your life as a kindergartener. Close your eyes if that helps you remember what it was like to be kindergarten you. How did you begin a typical Tuesday? What was your morning routine? When you went to school, what did you actually do there? What kinds of work and play did you do? What did you do after school? What did you eat for dinner? What was your evening like? What was your bedtime routine? (*Pauses between questions so students have time to think and remember.*)

Anyone want to share some memories of a typical Tuesday in kindergarten?

Let's think about a typical Tuesday in your life now. Not a special day—just an ordinary one. How do you ordinarily begin a Tuesday? What's your morning routine like? When you go to school, what kinds of work and play do you do? How do you socialize? What happens after school? Do you do anything to relax or have fun? What do you eat for dinner? What's your evening like on a typical Tuesday? What's your bedtime routine now?

How do your Tuesdays *now* compare to your Tuesdays back in kindergarten? What's better? What's worse? What's just different? What's the same?

Since we've thought about Tuesdays in the past and Tuesdays in the present, we're going to complete the picture by thinking about Tuesdays in the future. (*Distributes the "Typical*

Tuesdays Throughout My Life" handout *[figure 1.4].*) First fill out the *Kindergarten Me* and *Me Today* columns with what you do on a typical Tuesday. Be specific. Instead of just writing *school* for kindergarten and now, list what you actually did or do—like maybe *block corner* and *reading groups* for kindergarten and *physics class* and *drama club* for now.

Then, imagine what your Tuesdays will be like when you become an adult, when you're middle aged, and when you're elderly. I know it might be hard to picture a day in your life that far in the future, but try. Again, be specific. Instead of writing *work*, write what you imagine doing as part of your work day. Instead of writing *home*, what do you imagine doing at home? Instead of writing *dinner*, write what you'd make or where you'd go. (*Circulates and supports students as they make their schedules.*)

How do your Tuesdays now compare to your Tuesdays of the future? What do you look forward to? What are you not so excited about? What do you imagine staying pretty much the same?

If you look at these five eras of your life, what parts of your life become more and less important over time? What stays important throughout your life?

Which of the five Tuesdays seems like you're spending your time in a way that best reflects what matters to you most? What's stopping you from doing what matters to you most right now? What small changes can you make to your schedule for this coming Tuesday to make it better reflect what matters to you?

Let's each share one small change to make for next Tuesday.

Follow-Up

After the following Tuesday, the students can share whether they made any changes to their schedule. If they did, how did it go? If they didn't make any changes, what got in the way? If students bring up the fact that they don't have much control over their schedules and don't get to do preferred activities as often or for as long as they'd like, you can teach them mindfulness skills so they can savor the time they do have. Mindfully eating a piece of chocolate, or noticing their own breathing in and out, can help students experience good times more fully.

Even students who never get to choose what they do with their time always get to choose the qualities of their actions: *how* they do what they do. When they consider what they'll do with their time next Tuesday, *how* do they want to approach each part of the day? Students could make a schedule for the coming Tuesday that includes adverbs attached to each part of the day. (See the appendix, page 214, for examples of these sorts of adverbs.) You could later ask what they did to live those values.

If you teach writing, this activity could lead to an essay assignment in which students compare and contrast typical Tuesdays at different life stages and discuss which Tuesday best reflects what's important to them. Such an essay would give the students practice in making claims, organizing ideas, selecting relevant details—and discussing their values.

Variations

Instead of filling out schedules with lists of activities, the students could write about their Tuesdays in narrative form. They could even role-play in pairs: one student could pretend to be a loved one at home and ask, "How was your day, sweetheart?" and the other student could answer as his or her kindergarten self, current self, adult self, and so on. The student in the role of loved one could ask questions to elicit more information and storytelling. Then the students could switch roles. You'll probably have to model this process with a volunteer before asking the class to form pairs and do it themselves. Also, acting out various versions of themselves—and each other's caregivers and partners—might elicit some silliness and will take more time than filling out a schedule. At the same time, the role plays might help students remember their pasts and imagine their futures more vividly.

Challenges

Students might express frustration because they don't control their time. They might even become indignant about doing the activity: "Why are you making us do this? It's not like we can go back to kindergarten and play. This is just depressing." If students make statements like these, you have an opportunity to validate those feelings. Many people miss their younger days or look forward to bright futures. You can share some of your own fond memories and future hopes.

As you help your students notice what they miss about their pasts or long for in their futures, you can also refocus them on qualities of action they can choose right now. Do they miss building castles in the sandbox because they got to be creative and purposeful? How can they live creatively and purposefully now? Do they miss getting to run around and be outside? What opportunities do they have to live actively now? Are they impatient for a future in which they can choose to spend more time with friends? How can they behave more lovingly or appreciatively toward their friends now?

Your Exploration

When it comes to how we spend our time, we're not much better off than our students. Think back on the last couple of classes you taught. Did you spend every minute exactly the way you wanted? Do you have total control over what you teach or even how you teach it? Do you receive competing, changing messages about what's most important for your students?

We also have lives outside school that demand our attention, and we don't get to leave our ideas and worries at home when we come to work. As we try to teach, we deal with a million distractions: the heater kicking on, a siren outside, a colleague's voice from two doors down, our students' whispers and slightly distasteful remarks—we're not immune to any of it. Nor are we immune to feelings of boredom and frustration in our own classrooms.

The good news is that our inability to focus on what's most important can actually help our students if we're willing to admit to it. If we do these activities alongside the students, they'll be able to see that we, too, have to deal with demands on our time and energy. But we, too, can make values-informed decisions about how we spend our time (to the extent that we have that choice). We, too, can consider how we might enact our values in every part of our lives. These activities are not only opportunities for your students to explore their values; they're opportunities for you to explore yours. Your students will see that exploring values can be a struggle—and one worth having.

From Exploration to Motivation

This chapter's activities were about how students can explore their values. They notice how different situations, times, and people might influence the ways they can express their values—and how they're empowered to choose their values even in contexts where they have less control than they'd like. In the next chapter, students consider how they can bring their values into the context of school and use them as motivation to do their work.

E **M** P O W E R

Chapter 2

• • • • •

MOTIVATION

Empower Students to Make Their Values the Reason for Doing Schoolwork

When students find a task uninteresting (which, let's face it, happens fairly often), we sometimes tell them why it's important. *If* you do your history homework, *then* you'll get a good grade and the knowledge you need for the next unit. *If* you avoid your work, *then* you'll get a bad grade and unhappy parents. *If* you never do your history homework, *then* you'll lack the skills to get into a good college. We frame schoolwork as being a condition for something—an *if* that has a *then*.

But doing schoolwork isn't necessarily a condition for anything good to happen, just as avoiding work doesn't necessarily lead to anything bad. Some students do the minimum and still get excellent grades, charm their teachers (or at least escape notice), and go on to have brilliant careers. Other students complete every assignment to the best of their ability and still see few successes. When we frame an action—such as doing history homework—as a condition for achieving a specific goal, we feel satisfaction only upon achieving the goal, not from doing the action itself (Villatte et al., 2015). If Juan knows his history teacher will give a quiz tomorrow, he might do his reading tonight in order to get the grade he wants. Being satisfied with his grade doesn't mean he finds the act of reading history satisfying, and he might not do his reading again until there's another quiz.

However, if we frame actions not as conditions for achieving a particular outcome but as components of meaningful lives, we can find satisfaction in the actions themselves and feel motivated to keep doing them (Villatte et al., 2015). For Juan, a meaningful life includes connecting with people, understanding their lives, and helping when he can. If he sees how reading about history can increase his understanding of and ability to help others, he might do more of his homework!

Rather than trying to motivate our students by telling them what might happen if they do or don't complete their assignments, we can help each of them clarify what a meaningful life is and ask, "How does doing this assignment contribute to that kind of life?" This chapter's activities help students think about how their assignments and interactions at school contribute to the lives they want for themselves.

Grading Your Classes

After defining criteria for what makes school personally meaningful, students grade each of their courses based on these criteria and write about how they can increase their sense of meaning in class. Try this activity near the end of a marking period, when students are thinking about the grades they're getting.

Materials for Each Student

For this activity, each student will need a pen, notebook paper, and the "What Makes a Class Meaningful?" handout (figure 2.1).

Students sometimes make the following statements about what makes a class meaningful to them. What makes a class meaningful to you?

Instructions: Please choose the three factors that are most important to making a class meaningful to you. If the wording doesn't quite work for you, change the words so they do work, or write your own factors.

To me, a class is meaningful when it provides opportunities for me to:

- ☐ Learn about topics that matter to me personally
- ☐ Learn about topics that matter to my family
- ☐ Learn about topics that matter in the world
- ☐ Learn about myself, my identity, and my place in the world
- ☐ Use my creativity
- ☐ Explore, experiment, and ask questions
- ☐ Build relationships with my peers
- ☐ Build a relationship with my teacher
- ☐ Develop skills that help me in other classes or in life outside school
- ☐ Develop skills that will help me be a responsible adult
- ☐ Develop skills I need to get into a good college or get a good job
- ☐ Develop skills that will help me make a positive change in the world
- ☐ See new perspectives and develop empathy
- ☐ Belong to a community
- ☐ Show leadership
- ☐ Challenge myself
- ☐ _____
- ☐ _____
- ☐ _____

Figure 2.1: "What Makes a Class Meaningful?" handout

*Visit **go.SolutionTree.com/instruction** for a free reproducible version of this figure.*

Sample Script

The following sample script gives an idea of how this activity might work in your classroom.

Let's think about how schoolwork can be meaningful. Just to get started, we'll use a little food metaphor. In a few minutes, you'll see how it relates to making schoolwork meaningful. (*Draws a matrix on the board. Labels the columns* Yummy *and* Yucky, *labels the rows* Healthy *and* Unhealthy, *and asks the students to do the same. See figure 2.2.*)

	Yummy	Yucky
Healthy	Greek salad	Kale smoothie
Unhealthy	Chocolate mousse	Cheese puffs

	Fun	Painful
Meaningful	Swimming with my family	Getting my teeth cleaned
Pointless	Playing games on my phone	Folding laundry

Figure 2.2: Yummy versus healthy and fun versus meaningful.

*Visit **go.SolutionTree.com/instruction** for a free reproducible version of this figure.*

Yummy and healthy mean different things. For me, Greek salad is yummy and healthy, kale smoothies are yucky and healthy, chocolate mousse is yummy and unhealthy, and cheese puffs are yucky and unhealthy. (*Fills in the boxes accordingly.*) See if you can fill in your own charts with foods you like and dislike. Our tastes are going to be different. Anyone want to share what they wrote? (*Pauses.*)

Now that we've distinguished between yummy and healthy, we're going to distinguish between fun and meaningful. (*Makes a new matrix. Labels the columns* Fun *and* Painful *and labels the rows* Meaningful *and* Pointless.) Draw yourself another matrix like mine.

An activity can be fun and meaningful, painful and meaningful, fun and pointless, or painful and pointless. You're going to fill in your four boxes with activities, but first, just notice that something can be painful in all kinds of ways. It might be physically painful, but it could also be emotionally painful, like if it's boring or frustrating or scary or stressful or exhausting or embarrassing. With that in mind, fill in your boxes.

What do you notice this time? Can anyone think of a meaningful pursuit that's always fun or always painful? Is it easier to classify activities or foods? For me, even though I put swimming with my family as an activity I find fun and meaningful, there are days when going in the water is painful!

Now that we see that fun isn't the same as meaningful, let's talk about what makes a class fun. (*Calls on students to share and records their responses, such as learning about an interesting topic, playing games, having a funny teacher, being with friends, bringing food, or getting no homework.)*

If this is what makes a class fun, what makes a class meaningful? (*Calls on students to share and writes their responses on the board.*)

It might be hard to express what it is about a class that makes it meaningful, so here's a list of things students sometimes say. (*Distributes the "What Makes a Class Meaningful?" handout [figure 2.1, page 32].*) See if you can choose three factors that are most important for a class to be meaningful to you. If the wording doesn't quite work for you, feel free to change the wording or write your own factors. (*Pauses for students to write.*)

Now that you've come up with your three factors, see if you can recall a time when you had a classroom experience that was meaningful in one or more of the ways you identified. Maybe it was a particular lesson or project, or maybe a unit, or maybe it was the course as a whole. What happened during that experience? What was it like for you? (*Students talk or write about their meaningful classroom experiences.*)

How did it feel to talk about learning experiences you found meaningful? (*Students might share feelings of fondness; they might also share feelings of loss or frustration that they no longer have experiences like these.*)

Now let's move from the past to the present. Please make a list of all the classes you're currently taking. Beside each one, write what grade you'd give that class based on how meaningful it is, according to the criteria you've chosen. If, for example, you said a class is meaningful when it gives you opportunities to learn about topics that matter in the world, develop empathy, and show leadership, you'd give each one a grade based on how well it gives you those opportunities. (*Pauses for students to write.*)

How was that? What did you notice?

Now pick one or two classes that got disappointing grades. Not necessarily the *lowest* grades, but ones that disappoint *you*. Maybe you like the subject or the teacher, but you don't find the class meaningful in the ways you identified. Or maybe you were more excited about this class at the beginning of the year than you are now. How can you take better advantage of opportunities to make these classes meaningful, or make those opportunities yourself? For example, if you think it's important to develop relationships and you don't feel like Spanish class gives you many opportunities to do that, then how can you create ways to develop relationships with your teacher and peers? Maybe you could meet with the teacher outside of class, or maybe you could study harder so you can have conversations with your classmates and teacher in Spanish.

Even though your teachers come to class with lesson plans and assignments, you can decide how you're going to be in that class. Below the grades you listed, see if you can write two or three specific things *you* can do to make the classes that got disappointing grades more meaningful. (*See figure 2.3.*)

A class is meaningful when it gives me opportunities to:

- Learn about myself, my identity, and my place in the world
- Develop skills that will help me be a positive adult
- Challenge myself

My classes' grades, based on how meaningful they are:

mathematics	B
History	C
English	A−
Science	D
French	B+
Graphic arts	C+
Physical education	B+
Chorus	B

To make my classes more meaningful, I can:

- Save a few pages in my science notebook to write notes about how the topics we learn connect to me
- Read, on my own, about topics we're learning in science so I can go deeper
- Ask my graphic arts teacher how the skills we're learning relate to the real world

Figure 2.3: Example of a class report card.

*Visit **go.SolutionTree.com/instruction** for a free reproducible version of this figure.*

Follow-Up

After a few days or weeks, you can ask your students to talk about how their ideas for making class meaningful are working out, and whether they need help thinking of more ideas.

If students receive narrative feedback, either in their report cards or on individual assignments, another next step could be for students to look in these narratives for suggestions they could follow to make their classes more meaningful. Instead of obediently following the suggestions, rebelliously ignoring them, or feeling overwhelmed by them all, students can decide which suggestions match their values.

If students participate in parent-teacher conferences, they can present a portfolio of work that represents times when they've succeeded and failed to make school meaningful in the ways they identified. The conference can become a brainstorming session: How can the student make school meaningful in the future? How can you, in collaboration with the parents or guardians, support the student's efforts to make school meaningful?

You can repeat this activity as often as grades come out. Students can revisit their factors for what makes a class meaningful and make adjustments, because what is important to them might change. They can give their classes grades every marking period—just as they get grades in each class—and come up with new ideas for making class meaningful.

Variations

We designed this activity for students who get letter grades; if your students get numeric scores or a rubric, they can evaluate their courses accordingly. The students could also grade assignments or units rather than grading the entire course.

Challenges

Some students won't know what motivates them. For them, this activity is a chance to play with ideas—just as they're playing with clothing styles, food choices, musical tastes, career aspirations, and romantic interests. Others might have a sense of what makes learning meaningful, but they won't be able to find words for it on the list or make up their own. You can acknowledge the limits of language—that the vitality that comes with doing meaningful work is *felt*. In this activity, getting the phrasing exactly right isn't the point. The point is to become aware of what makes school meaningful so they notice and seize opportunities to do what matters.

Some students might sense a disconnect between the grades and their experiences. Perhaps the grades don't "feel right" to them. This can happen for several reasons. Some might have chosen factors that don't actually capture what's most important to them. They can rethink their factors.

Others might feel awkward if they like certain teachers but don't find their classes all that meaningful. You can point out that the grades students *get* aren't based on how much their teachers like them but rather on how well the students are doing in areas those teachers deem important. You can also review the difference between liking something and finding it meaningful. They're not grading how much they like the teacher or even the class; they're basing the grades on how meaningful the classes are to them, according to their own definitions of *meaningful*.

Giving a class a good grade might feel distressing to students who don't feel like the teacher values *them*. Teachers certainly aren't immune to bias, and some students might feel invisible or invalidated on the basis of race, gender, gender-nonconforming behavior, physical appearance, first language, mental or physical health conditions, or a variety of other factors. Let's say Kumar values learning about topics that matter in the world, using his creativity, and belonging to a community. In his history class, he does feel he's learning about important events, doing projects that allow him to be creative, and sitting with three girls who have become his intellectual companions and friends. However, his history teacher often mistakes his playfulness for disrespect while ignoring similar behaviors in his white classmates, and never calls attention to his strengths. Therefore, even though the class itself provides many opportunities for Kumar to put his values into action, he feels conflicted about giving it a good grade. We hope this activity will empower students to see their classes as a context for enacting their own values, even in the face of unfair treatment.

Finally, many students get stuck during the last part of the activity, when they're asked to think of ways they can make their classes more meaningful. They're so used to receiving directions and rules that they might struggle when you ask them to think critically and creatively. To inspire students who are having difficulty, you can ask those who *do* come up with ways to make their classes meaningful to share their strategies. You can also invite older students or alumni to talk about ways they made school meaningful, and encourage students to ask trusted adults for ideas. Even if some students aren't ready to try anything new, this activity can begin a conversation.

Focus Stickers

Sometimes students genuinely want to change the way they behave but have trouble carrying out a new behavior because they're so accustomed to an old one. This sort of thing happens in day-to-day life all the time. Perhaps we truly want to go running after work, but we're used to flopping down on the couch, and by the time we remember that we'd set the intention to run, it's too late at night.

People are more likely to make values-consistent changes to their behavior when they direct attention toward them (Fitzpatrick et al., 2016; Verplanken & Holland, 2002). In this activity, students make icons to represent values-consistent actions and use the icons as visual cues to fulfill the actions at times when it's usually hard. It works well in the middle of the school year, once students have established their routines and a sense of who they are in each of their classes.

Materials for Each Student

For this activity, each student will need a pen, paper, three to six dot stickers, and a black permanent marker.

Sample Script

The following sample script gives an idea of how this activity might work in your classroom.

> Think of a time when a learning experience went really well. It could be a class, an assignment, or an out-of-school learning experience—maybe on a team, in a club, in a religious or after-school class, or even at home. Try to think of something recent, but it's okay if you have to think back.
>
> What were you doing, physically and mentally, during that experience? For example, if you took a really great cooking class, maybe you were washing sweet potatoes, shredding kale,

using the blender to make sauce, and frying tofu. And maybe you were also listening really carefully about how to cut the sweet potatoes properly and how to make the barbecue sauce. Maybe you were imagining how your family would react if you made them the garlicky greens for dinner. And maybe you were asking a lot of questions and talking to different people in the class about what you were doing.

Describe in as much detail as possible what you were doing during that learning experience—not what someone else was doing, not what you weren't doing, and not what the experience was like. Mental actions, like thinking and wondering, count as doing something. (*Students write their descriptions; some might wish to share what they wrote.*)

You've now described some of the things you did in a particular learning situation. Some of those actions are probably appropriate to that specific situation but wouldn't be appropriate in learning situations at school. Washing sweet potatoes makes sense in a cooking class, but you obviously wouldn't be able to wash sweet potatoes in math class. But if you also wrote that you were helping other people, listening really carefully, imagining possibilities, asking a lot of questions, talking to different people—these are all things you could do in math, English, gym, or Spanish—really any class. Go back through your description and underline actions you could do in several of your different classes, or while working on different kinds of school assignments.

Now pick one of the actions you underlined. Find something you think is particularly important, not just in the context of the learning experience you wrote about but in other situations, too. Circle that action. Would anyone like to share what you picked?

And now you're going to create a very simple icon to represent the behavior you picked. Make it a simple shape—something you can draw pretty quickly and easily with just a few strokes of a pen. Draw a circle around your icon. (*Students draw their icons. Some might wish to share them by drawing them on the board and labeling them with the behaviors they represent. See figure 2.4.*)

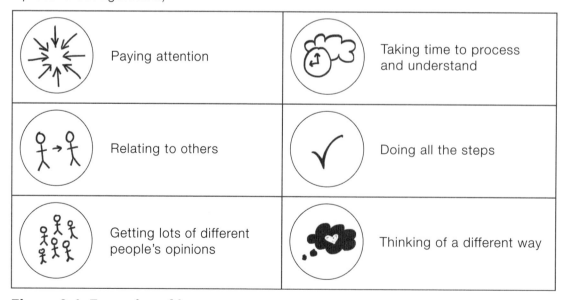

Figure 2.4: Examples of icons.

Now I'm going to give you a black marker and three dot stickers. With the marker, draw your icon on each of your dot stickers. (*Draws icons on stickers and shows them to the class as models.*)

Put these stickers in places where they'll be visual reminders for you to do the behaviors they represent. For example, if your behavior is asking questions, maybe you drew a question mark. If you hardly ever ask questions in English class, but you want to, maybe put the sticker on your English notebook.

You might put your stickers on your materials for a particular class, like your history binder, your science text, your music folder, or your calculator. You might put them on materials you bring to all of your classes, like a laptop. Your locker, phone, or homework area could all be helpful places. The best place is wherever you might look when you need a reminder to engage in the behavior. Who would like to share where you're putting your stickers?

Follow-Up

After a few days or weeks, you can ask if the stickers ever prompted the behaviors they represent. How did it go? How did it feel? Are there other places the students want to put stickers? Are there other behaviors they want to try making icons for (perhaps using a different color dot sticker)? You can keep a supply of dot stickers on hand and occasionally ask students if they want to share stories, make new commitments, or renew old ones.

Variations

You can ask your students to think about how they can incorporate their valued behaviors into processes they learn in your class, such as the writing process, the process of analyzing a primary source document, or the process of doing a lab experiment. Students can share their behavior targets with one another to help hold themselves accountable to their values.

If you don't have dot stickers, you could use sticky notes or have the students draw their icons directly on their materials in permanent marker.

You can suggest that students hide their icons so they find them in the future. For example, a student who wants to listen more actively could draw her ear icon on random notebook pages. On days when she gets to these pages, she'll rediscover the icons and remember to listen more attentively during those class periods.

You can also use this activity to help students think about how they want to behave during less structured parts of their day. Instead of asking them to recall a time when they were engaged in learning, ask them to recall an experience when they were their most compassionate, kindest, or most respectful selves. They can list the things they were doing during this experience and make an icon that represents and prompts the behavior. This version puts group values ahead of individual values while letting students choose how they enact those values.

Challenges

Students who dislike drawing might resist making icons, and some might need help thinking of visual representations. Others might complain that their icons aren't creative enough: "I want to ask questions, but a question mark seems so obvious." Still others might create icons that don't connect to the behavior; a student who draws a line to represent asking questions (because asking a question is like crossing the line from curiosity into knowledge, perhaps) might forget the icon's meaning. Then it won't prompt the behavior. These kinds of struggles could be great opportunities for your students to help each other, and also to notice that the point isn't perfection but workability.

We've found that this activity works best if you have your students immediately put their stickers into place. Otherwise, the students most in need of reminders will be the ones who lose their stickers.

Some students might choose behaviors that are already easy for them, or that aren't that important, or that they can most quickly figure out how to represent with an icon. After some time has passed, ask your students to think about whether their focus stickers are reminding them to behave in ways that genuinely matter to them. If not, they can make new stickers that better reflect their values.

For some students, the stickers won't serve as effective cues. If the sticker isn't working, you can help that student brainstorm other kinds of reminders that might work better.

How I Want to Be in a Group

Students spend a fair amount of their time in groups, whether they're assigned a partner for a project, having lunch with their friends in the cafeteria, playing on a team, or just being members of different classes. Any of these group situations can feel threatening. Students might worry about looking stupid or uncool, getting a bad grade because of someone else's mistake or lack of effort, being excluded, and all sorts of other unwanted outcomes.

When we feel threatened, our behavioral repertoire tends to narrow (Wilson, 2009; Wilson & Murrell, 2004). We fight back, run away, or freeze up—and in the process, we sometimes subvert our values. Think of a student who wants to treat others compassionately but rewrites his partner's half of their essay because he's afraid it will bring their grade down. Or a student who wants to express herself creatively but stays silent during a brainstorm session because she's sure her peers will laugh at her ideas. Or students who want to treat themselves kindly but skip lunch for fear of getting bullied in the cafeteria. This activity's aim is not to get students to behave a certain way, but rather to help them take stock of their options so they can act more flexibly in the face of a perceived threat.

This activity works best when groups are forming: on the first day of a group project or when a class, team, club, or ensemble first comes together. You can repeat it every time a group forms.

Materials for Each Student

For this activity, each student will need a pen, writing paper, "Being in a Group" handout (figure 2.5), and the "Examples of Values" handout (page 214).

Qualities of action that matter to me	
What I want to do in my group (but that might be challenging for me)	1. 2.
What I need my group members to do	1. 2.
What my group members need me to do	1. 2.

Figure 2.5: "Being in a Group" handout.

*Visit **go.SolutionTree.com/instruction** for a free reproducible version of this figure.*

Sample Script

The following sample script gives an idea of how this activity might work in your classroom.

Think about some of the groups you've worked with. It could be a class, a sports team, an ensemble for a performance, a religious group, or maybe something less formal like a team for a class project or even a group of friends. When all goes well, what can be really great about working in a group? (*Students suggest benefits of group work, such as hearing more perspectives on problems, creating solutions together, making new friends, sharing burdensome work, learning from each other, and playing to each person's strengths.*)

We've probably all experienced some of the things that don't go so well in groups. What can be really horrible about working in a group? (*Students suggest drawbacks such as arguing, being unable to compromise, distracting each other, having different standards for the final product, having a boring task, getting left out, getting bossed around, and having some people not contribute enough.*)

What can we do when we're in our groups to maximize the benefits and minimize the drawbacks? Let's try to give *dos* instead of *don'ts* so that we know what to do rather than what not to do. (*Students suggest behaviors such as taking turns speaking and listening to all perspectives before making a decision. If students suggest don'ts, like don't micromanage, ask what the do is: "If you're not micromanaging, what are you doing?"*)

Sometimes people don't like working in groups because of these drawbacks that are outside their control. So today I'm going to ask you to think about what *is* in your control. (*Distributes the "Being in a Group" handout [figure 2.5].*)

When you think about how you want to behave in your group, what words come to mind? How do you want to interact with your group members? How do you want to do the work? How do you want to solve problems? Since we're talking about how we're behaving, we need adverbs. For example, if it's important to me to be real, I might write *genuinely*. If I want to act kindly toward the people in my group, I'll write *kindly* on my chart. What qualities of action are important for you? Write them in your chart. (*Students write their adverbs. For ideas, they can look at the "Examples of Values" handout [page 214].*)

Notice that these qualities of action are available to you all the time. I have the potential to act kindly in class, at the lunch table, at home with my family, and at the supermarket when I'm talking to the checkout clerk. Even when I'm alone I can act kindly toward myself. Acting kindly is an important value for me, and I can look for ways to act kindly wherever I am. Notice that whatever adverbs you wrote down are available as qualities of your actions when you're with your family, when you're with your friends, and even right now. And they'll also be available to you when you're working in your group.

Look over the list of behaviors we made a few minutes ago. Choose two that are an important part of living according to the values you wrote down—but that might be sort of challenging for you to do. Maybe it's something you haven't done and you're curious to try it. Or maybe it's something you *have* done, but not as much or as often as you'd like. Or maybe it's something you tried and didn't do so well, but you're willing to give it another shot. See if you can find two behaviors that seem important but that are hard for you, and write them down in your chart.

Now think about the behaviors you need your group members to exhibit in order for you to work effectively. Maybe these are some of the same behaviors you chose for yourself, or maybe they come easily to you but not to everyone. Maybe they're related to some of the ways groups haven't gone so well for you in the past. Pick two behaviors that seem most important for your group members to do for you, and write them in your chart.

I'm about to put you into your groups. You'll share the behaviors you need your group members to do, and you'll listen to what your group members say they need from you. Then you'll pick two of the behaviors they need from you, and write them at the bottom of your own chart. Put your chart with the rest of your materials for this group project so you can refer back to it.

Follow-Up

The behaviors that students choose for themselves, along with the behaviors their group members choose for them, could become a rubric for students to use throughout the project. Each day, they could rate their own behaviors and then make a plan for the next day. What can they do more, the same, and less?

At the end of the project, students can journal about their experiences: How did it go in your group? What are some things your partner does well, as a student and as a group member? What are some behaviors you want to work on the next time you're in a group?

If you collect the behavior statements, you can redistribute them later in the year and see if students are still working on these behaviors. If you give another group assignment, you can invite students to decide whether to recommit to the behaviors they identified last time, try bigger or smaller versions of these behaviors, or explore entirely new behaviors. You could even use the behavior statements to *make* groups (for example, by pairing a student who wants to listen more thoroughly with a partner who wants to participate more actively).

Variations

You could ask the students to reflect more deeply by having them write stories about specific experiences they've had in groups. What was the situation? How did they feel? How did they respond? How did that way of responding work out for them? You can offer to collect these stories so students who want to share them with you can.

To help your students be authentic and vulnerable, you can tell a story about a time when you were in a group—maybe an academic department, grade-level team, task force, or committee—and didn't act in accordance with your values. If students see that you're willing to be vulnerable by sharing times when you've strayed from your values, they might open up, too. If nothing else, they've learned that values-consistent action is a lifelong but worthwhile struggle.

If your school has a homeroom or an advisory period, your students can use that forum to discuss the benefits and drawbacks of group work, clarify their values, and identify important but challenging behaviors they want from themselves and need from others. This way, a group project in any class requires only that students share their behavioral commitments and needs and then make their rubrics. This approach not only saves time in the academic class but also helps students see how they can choose values-consistent behaviors across contexts.

This activity can also help a whole class consider how their behavior toward each other matches their values. Each student's own statements about what he or she wants to do in the group become that student's personal commitments. From time to time, students can write or talk about their satisfaction with their own behaviors in terms of their commitments. Statements from all students about what they need from the group, compiled into a list, can become a classroom behavior guide. When necessary, students can discuss the entire class's behavior in terms of the list of needs: As a group, are we meeting the needs of our members? Which behaviors are helping our classmates? Do we want any of our behaviors to change? Why? Does anyone want to make a behavior commitment for the sake of your classmates? Questions like these can help hold students accountable for their behaviors, not because they'll get in trouble for breaking rules, but because they're living up to their values.

Challenges

Inevitably, some students will choose values without much thought; they've learned to get through school tasks as quickly as possible—even when the task's purpose is to help them see that they don't have to see school as something to be gotten through. Other students will say whatever they think will make them look cool, repeat what they've heard at home or from their friends, or refuse to expose their true feelings and behaviors. And even those who articulate exactly how they want to behave won't stop their unhelpful power-seeking and self-protective group behaviors. These are all ways of avoiding discomfort.

As frustrating as these behaviors are, this activity's goal is not to limit a student's behavioral repertoire but rather to expand it. If you shut down unhelpful behaviors, *you're* the one in control. Instead, try asking students how satisfied they are with the choices *they* made. "Does this feel important to you? Is this helping you become the person you want to be?"

Your Motivation

When we work hard, we expect a payoff. For many students, the payoff of working hard at school is too small, too far in the future, and too abstract to feel worth the effort expected of them. They might believe in working hard and understand that their efforts will lead to outcomes they want, but moment to moment, their motivation can falter. Grading their classes, making cute stickers, or listing what they want to do in a group won't suddenly change the way students behave, but the activities themselves aren't the point. The point is to help students begin a process of connecting their work to their values—of transforming what their work means—so that their work becomes worth the effort. To maintain that motivation, the students will need opportunities to keep discussing what makes school meaningful. What are they doing to connect their assignments to their values? What happens when they do? What are the benefits and costs? How does it feel? Would they like to try something different? What else is there to try? The follow-up to the work *is* the work.

All of this can be very frustrating, because we usually define our success in terms of student outcomes: observable, measurable improvement in a student's skill level or understanding. If we frame our actions as conditions for achieving a specific outcome—*if* we do these activities, *then* students will discover what makes school meaningful and find more motivation to do their schoolwork—we'll feel satisfaction only if and when we achieve that outcome. However, if we frame our actions as components of meaningful teaching—these activities are *part of* a process that empowers students—we can find satisfaction in the process and feel motivated to keep at it, even when we struggle and fail.

From Motivation to Participation

Schoolwork doesn't have to be all about getting the grade, the test score, the college acceptance letter, the competitive job, the big money, or some other unguaranteed outcome that provides only temporary satisfaction. Schoolwork can also be about building behavior patterns that make life meaningful. The activities in this chapter empower students to find a different kind of motivation to do their work and are an opportunity to enact their values. The next chapter goes a step further: students make their own opportunities to enact their values at school.

EM**P**OWER

• • • • •

Chapter 3

PARTICIPATION

Empower Students to Create Opportunities to Enact Their Values

Have you ever found yourself saying something like, "It's March! Don't you know by now that you should be taking notes?" If you say on Monday, Tuesday, Wednesday, and Thursday to take notes, you might think that by Friday, they'll all take notes. But if you're a teacher, you know that some students will still need this reminder on Friday. Even if you've told the students in the past that they should take notes, even if they've taken notes every day, and even if they've experienced the rewards of note taking, some won't take notes unless you tell them to. That's not because they're unintelligent or irresponsible. It's because they're so used to being told what to do that when they're *not* explicitly told to do something, they don't do it.

It turns out that verbal instructions tend to make learners more likely to follow the instructions and less likely to notice cues in their environments that might suggest a different course of action (Haas & Hayes, 2006; Hayes, Brownstein, Haas, & Greenway, 1986; Hayes, Brownstein, Zettle, Rosenfarb, & Korn, 1986; Hayes, Strosahl, & Wilson, 1999). Telling students to take notes will lead to note taking more quickly than waiting for them to figure out how to take notes in a way that helps them remember and process information. But it will also make them more likely to wait to receive orders to take notes—in other classes, and even on other days in your class—and less likely to notice when note taking is helpful and when it's pointless. Over time, following so many instructions leaves students less able to take charge of their own learning.

If we really want to develop our students' critical and ethical capacities, we can help them question *all* the ways we predefine what success means—even when we're the ones doing the defining. They can learn to formulate questions like, What is this assignment for? What is this class for? What is the room set up for? Who is it for? Who isn't it for? Is it for someone who looks like me? Someone who learns like me? Someone who cares about the things I care about? If not, is there a way I can transform it, or transform the way I approach it?

This chapter's activities create contexts in which students can shift their understanding of school from a place where they do what they're told to a place where they can construct meaningful opportunities for themselves.

Behavior Brainstorm

This activity harnesses the power of the group to help each student think of values-consistent behaviors. It's a good activity to do once students have settled into the groove of the school year—around October or November. It's also a good one to repeat once or twice later in the year, when it seems like students are a little *too* settled into a groove, so they can reaffirm commitments to values-consistent behavior instead of going through the motions.

Materials for Each Student

For this activity, each student will need six sticky notes, a pen or pencil, the "Examples of Values" handout (page 214), and the "Values-Guided Behavior Brainstorm" handout (figure 3.1).

In my school life, I choose to _____.

Because it's important to me to _____ at school, this week I will _____.

Figure 3.1: "Values-Guided Behavior Brainstorm" handout.

*Visit **go.SolutionTree.com/instruction** for a free reproducible version of this figure.*

Sample Script

The following sample script gives an idea of how this activity might work in your classroom.

What could a meaningful life actually look like day to day, here at school? For example, if treating people kindly is what makes school meaningful for you, what might that look like in math class? Or in music class? Or at lunch? Sometimes it's hard to think specifically, so this activity will help us come up with behaviors that will serve our values. (*Distributes the "Values-Guided Behavior Brainstorm" handout [figure 3.1].*)

Where it says, "In my school life, I choose to," you're going to fill in the blank with some way of acting that would make your school life meaningful. How do you want to do your work? How do you want to relate to your friends? How do you want to relate to your classmates and teachers? How do you want to go through your day?

If we can get grammatical for just a moment, you're going to list a verb and an adverb, like *listen attentively*, *think creatively*, or *work productively*. You might have some other stuff in there too. For instance, you might write something like *express myself authentically* or *treat people compassionately even when I don't agree with them*.

Since it might be a little hard to think of adverbs to describe how you want to approach school, you can use the "Examples of Values" handout. But the sheet is here to help you, not to limit you. (*Gives out copies of the "Examples of Values" handout [page 214] and waits for all students to fill out their statements.*)

I wrote that I want to teach attentively. Sometimes, I get so focused on what I want to say that I don't listen well, or I get caught up in some personal issue and I'm not fully present. What could I do this week that would help me teach more attentively? (*Takes and responds to suggestions. Listens for vague suggestions like "Pay attention" and asks for more specifics: "How could I do that? When?"*)

Thank you for those suggestions! Now you're going to do something similar for each other. Each of you will get no more than six sticky notes. (*Passes them around.*) You'll leave the paper with your value on your desk, and then you'll walk around the room and look at each other's papers. If you can think of a suggestion for what someone can do this week that would match up with his or her value, you'll write it on a note, sign your name, and stick it to your classmate's paper.

A couple of things before we get started. We're going to make our suggestions concrete and specific, not abstract and vague. We want to help each other imagine actual physical behaviors, like making eye contact with students who are talking, not vague states of being, like being fully present. If you can picture exactly what a behavior looks like, then you know exactly what to do. You can also see it when it's happening in real life, so you know you've successfully done it. Can someone else think of a concrete, specific behavior? (*Takes suggestions; points out how they're concrete and specific or asks, "What could that look like?" if suggestions are too abstract or vague.*)

Another thing we want to do in this activity is give each other positive suggestions—*dos* instead of *don'ts*. Someone might suggest that to teach attentively, I should not look at my computer screen. That's a *don't*. Can anyone give an example of a *do* for teaching attentively? (*Takes suggestions and offers further explanation if necessary.*)

Finally, we'll try to give each other a wide variety of choices for how to pursue our values. As this activity goes along, you'll have to read what's already on someone's sheet and think of something different from what's been suggested already. Let's see if each of you can give away six suggestions. If everyone does that, then everyone will get six suggestions. Let's try this! (*Students walk around, look at each other's sheets, write suggested behaviors on sticky notes, and leave them on each other's sheets. The activity continues until most students have used up all of their notes, and most sheets are full.*)

Now let's go back to our own desks. As you read the suggestions, rate each one on a scale of one to ten for how important it feels to do this behavior. A ten means that this idea sounds like a critically important part of living by your value. A one means it doesn't matter if you do this or not. Write your ratings underneath the lower-left corner of each sticky note, so the notes cover them.

Next, you're going to give each behavior another rating, this time based on how confident you are in your ability to do it. A ten means you're totally confident you can do it, and a one means you're not at all confident. Write these ratings underneath the lower-right corner of each sticky note.

Now choose a behavior that you're interested in trying this week. Peel off the corresponding sticky note and just hold it in front of you. Notice any thoughts and feelings that come up. Is your mind cheering you on? Or maybe telling you that you can't do it? Are you excited? Or sort of dreading it? Maybe feeling a little nervous or awkward? Whatever thoughts and feelings you're having, jot them down in the space that was underneath the note you're now holding.

Also, look at each note you didn't choose. Notice any thoughts and feelings you have about not choosing them. Maybe you feel relieved for certain ones. Or proud that you chose something more challenging. Or maybe your mind is telling you that you should have chosen something else. Again, whatever thoughts and feelings you're having, write them down underneath the notes. (*Gives students time to write and ask any questions.*)

Anyone want to share thoughts or feelings that came up? Do the thoughts and feelings we shared have anything in common?

At the bottom of your paper, you'll see another statement with blanks. The first blank is for your value; you can copy exactly what you wrote at the top of the other side of your paper. The second blank is for a specific behavior you're committing to doing. The behavior might come directly from a note, or it might be a variation. Mine is, *Because I value teaching attentively, this week I will start conversations with three students who don't usually talk in class*. Write yours. (*Pauses to let students think and write.*)

Let's read our statements out loud. (*Repeats the commitment statement and then invites each student to read his or her own statement.*)

I'm going to collect your papers, and next week we'll share how we did at keeping our commitments. Any negative thoughts and feelings that came up today might come up again, or new ones might come up, and that's normal. Do those thoughts and feelings have to decide what you do? Or can *you* decide? (*See an example brainstorm in figure 3.2.*)

In my school life, I choose to <u>listen attentively</u>.

Make eye contact.

Take notes to help you stay focused in class.

Turn off your phone.

Sit at the front of the room.

Sit next to people you don't know that well so you can listen in class.

Get exercise so you can pay better attention.

Because it's important to me to <u>listen attentively</u> at school, this week I will <u>get more exercise so I can pay attention better in class</u>.

Figure 3.2: Sample values-guided behavior brainstorm.

Follow-Up

After a few days, you can give back the papers and have your students write about their experiences. For those who kept their commitments, what was it like? What happened? How do they feel about themselves as a result of doing something that matches their values? For those who broke their commitments, what got in the way? The point isn't to elicit guilt or shame but rather to get the students to notice barriers.

Students can then make new commitments. Those who kept their commitments might want to think of bigger or higher-stakes versions. For example, a student who successfully helped his friend with homework might try forming a study group, or a student who raised her hand once in mathematics class could try raising her hand in every mathematics class that week. Those who didn't care about their commitments can choose behaviors they do care about. Those who didn't keep their commitments because they seemed too overwhelming, scary, exhausting, or awkward can think of smaller or lower-stakes versions. A student who said she'd raise her hand once but didn't do it could commit to asking her teacher a question after class.

To explain this idea of bigger and smaller versions of behaviors, you could use a metaphor by asking, "If this action is a stone, what's a pebble-sized version of it? What action would be a grain of sand? And what's a boulder-sized version? How about a mountain?" You can use a metaphor that connects to your subject: "If your action fills this test tube, what's a version of it that would fill this dropper? What about this micropipette? And this flask? This beaker?" Metaphors can help people see their situations differently and overcome obstacles to values-consistent behavior (Villatte et al., 2015).

The idea that they can take action on a variety of scales to make school meaningful might inspire some students to work toward bigger goals, but bigger isn't necessarily better. Just as a beaker and a micropipette have different important functions in a lab, big and small actions have different important functions in a meaningful life.

Variations

For students to be able to suggest specific behaviors, they need to be somewhat familiar with each other's daily lives. If your school is large, or if your students don't know each other that well, you might have them put their daily schedules on their desks next to their brainstorm sheets so that their classmates can more vividly imagine the specific contexts in which they enact their values. If a student is struggling to come up with a suggestion for a particular classmate, you can say something like, "Let's see what classes she takes. How can you imagine her behaving generously in Mr. Bassett's American history class, or during Coach Wu's soccer practice?"

Instead of writing their suggestions, students could draw them as cartoon panels. Where words can be vague, a drawing captures a specific image. For example, if a student said he values treating people kindly, his sticky notes might say things like, "Respect the teacher" or, "Be nice to other kids." What exactly does it look and sound like to show respect or be nice? Drawing also helps students suggest *dos* instead of *don'ts*. It's fast and easy to write *Don't make mean comments,* but drawing a kid making a mean comment and putting a slash over the drawing takes enough time that you're more likely to notice it and remind the student to think of a positive behavior instead.

Challenges

Since students will see each other's values and suggested behaviors, they might write responses they think will impress or amuse each other, or they might hold back from writing what they really think for fear of judgment. The best you can do is to invite students to be creative, kind, and honest. You can also emphasize how there are many ways people can live their values, and you're not hoping for or expecting any particular response.

If a student isn't taking this activity seriously, you can pull him or her aside to try to figure out why. What's getting in the way of thinking about how school can be meaningful? What's more important right now than helping classmates find values-consistent behaviors to do at school? If it seems like the student is just trying to get attention, then you're probably best off saying something like, "This isn't what we're doing right now" and asking the student to articulate the activity's directions and purpose.

A Walking Tour

This activity helps students notice that even though the different physical places in which they spend time are constructed around particular definitions of success, they still have the ability to choose their own definitions of success to live by. This activity is a good one to do between units or when you have a day before a school vacation when you don't want to start something new but do want to do something meaningful.

Materials for Each Student

For this activity, each student will need a pen, paper, clipboard, and the "Exploring Spaces" handout (figure 3.3).

	Space where I feel successful	Space where I feel unsuccessful	Space where I feel neutral
List specific features of this space that catch your attention.			
List questions you have about the space or anything in it.			
What does this space communicate about what success means within it?			

Figure 3.3: "Exploring Spaces" handout.

*Visit **go.SolutionTree.com/instruction** for a free reproducible version of this figure.*

Sample Script

The following sample script gives an idea of how this activity might work in your classroom.

Today we're going to think about how the space we're in affects us. We're going to start with this classroom. First, list specific features in this room that catch your attention. Look at the furniture arrangement, the walls, the things in the room—everything. (*Students list observations such as the scuff marks on the orange tiles, the teacher's desk at the back of the room, the student desks in a U shape, the fire exit sign by the door, and the unplugged pencil sharpener.*)

Let's have a few people share their lists.

Now list questions you have about the space or anything in it. You might have questions about things you just wrote down or things you just heard your classmates share, and you might have questions about other things you notice as you continue looking around the room. You might have guesses about the answers to your questions. You might have multiple questions about some things, and you might have no questions about other things. (*Students list questions such as, How did the scuff marks get on the tiles? Why is the teacher's desk at the back of the room? Why are the desks in a U shape? Why are there desks at all? Who unplugged the pencil sharpener? Why is it unplugged?*)

Let's have a few people share their questions. (*Students share.*)

Finally, based on your observations and questions, what does it mean to be successful in this space? For example, if you look at how the desks are arranged, what does it seem like it means to be successful? What assumptions are communicated by the fact that there are books in the room? What do the scuff marks on the floor tell you? We'll spend a few minutes writing about what this space communicates about what success means within it.

We'll come back to your writing about success in this space, but first we're going exploring! Take thirty minutes and go to three different locations in school where you spend time. Choose one place where you feel pretty successful, one place where you feel sort of unsuccessful, and one place where you feel neutral—neither successful nor unsuccessful. You'll write about each location using the same writing prompts we just used: listing images, listing questions, and writing about how the space communicates what it means to be successful within it. Here's a handout to help you remember the prompts. You can write on it or you can use your notebook if you prefer to have more space. (*Distributes the "Exploring Spaces" handout [figure 3.3, page 51] and students go analyze spaces in the school.*)

Anyone have any interesting observations to share about the places you visited? What are some of the interesting messages that the spaces in our school communicate? Did anyone discover anything surprising about themselves or the spaces in our school? How do the places in our school influence how we think, learn, and interact? How do different places influence our actions in different ways? What else influences our actions? Can you choose how you behave in different spaces? (*Pauses between questions so students can respond and discuss their ideas.*)

> Even if the spaces are different and the messages about success are different, you get to define what success means for yourself, according to your own values. What qualities do you want to bring to your actions and interactions in these spaces? Let's close by writing about how we want to act in each of these different spaces.

Follow-Up

You could collect the students' writings and, a week or so after doing this activity, return them and start a discussion about how students have acted and interacted in the different spaces they wrote about. How are the places' messages about success influencing them? Are they able to notice those messages and continue to pursue their own values?

Conversations about how a place can communicate might stimulate some students' interest in how they can redesign their own living and learning spaces to inspire valued behaviors. For example, students who value living inclusively might examine how certain spaces invite connection and participation while others more easily allow for isolation and segregation, and they might even want to rearrange or rebuild school spaces so they create community. Students who value living peacefully might learn about how spaces can create or reduce stress, and then take action to make school spaces promote peace within and among students. They might consider starting a community discussion on whether and how the design of school spaces promotes (or subverts) school values. Students in geometry, engineering, or architecture classes could even redesign spaces so they better reflect school values.

Variations

Students could do their walking tours in small groups, with each person choosing one location to visit. If they have access to cameras, they could take photos of different locations at school and create captions about the definitions of success that their photos suggest. They could post their photos on a class website (or print them and put them on the walls) and view each other's work to get a broader sense of how their peers think about success at school. In comments on the photos, they could write about how they could live by their own values in these spaces.

Students could also do a tour of the virtual spaces they inhabit. In which online locations do they feel successful, unsuccessful, and neutral? What are the features of these online spaces, what questions do students have about them, and what do the spaces communicate about what it means to be successful? What qualities do students want to bring to their actions in these spaces? How can they enact their values online?

Challenges

Your school might not have the kind of culture that welcomes groups of students walking around the building and grounds during class time. You'll probably want to notify your colleagues about this assignment and make sure the students have watches or clocks so they know when to return to class. If allowing your students to walk around the school unsupervised is a problem, you can limit them to a particular area.

Some students might take the idea of messages about success very literally; perhaps some classrooms have posters with verbal messages about success, like rubrics or inspirational quotations. You might need to give multiple examples of how a space communicates messages about what it means to succeed there.

Hacking the Curriculum

To *hack* is to modify a computer program in a clever way—like recoding *Super Mario Bros.* so that instead of Mario and Luigi, Princesses Peach and Daisy become the protagonists, thus "giving women more active, heroic, playable roles" (Kishi, n.d.). It has also come to mean, more figuratively, a clever method of solving a problem, such as putting a stocking over the end of a vacuum cleaner tool to suck the change out from under your dresser (Lee, n.d.). You can hack anything that contains a code, which we can take to mean any set of rules, expectations, and meanings, not just literal computer code. And hacking is democratic. Anyone can recode the world they're given. What would it mean for students to hack the curriculum? This lesson helps students make more intentional choices about whether and how to engage in the curriculum as it's presented or to hack it so it serves their values in addition to the school's.

Materials for Each Student

For this activity, each student will need a pen, paper, the "Examples of Curriculum Hacks" handout (figure 3.4), and the "Hacking Your Assignment" handout (figure 3.5).

Mateo, a sixth grader, is learning about medieval societies in social studies. As a final project, the teacher assigns each student a different topic about which they write a research report. Mateo has completed all of his research about his topic, medieval food. Instead of writing his report, he borrows his dad's voice recording app, and in his best newscaster voice, he reports "live from medieval times" on how foods are grown, prepared, and eaten. On the day the report is due, when all of his classmates are turning in their reports, Mateo emails his teacher the recording.

Aliyah, an eighth grader, sometimes feels like her science class goes too slowly. She decides to use the right-hand pages in her notebook to take down the class notes she's supposed to be copying from the board, and use the left side for her personal questions and mind wanderings related to the day's topic. One day, the class is learning how to draw a Punnett square, a diagram that shows an organism's genotype (which genes it inherits) and phenotype (what it ends up looking like). As the teacher demonstrates how to draw Punnett squares that show genotypes and phenotypes of pea plants, Aliyah draws her two favorite video game characters and makes Punnett squares to show what their biological children and grandchildren might look like. She also writes the questions, *When people say I act just like Dad used to, is that genetic? I look nothing like my sister but we both look like our parents. How is that even possible? How am I like my grandparents and great-grandparents?*

Marisol is in ninth-grade honors English. Her class is reading J. D. Salinger's *The Catcher in the Rye*, and she is supposed to write an essay about the book that introduces an arguable thesis, supports it with clear reasoning and specific evidence, and adheres to conventions as specified by state standards. Marisol understands *The Catcher in the Rye* and appreciates

Salinger's writing style, and she has a few good ideas for her essay, but what's really on Marisol's mind is the fact that one of her close friends has an eating disorder and another of her close friends has been cutting herself. Although she's a little afraid of what her English teacher will say (especially because he loves *The Catcher in the Rye*), Marisol has decided to write an essay arguing that Holden from *Catcher* models terrible coping skills, and that today's teenagers need better coping skills so they don't resort to self-harm.

Theo is a junior in high school. Between his advanced classes, running varsity track, and his close-knit group of friends, he feels like he has a pretty great life. One day during practice, he overhears a few of his teammates talking about how their mathematics teacher hardly ever talks to boys of color except to yell at them. Theo is white and thinks of himself as color-blind. He has a diverse group of friends and doesn't think he pays attention to race, but he can't stop thinking about his teammates' discussion. The next day in mathematics, Theo starts tallying who the teacher calls on and scolds, broken down by race and gender, and he's surprised to find that his teammates might be right. He tries the same thing in the rest of his classes, and by the end of that day, he's decided that his science fair project will be a study of whether there are race and gender biases among teachers at his school.

Figure 3.4: "Examples of Curriculum Hacks" handout.

Visit go.SolutionTree.com/instruction for a free reproducible version of this figure.

1. Write the assignment.

2. List purposes of the assignment, as far as you can tell. Most assignments are intended to help you learn about a topic (What's the topic?), practice a process (What's the process?), or test your abilities (To do what?). Be as specific as you can.

3. In the list you made, circle what you think is the assignment's most important purpose.

4. Imagine other things you could do that would fulfill the assignment's most important purpose while also fulfilling some of your own purposes. That might mean exploring a topic or learning a skill that matters to you. Write your ideas for alternative assignments here.

Figure 3.5: "Hacking Your Assignment" handout.

continued ⇨

Visit go.SolutionTree.com/instruction for a free reproducible version of this figure.

5. Analyze the costs and benefits of doing an assignment you made up and the assignment your teacher gave you. Try to consider positives and negatives.

	If you do the assignment you made up:	If you do the assignment your teacher gave you:
How would this affect your grade?		
How would this affect your relationship with your teacher?		
How would this affect your classmates?		
How would this affect your learning?		
How would this affect you as a person?		

6. Plan how you might discuss your decision with your teacher. What reasons might you give for wanting to hack an assignment? What questions might you ask? How will you make sure you're serving your values as you have this conversation? What will you do if your teacher says no or gets upset? If you do the hacked version against your teacher's wishes, what might the consequences be? How do you feel about those consequences?

7. Hacking an assignment to serve your values is not the same as avoiding challenging work, showing your teacher that you're smarter, or rebelling. The point of hacking is to incorporate into your school experience the content and skills that matter to you. List some people who can help you make values-based decisions about whether to do the teacher-assigned version or your hacked version.

Sample Script

The following sample script gives an idea of how this activity might work in your classroom.

How many of you have heard of hacking? In computer programming, hacking means to change some of the code so the program does something in a different way. Today, we're going to think about what it could mean to hack the curriculum at school.

Before hackers can change the code, they need to understand what's already in it. So let's think about what's in the curriculum at our school. If you think about everything humans know and can do, you could divide that knowledge into two categories: stuff you learn about in school and stuff you don't learn about in school. (*Gives examples from personal experience: knowledge and skills that were and weren't acquired in school.*)

Take a moment to list a few things you have learned in school and a few things you haven't learned in school.

There's another way you can divide all of human knowledge: stuff that's important for you to know and stuff that isn't. Notice that what you consider important will not necessarily be what the student sitting next to you thinks is important, or what I think is important, or what your family thinks is important. What you think is important depends on you.

If we think about dividing all of human knowledge according to what is and isn't taught in school, and according to what is and isn't important, we could create a matrix. (*Draws a matrix like the one shown in figure 3.6.*)

	Stuff we learn in school	Stuff we don't learn in school
Important for me to learn		
Not that important for me to learn		

Figure 3.6: Knowledge matrix.

Please divide one of your notebook pages into four boxes and see if you can come up with examples of topics, issues, ideas, or skills that would fit into each box for you personally.

Some knowledge might be important to us because it relates to us. (*Writes or projects a list of social identifiers.*)

- Your abilities
- Your age
- Your ethnicity
- Your family composition
- Your gender
- Your geographic origin
- Your languages
- Your passions
- Your political beliefs
- Your race
- Your religion
- Your sexual orientation
- Your socioeconomic class

These are social identifiers, or ways that people sometimes think about themselves and each other in groups. Some of these might feel very important to you and some might feel less important. I'm going to share some that are important to me, and then it will be your turn to list some of your own important identifiers. (*Shares some personal identifiers and then invites students to list their own identifiers, which are kept private.*)

I can divide my list of identifiers into stuff I learned about in school and stuff I didn't learn or barely learned about in school that would have been important or helpful for me. (*Gives specific personal examples.*) Please put your important identifiers into your own charts.

If there's a topic you think is important to learn about but you don't learn about it in school, you might have questions about it. (*Gives examples of genuine questions related to a personal identifier.*) Write your own questions about a topic you don't learn about in school that's important to you.

Now, please choose one question that you're willing to share with the class, and we'll go around the room and hear them.

How does it feel to hear these questions?

Of course our school has the responsibility to deliver a meaningful curriculum, but that doesn't necessarily mean school always provides the curriculum that's most meaningful to you personally. So how can you get something when it isn't provided? You can make it yourself! Which brings us to hacking. You can hack anything that has rules, expectations, and meanings. A curriculum has a set of rules, expectations, and meanings, so you can hack it. Let's look at some examples of students hacking the curriculum. (*Distributes the "Examples of Curriculum Hacks" handout [figure 3.4, page 54]; students read and discuss them.*)

Hacking the curriculum begins with identifying the assignment's purposes. Believe it or not, every assignment has multiple purposes. Imagine that for your Spanish homework, you get some sentences and you have to fill in blanks with past-tense conjugations of different verbs. What might be some purposes of that assignment? (*Lists responses on the board, such as to give an opportunity to practice a skill they'll need for more advanced work, to allow the teacher to assess understanding quickly, to provide a written record of students' progress, and to give students something to do after school.*)

What might be the most important purpose? (*Circles the most important purpose after students come to consensus.*)

Now let's see if we can think of other ways to fulfill the most important purpose. What else could a student do to practice conjugating Spanish verbs in the past tense? (*Students offer responses, such as have a conversation in Spanish about something that happened in the past, write a story that takes place in the past, and make flashcards with verb infinitives and their past-tense conjugations.*)

Next, we need to consider the positive and negative consequences of doing one of our hacks instead of the given assignment. If you choose to have a conversation in Spanish about something that happened in the past instead of doing your handout, how might that affect your grade? How would it affect your relationship with your Spanish teacher? How would it affect your classmates? How would it affect your learning of Spanish? How would it affect you? (*Pauses between questions to give students an opportunity to respond and ask their own questions.*)

What if you did the Spanish homework as assigned? How would that affect your grade? How would it affect your relationship with your Spanish teacher? How would it affect your classmates? How about your learning? How about you as a person? (*Pauses between questions to give students an opportunity to respond and ask their own questions.*) Notice that there are good and bad consequences of doing the hacked and assigned versions.

That's the process of hacking the curriculum: identifying the purposes of an assignment, thinking of an alternative version that would serve some of the same purposes and also some of your own purposes, and analyzing the good and bad consequences of both assignments. Let's try the hacking process again, but with an assignment you actually have right now. It could be a major assignment, like your history project. It could be a small assignment, like that Spanish homework sheet, or it could be something you do every day in a class, like take notes. (*Distributes the "Hacking Your Assignment" handout [figure 3.5, page 55] and guides students through it.*)

Any final thoughts?

Follow-Up

Hacking is hard. Inventing a podcast assignment, and then actually creating the podcast, is a lot more work than following a teacher's guidelines to write a report. Students who are already turned off school won't want to do *more* schoolwork. You can be one of the caring people who helps students understand that every action will have costs and benefits. Writing the report might have benefits, but it also has costs for a student who thinks it's boring and pointless, or that the only reason to do it is to get a good grade and please the teacher. Making a podcast instead might have costs—less writing practice and perhaps a lower grade on the assignment—but it also has benefits for a student who finds it meaningful.

If you wanted to go further, you could show exemplars of work that meets criteria for excellence on the given assignment *and* work product from a hacked assignment: a great medieval food report, a great medieval food podcast, and a great medieval food collage. Imagine students' reactions! "Wait—we can do that?" You could discuss the underlying purpose of the assignment, show alternatives, and analyze the costs and benefits of different choices. Then the students can decide what they'll do.

To go further still, you could host a curriculum hackathon. Organizations, universities, and corporations bring computer programmers together to play with code, explore its possibilities, and invent collaboratively. Why shouldn't students come together to play with the curriculum, explore its possibilities, and invent collaboratively? Like any hackathon, yours would need clear procedures, thoughtfully constructed groups, and time limits to ensure values-consistent work instead of a free-for-all waste of time.

Variations

After students fill out their knowledge matrices, you can give them markers and have them cover the board or a sheet of butcher paper with what they said is important for them to learn but that isn't taught in school. Doing this allows them to share their own interests and learn about each other's.

Instead of identifying one assignment to hack, students could choose one aspect of their identities they want to learn more about, list all the assignments they're working on, and brainstorm how each assignment could possibly lend itself to their learning about that aspect. Some aspects will be hard to connect to some assignments, or to any assignment, but the attempt will help students think flexibly about how their schoolwork can connect to topics that matter to them.

Since hacking the curriculum presents a wonderful opportunity for students to talk to their teachers about their values, they could try role playing those conversations. How might they present a hacked assignment to the teacher who wrote the original? How might the teacher respond? What qualities of action do they want to bring to their conversations? Role playing not only gives students a chance to practice what they might say but it also allows them to practice enacting their values when relating to their teachers.

If this entire exercise seems too risky to do with your students, you could use it on your own. Try imagining how some of your more challenging students might hack each of your assignments. While hacking your own curriculum won't give your students the opportunity to hack it themselves, you might come up with creative ideas for your class that better respond to your students' needs and interests, and that's not such a terrible outcome.

By definition, hacking the curriculum calls for variations from the traditional plan. By all means, hack this activity! Hack this entire book!

Challenges

Probably the biggest challenge in giving a lesson on curriculum hacking is how we feel about encouraging students to hack assignments. We might feel strongly that our own assignments are worthwhile and that our students just have to do them, much like we just have to do parts of our jobs we don't like. But would we rather see our students work for the reward of a good grade, someone's approval, or the relief of being done? Would we rather see our students say, "Yes!" to a hacked assignment or shrug at one we hand them? The curriculum exists before students come to class, but they're the ones who decide what aspects of the lesson they engage with, how deeply they think, and whether they put forth the mental effort to connect their learning to their lives—in short, how meaningful they want class to be.

There's also the matter of other teachers and administrators, who might disapprove if *their* assignments get hacked. We highly recommend discussing this activity with your colleagues and sharing why you want to do it. You might be surprised to find support from colleagues—or at least curiosity. If nothing else, their reactions are information you can use to help your students weigh the risks and benefits of hacking assignments in different classes.

But what about grading? If you ask a student to write a report and he makes an excellent podcast instead, what grade should he get? An A for the quality of the podcast? A C because he met some expectations but not others? An F because the assignment was to write a report and he didn't do that? A standards-based rubric would provide some clarity; rather than giving a single letter grade, you could evaluate the students' work (whether they followed the assignment or hacked it) as evidence that they've mastered the specific concepts and skills on the rubric (Guskey, 2015). If the hacked assignment fulfills at least some of the original's purpose, then you should be able to use the same rubric to evaluate at least those aspects. But some aspects of work product from a hacked assignment might demonstrate capacities that the standards do not reflect. The very fact that a piece of student work can be excellent in ways not mentioned in academic standards illustrates the limitations of the standards themselves. Creating a set of standards means identifying the concepts and skills that are most important for students to master, and what's deemed most important depends on values (Porosoff, 2014). Why shouldn't the curriculum serve the students' values, too?

Your Participation

Asking students to participate in crafting their experience of school can be uncomfortable—not only for students but for teachers. We're asking students to transform the functions of their school experiences so they serve their own values rather than only the system's, and we're agents of that very system. Not only are we contractually and financially bound to our schools, but we often have networks of collegial relationships and friendships that we don't want to disturb. While enlightening students about the politics among your colleagues isn't likely to empower anyone, you might share any discomfort you feel in encouraging them to question school-constructed definitions of success—and why that discomfort is worthwhile for you because it's in the service of their empowerment. If you think sharing these feelings will make your students feel guilty, angry, or some other unproductive reaction, then doing so might not be in their best interest.

We might also tell ourselves there will be time for students to create their own opportunities to enact their values once they've graduated from high school, gone through college, and earned the freedom to live the way they want to. Teachers who work with populations that are subject to injustices (low income, language barriers, disabilities, racism, job insecurity, food insecurity) might very reasonably think it's their job to acculturate their students to the school system—to help them learn to play by its rules rather than putting themselves at a further disadvantage by refusing to do so.

Encouraging our students to craft their own education in accordance with their values might come at a cost. But consider the cost of *not* teaching them to make school match their values. What's important to you in your classroom? When you enforce school rules and standards, does that move you toward what's important to you? Does it move your students toward what's important to them? Is there a cost in terms of your values or theirs? What else can you try? Who can help?

From Participation to Openness

This chapter's activities empower students to redefine success at school in terms of their own values, and to pursue those personal ideas of success when they're different from, or even in conflict with, the school's ideas of what success means. This isn't about rebellion for its own sake; it's no more empowering for them if they always disobey directions than if they always obey them. What's empowering is the act of choosing their values and doing what's meaningful to them, even when that's hard. It can be hard just to talk about the things that genuinely matter and risk looking stupid, weak, or uncool. The next chapter's activities help students share their genuine selves, stories, and vulnerabilities so they can build a community in which everyone supports each other in serving their values.

EMP**O**WER

• • • • •

Chapter 4

OPENNESS
Empower Students to Share Their Values

School is supposed to be a place of learning. We know that learning necessarily involves mistakes, false starts, confusion, misconceptions, incorrect assumptions, and saying things that make no sense—and we expect students to do all of these things in front of each other? Many students will play it safe, go along with their peers, remain silent, and otherwise avoid the shame of being imperfect. If we want to help students learn in a deep, lasting, and meaningful way, we need to teach them how to be vulnerable in front of each other.

Brené Brown (2010), whose research professorship is about vulnerability, tells a story of a mom who got stuck in traffic and arrived late to her child's school performance. The mom was stressed out and upset, and while one fellow mom rolled her eyes judgmentally, others came up to her and shared their own stories of similar failures. One completely forgot about the previous performance, and another failed to dress her son for pajama day. According to Brown (2010), "The moms who stopped and shared their stories of imperfection and vulnerability were practicing courage . . . . Every time we choose courage, we make everyone around us a little better and the world a little braver" (p. 15). Storytelling allows us to understand our mistakes so we can grow, and it invites others to share their stories so they can grow, too. When we share, we help ourselves and each other.

The activities in this chapter create contexts in which students can tell the stories of the worries, mess-ups, confusions, and other vulnerabilities that are an integral part of learning (and humanity), not only so they can learn and grow in ways that matter to them, but so they can begin to create a kind, nurturing, and courageous community.

Concern Cards

Many teachers ask students to anonymously submit comments or questions on index cards. In this version, students write a concern, which the teacher reads to the class without anyone knowing who wrote it. Students then respond with their own similar stories, helpful suggestions, and expressions of caring for their classmate. Use this activity any time you sense there might be unspoken concerns among your students.

Materials for Each Student

For this activity, each student will need an index card and a pen.

Sample Script

The following sample script gives an idea of how this activity might work in your classroom.

> Today we're taking a few minutes to help each other think about some of the things that are on our minds right now.
>
> I'm going to give each of you an index card. (*Distributes them.*) On the card, you'll write something that is a concern for you at the moment. It could be a major worry or fear in your life, or it could be something smaller that's just sort of stressing you out or bugging you or taking up space in your head. It could be an academic concern, a social concern, or a family concern. It could involve your physical body, your friends, your community, or the whole world. And it doesn't necessarily have to be a bad thing or a good thing. It could be both, or neither. Whatever is your concern at this moment.
>
> When you write your concern, you won't put your name on your card. I'll collect all the cards and read one out loud, and then together we'll have a discussion about that concern without knowing who wrote it. So this is an opportunity to share something that's on your mind and get your classmates' help without identifying yourself. It's also an opportunity to help your classmates. If we have time, we'll do a few rounds of these.
>
> One last thing: please don't include any identifying details about yourself or anyone else. For example, if your concern is that you're having a conflict with your friend Jordan, just put that you're having a conflict with a friend.
>
> Okay, let's make our cards. When you're finished, just put the card face down in front of you. (*Waits for all students to finish writing and then collects and mixes up the cards.*)
>
> I've shuffled the cards, and I'm going to read the one that happens to come out on top. (*Reads the top card, paraphrasing if necessary to protect the identity of the person who wrote it.*)
>
> Who has a response to that? (*Leads a discussion of the concern. Can repeat the process of reading a card and discussing the concern, but the goal is not to get through all the cards in one sitting.*)

If you were one of the people whose concern I shared today, take a moment and silently notice how that felt. Notice where you felt it in your body when you heard me read your words out loud. Notice some of the thoughts and feelings that came up as you heard me read. And notice how it felt to listen to your classmates talk about your concern. Let's all appreciate what our classmate might be thinking and feeling right now. (*Pauses between prompts to give students an opportunity to notice their thoughts and feelings.*)

If I did not read your card, notice how it felt when you heard a card and it wasn't yours. A little relieved, maybe? Or a little disappointed? Some of both? Something else? And notice some of the thoughts and feelings that came up as you heard your classmate's concern. Did it resonate with you? (*Pauses so students can continue noticing their thoughts and feelings.*)

Does anyone want to share?

Follow-Up

Depending on how much time you have, your students might get to talk about only one of the cards. You can keep the cards and pull them out over the next few days when you have more time. Or, you could keep the cards for a few weeks, read them all aloud to the class, and ask students to raise their hands if they either no longer have the concern or can't remember which concern was theirs. That would serve as a reminder that some worries are fleeting and some aren't, and regardless, the choice to open up about a genuine concern is an act of strength.

Variations

Reading only the top card aloud means the group can't judge some concerns as more important than others. Comparing concerns can lead to unhelpful self-judgments like, "I'm selfish and stupid for worrying about something so small," or, on the flip side, "My life is so messed up and weird." The assumptions in this activity are that any concern is a big deal, anyone can benefit from sharing what's on his or her mind and getting validation, and the group can offer compassion and help to anyone.

That said, another way to do this activity is to read aloud all the cards quickly and then ask the students if they noticed themes or connections among them. You might discuss a concern that comes up a lot, or you might draw the group's attention to a concern that only came up once. Depending on what the cards say, you might ask questions like, "How does it feel to know you're not alone in your concern?" or "How does it feel to be part of a group that has so many different concerns?" You can also ask, "How can we treat each other, knowing we all have stuff on our minds that we might or might not be talking about?"

You could limit this activity to concerns about a specific topic, such as an upcoming school event or a recent tragedy, or a specific domain, such as the students' academic, social, or online lives. You could look for patterns among the concerns and use them with your colleagues to identify issues that you need to address at the school level.

As an alternative to index cards, you might have students text or email their concerns to you, although some students might be less open and honest when they have more time to compose their concerns and when you'll know whose concerns are whose.

Challenges

Often when students hear each other's concerns, they immediately go into problem-solving mode. They might suggest several solutions and debate the merits of each one. If this happens, you can acknowledge the instinct to solve the problem as a kind gesture, and you can also point out that the person who's having this problem is in the room and might not need a solution but rather some other kind of response. You can prompt expressions of caring with questions like, "How does it feel to know someone in this room is having this concern? Even though we don't know which person it is, how can we all take care of each other? Knowing that someone in this room has this concern, is anyone willing to share a story about something similar that happened to you? Does anyone want to say something to this person, not knowing who it is but knowing he or she is in this room?"

Sometimes students might try to argue that the concern isn't valid: "Whoever wrote this, I don't think your teachers actually hate you." If you hear this sort of statement, you can point out that the concern is real for the person who's experiencing it, and his or her feelings about it are also real. You can ask students, "Has anyone else ever felt this way? What was that like? What did you need at the time?"

If you've framed this activity broadly and open-endedly, you might get a wide range of concerns, including everything from, "I'm worried I'll get in trouble for not doing my Latin homework," to "I didn't make the basketball team," to "All of my teachers hate me," to "I don't eat enough," to "I'm afraid my mom will never come home." Some students might hear each other's concerns and feel like they did the activity wrong because their concern either was too big or not big enough. You can keep acknowledging that there's a wide range of concerns in each person's life and that our concerns change from day to day and moment to moment.

If the concern is particularly painful, then you might get a few moments of silence as students search for their words or struggle with their own feelings. We think it's important to resist the urge to fill that silence with your own words or, even worse, move on to the next card. Psychologist Kelly Wilson (2009) discusses how hard it is to allow ourselves to get close to other people's suffering:

> We so want suffering to be an abstraction, to be about someone else, somewhere else, or at least somewhen else. . . . We all bear some responsibility and possess some ability to respond. But we remain silent about our own suffering. And, in sometimes subtle and sometimes not-so-subtle ways, we conspire to silence suffering around us. (p. 5)

Concern cards are intended to acknowledge and alleviate suffering, not silence it.

Finally, any time students can submit concerns anonymously, there is the possibility that someone might express concerns about self-harm or threaten others. If this happens, immediately contact the school psychologist, who can meet privately with each student and ask him or her to identify his or her own card. This process would preserve the students' anonymity while allowing the school psychologist to identify the student who threatened harm.

Help Seeking

Help can benefit everyone, but not all students ask for it, and some actively avoid it. It turns out that when students have status goals—like high grades or a good reputation—they tend to *avoid* help for fear of looking stupid and dependent, but when students have learning goals, they tend to *seek* help so they can grow (Karabenick, 1998; Karabenick & Newman, 2011; Ryan, Hicks, & Midgley, 1997).

Students often have both kinds of goals simultaneously; as Maria is working on her essay for English class, she might want to get better at writing *and* get a good grade. Or a student might have different goals in different contexts. Maria might think about growing as a writer when she's in English class, but in history she's uninterested in her paper topic and just wants a decent grade, and in science she's writing a lab report with the boy she likes and is focused on impressing him. Students aren't entirely in control of outcomes: Maria could work hard to get an A on her history paper and try to impress the boy in science, and she could still end up with a B– and no boyfriend. But students *are* in control of how they approach their learning.

In this activity, students distinguish "getting and maintaining" goals from "learning and improving" goals. After identifying their own goals, they practice help-seeking behaviors that might feel uncomfortable in the short term but that move them toward the longer-term satisfaction that comes from learning what matters to them.

Materials for Each Student

For this activity, each student will need the "Case Studies on Getting Help" handout (figure 4.1), two or three help-seeking email examples, pen, paper, and an email account. (See the variations [page 70] if students do not have email access.)

> Ryder isn't the biggest reader, but he does like to discuss books. In English class, he contributes lots of ideas and enjoys hearing different interpretations from his classmates. After each book, the teacher always assigns an essay. Ryder very much wants to get an A in English, so during work periods he asks his teacher a lot of questions, such as, "Is it okay if all of my quotations are in the second paragraph?" or, "What do you think my title should be?" After the teacher grades his essays, the comments always say that his thesis is too vague and that he needs to support his points with more evidence. The teacher has just assigned him another essay.

Figure 4.1: "Case Studies on Getting Help" handout. continued ⇨

- What goals does this student seem to have?
- What kinds of help would benefit this student in achieving these goals?
- Who are some possible sources of help?

Ayanna has always loved music. When she was little, she picked up guitar and cello very quickly, and she's just started to teach herself bass. But Ayanna hates her music class. The other students don't really practice or listen, so the teacher has to go painfully slowly and spends a lot of time admonishing the class. Ayanna figures she can just coast through to the winter concert and get an easy A. She's started to do her mathematics homework during music class so she'll have more time after school, and twice she's pretended to have a stomachache and spent music class in the nurse's office.

- What goals does this student seem to have?
- What kinds of help would benefit this student in achieving these goals?
- Who are some possible sources of help?

Sondra is having trouble in her physics class. She understands the concepts when she watches a demonstration, but all the variables and formulas confuse her. She feels like her teacher goes too fast and doesn't explain the material clearly. She ends up staring out the window or whispering to her friends in the class. Her teacher has pulled her aside several times and asked her to stay focused. Sondra is afraid that if she asks her teacher to slow down and give more examples of how to solve the problems, the teacher will just think she's being even more disrespectful and maybe even lower her grade.

- What goals does this student seem to have?
- What kinds of help would benefit this student in achieving these goals?
- Who are some possible sources of help?

Sample Script

The following sample script gives an idea of how this activity might work in your classroom.

Lately your schoolwork has been getting more challenging—maybe not just in this class. I've noticed that even though everyone can benefit from help, some students don't ask for it. What do you think stops students at our school from asking for help? (*Students might say things like they're embarrassed to ask in front of their friends, they're afraid of sounding stupid, they think the teacher will think they weren't listening, or they don't think they need help.*)

How many of these barriers involve feelings or thoughts we don't like having?

Let's look at why asking for help might be worthwhile even if it means having unpleasant thoughts and feelings. (*Hands out the case studies. Students form small groups, read the case studies, respond to the questions, and share with the class. See figure 4.1.*)

Now that we've seen how made-up people could achieve their goals with help, let's think about our goals. One kind of goal involves either getting something or keeping something you already have. For example, in French class you might want to maintain a test average of 85 percent or higher. Or you might want to get higher grades than your friends, or keep the respect of your classmates. These kinds of goals might begin, *I want to get . . .* or *I want to maintain . . .* or *I want to have . . . .* (*Writes these phrases on the board.*)

What are some more examples of getting or maintaining goals?

Most people have getting and maintaining goals. Of course we want to be successful, and we want people to like and respect us. But goals that are about getting and maintaining can become barriers to seeking help. If a student doesn't ask for help because she's afraid the teacher will think she wasn't listening, her goals are to *maintain* the teacher's respect and *get* a good grade. Someone who doesn't ask for help because he's embarrassed has a goal to *maintain* his image as someone who knows a lot. If we're focused on getting and maintaining, we probably won't ask for help.

Let's look at another kind of goal. This kind involves learning more about something or getting better at doing something. If you take French, you might want to learn how to speak fluently, or at least get the general idea of what your French-speaking grandmother is telling you on the phone. If you take music, you might want to learn how to read musical notation or play your favorite song on the guitar. These kinds of goals might begin, *I want to know more about . . .* or *I want to be able to . . .* or *I want to get better at . . . .* (*Writes these phrases on the board.*)

Who has another example of a learning or improving goal?

If we're focused on learning and improving goals, we probably *will* ask for help. If I want to improve my French speaking, then sure, I'll ask my French teacher for help. Why not? I can listen to him as an example of how to speak it well. If I speak French to him, I'm practicing my skills and getting his feedback. I might not *want* to ask for help; I don't like the idea of taking up his time and I'm embarrassed by my bad French, but if I truly want to learn to speak better, then maybe I'm willing to feel that awkwardness and embarrassment.

Now let's write some of our learning and improving goals. Make a list of your classes. Think about what you want to learn more about, or be able to do, or get better at in some of them. Write goals you genuinely have for yourself. It shouldn't be someone else's goal for you, because then *your* goal is to get or maintain that person's approval. (*Gives students time to write their learning and improving goals and circulates to make sure students aren't writing getting and maintaining goals.*)

Focus on one of these goals—something important to you. Generally, when we have a learning or improving goal, it helps to see examples of what to do, practice, and get feedback. What examples of excellence could you look at? What could you do to practice? What kinds of feedback could you get? Write your ideas.

Next, who are some people who could give you the kinds of help you listed? It could be the teacher of that subject, but also think about less obvious sources of help—teachers of other subjects, people who work at our school but aren't teachers, your peers, family members— really anyone. Write the names of people who might be able to provide the help you listed.

Finally, let's think about how to ask for help. I ask for help all the time, and I want to show you some help-seeking emails I've sent. (*Projects or hands out a help-seeking email, gives context, and reads the email aloud.*)

What do you notice about this email?

How do you think I felt when I was sending this?

You're right—I did feel sort of uncomfortable! Why do you think I sent the email anyway?

Let's look at another one. (*Shares one or two more help-seeking emails. For each, asks what the students notice and shares any uncomfortable thoughts and feelings that came up when sending the email.*)

Let's see if we can name the features of a help-seeking request. (*Elicits or shares that help-seeking emails generally give context about the problem or issue, ask for a specific type of help, use an appropriate tone given the relationship the sender has with the recipient, show appreciation for the person's time and effort, and are proofread as a sign of respect. Lists these features on the board.*)

Now that you've seen some of my help-seeking emails, your assignment is to choose someone on your list who can help you fulfill a goal that matters to you, and send an email asking for help that would benefit you.

You might feel uncomfortable sending the email. Maybe you're having some of the same thoughts I did, like, "What if they don't respond?" or, "What if they think I'm weird?" or, "I'm going to look like an idiot," or just, "I hate this!" Take a moment to really listen to the thoughts you're having. Are these thoughts making it more or less likely that you'll accomplish a goal that matters to you? Will these thoughts and feelings stand in your way? Can you have these thoughts and feelings and still send the email? Why would you want to send the email anyway?

Follow-Up

Students can forward you their emails, both so you know they wrote them and so you can coach them on more effective ways to ask for help. In the next class, you might have them discuss their experiences writing the emails: thoughts and feelings they had, how it felt to receive or not to receive a response, what the response was, and what next steps they're planning.

Variations

You can use the case studies in figure 4.1 (page 67), but you're probably better off writing your own based on common struggles in your class. After reading and responding to the case studies you wrote, students can write their own case studies and respond to each other's. If you're pressed for time, you can skip the case studies entirely, but we recommend doing them. Asking for help means being able to put learning goals ahead of achievement goals and accept feelings of discomfort—and that's hard! It's a little easier if they practice on a fictional character. Reading multiple case studies shows students that asking for help doesn't mean they're deficient, and that struggling in class is normal.

Instead of sharing your own help-seeking emails, you can write one as the students watch so they can see the process. They'll get to see you struggling with your word choices and expressing any hesitation you might feel.

If your students don't have email access, they can ask for help in person, on the phone, or via text message and report their conversations to you.

Challenges

Some students will say they don't have any goals, or that their only goal at school is to survive the day and go home. In that case, you can empathize: "I get it. You didn't ask to be here." Then, you can suggest making the most of their time at school: "But as long as you're here, is there anything you want to learn more about or get better at?"

Other students will find ways to subvert the intentions of this assignment. For example, they'll say in their emails that they're asking for help only because of a class assignment, or they'll email people who are already giving them the kind of help they're asking for, or they'll choose goals they think are easily achievable so they look smart and capable to their helpers. These behaviors are usually signs that the student is trying to avoid the uncomfortable feelings associated with help seeking. You can gently say that it's understandable to want to avoid feeling uncomfortable. Then you can ask these students to talk about why their goals matter, and how help would move them toward achieving their goals. Particularly resistant students would benefit from the Passengers on the Bus activity in chapter 5 (page 85), which is about overcoming unwillingness.

Another challenge is the inherent contradiction between a class assignment and a chosen commitment. Some students might be excited to write a help-seeking email, but others will think it's just another burden or even feel offended that you're forcing them to ask for help. The point of this activity is to give students practice doing the sort of behavior that might transform school into a place where they can serve their values.

Investigating Your Study Practices

Making school meaningful can be immensely rewarding for students, but it's also hard. Just as it helps us to have supportive colleagues—to share our passions for the work, push back when we make self-limiting statements, provoke us with their insights, and help us hold ourselves accountable to our values—it can be helpful for students to have each other's backs.

In this activity, students are invited to join study groups. Traditional study groups work together to master the academic content, which already requires some vulnerability. These groups go a step further;

they become a forum for members to share their struggles, analyze how their schoolwork matches up with their values, and think of new and creative ways to make school meaningful.

In these study groups, students use protocols adapted from the School Reform Initiative (www .schoolreforminitiative.org) and the National School Reform Faculty (NSRF; www.nsrfharmony.org). The protocols structure conversation in a way that encourages focus, inclusivity, and trust as teachers seek and receive each other's feedback (McDonald, n.d.; NSRF, n.d.). Since protocols are such an effective way for teachers to make themselves vulnerable in the service of their values, we've adapted two of them for students to use.

These groups are most effective if students have thought about values-consistent behavior, for example through the Grading Your Classes (chapter 2, page 32) or Focus Stickers activities (page 37) or Behavior Brainstorm (chapter 3, page 46). You could do a values clarification activity before introducing the idea of study groups or as an activity for all the groups to do together once they've formed.

Materials for Each Student

For this activity, each student will need the "Examining Your Work" handout (figure 4.2) and the "Exploring a Genuine Question" handout (figure 4.3, page 74).

Every time you do an assignment—from a quick do-now to a long-term project—your teacher has a set of expectations. These expectations might come from the teacher, your school or district, or national standards. But other people's expectations are not the whole story. Your own values matter, too. This protocol is a structured way for you to get feedback from your peers about how much your work matches up with your teacher's expectations *and* your own values.

You need:

- Schoolwork that you created (like an essay, poster, slide deck, study guide, or artwork)
- A copy of the assignment that led you to create this work (like a checklist or rubric if there was one)
- Three or four trusted peers
- A facilitator (another peer, a more experienced student, or a trusted adult)

What happens:

1. Share information about your work while everyone else is silent and takes notes. (Five minutes)

    - What was the assignment?
    - What were some of the teacher's expectations? Is there a checklist or rubric you can show the group?
    - What were the steps you went through to do this assignment?
    - What are some things that make school meaningful for you? How do you want to approach your work?
    - What do you want from today's session? Is there a particular question you want the group to answer or a goal you have?

2. The group asks questions to get more facts about the work. (Four minutes) The facilitator makes sure that the questions are about facts, not opinions. Some examples follow.

   - How long did it take you to make this?
   - What unit was this assignment a part of?
   - When during the unit did you do this?
   - What lessons were there to teach you how to do this?
   - What did the teacher expect you to already know how to do? What did you have to figure out for yourself?
   - Did you do this in class or at home?
   - Did anyone help you?
   - How many times have you done something like this before?

3. The group silently studies your work. Participants write notes about where the assignment seems to match up with what you said makes school meaningful and how you want to approach your work. They also note where the assignment seems disconnected from what matters most to you at school. (Five minutes)

4. The group pauses to think about the feedback they're about to give. (One minute)

5. You are a silent observer while the group discusses your work. They begin by identifying ways it seems to match what matters most to you at school and continue by identifying possible problems or disconnections. You may wish to take notes. (Seven minutes)

   During this discussion, the group refers to you in the third person and does not address you directly. For example, if your name is Steve, the group will say things like, "Steve wrote about his family," rather than "You wrote about your family." This can feel a little weird, but it keeps the conversation about the work and not about you or your reactions.

6. The facilitator returns your work. The group does not offer any more feedback after this point.

7. You share what you're thinking after hearing the group's feedback. Try not to defend yourself. Use the time to reflect upon interesting ideas that came out of the discussion. (Five minutes)

8. The facilitator leads a brief discussion about this experience. (Three minutes)

   - How did you, the presenter, feel?
   - How did the group feel?
   - What did the group learn that might make their own schoolwork meaningful?

Source: Adapted from McDonald, n.d.; NSRF, n.d.

Figure 4.2: "Examining Your Work" handout.

*Visit **go.SolutionTree.com/instruction** for a free reproducible version of this figure.*

If you've started to think about what makes school meaningful for you, you might have questions about how to do that. This protocol is a structured way for you to get feedback from your peers about how you can make your work at school more meaningful.

You need:

- A question about how to make school meaningful
  Here are some sample questions. They're just examples and shouldn't limit you! If you want to ask the question about a specific class, just add the words *in* _____ *class*.

  - When can I learn about topics that matter to me personally?
  - How can I use my creativity more often?
  - How can I contribute to more discussions?
  - How can I build better relationships with my classmates?
  - How can I build a better relationship with my teacher?
  - How will the skills I'm learning help me outside school?
  - How will the skills I'm learning help me when I'm an adult?
  - How can I see more perspectives?
  - How can I take a leadership role?
  - How can I challenge myself more?

- Pieces of work, assignments, written feedback from teachers, or anything else that will help your group understand why you're asking your question

- Three or four trusted peers

- A facilitator (another peer, a more experienced student, or a trusted adult)

What happens:

1. Explain what led you to ask your question. Describe particular situations or show pieces of your work, assignments, and teacher feedback. (Eight minutes)

2. If necessary, pause so your group members can examine anything you've shown them. (Three minutes)

3. Ask your question.

4. The group asks questions to get more information. These questions should have answers that are facts, not opinions or judgments. If someone asks an opinion or judgment question, the facilitator points that out and you don't answer the question. (Four minutes)

5. The group asks questions to help you think differently about your situation. You can answer them if you have an answer, or you can simply say, "I don't know," or, "I'd have to think about that." The group does not discuss your responses. The group could use these question stems. (Eight minutes)

   - What would be different if . . .?
   - What are you doing when . . .?
   - What else is happening around you when . . .?
   - Have you tried . . .?
   - What would be a different way to . . .?
   - What would be a smaller/bigger version of . . .?
   - What assumptions are you making about . . .?

6. The facilitator asks you to restate your question.

7. You are a silent observer while the group has a discussion in response to your question. Possible discussion questions follow. (Eight minutes)

   • What did we hear?

   • What stood out?

   • What do we wonder?

   • What do we think?

   • What might we do or try in this situation? What have we done in similar situations?

   The goal is to talk about the problem or issue rather than quickly coming up with solutions. If someone has a solution, he or she should frame it as a suggestion, rather than an answer.

   During this discussion, the group refers to you in the third person and does not address you directly. For example, if your name is Steve, the group will say things like, "It sounds like Steve has already tried to meet with his teacher," rather than, "It sounds like you have already tried to meet with your teacher." This can feel a little weird, but it keeps the entire conversation about the question.

8. Pause so you can reflect on what you have just heard. (One minute)

9. Share what you're thinking after hearing the group's discussion. You might identify next steps you want to take or share your reactions to the ideas that came up. (Five minutes)

10. The facilitator leads a brief discussion about this experience. (Three minutes)

    • How did you, the presenter, feel?

    • How did the group feel?

    • What did the group members learn that might help them make their schoolwork meaningful?

Source: Adapted from McDonald, n.d.; NSRF, n.d.

Figure 4.3: "Exploring a Genuine Question" handout.

*Visit **go.SolutionTree.com/instruction** for a free reproducible version of this figure.*

Sample Script

The following sample script gives an idea of how this activity might work in your classroom.

Today I'm going to tell you about an opportunity to work with other students who share the goal of making academic experiences more meaningful. It's totally optional, and I think some of you would get a lot out of it.

Here's how it would work. You'd be in a group with three or four other students who are also interested in making school more meaningful. You'd get together about once a month to talk about your work, and there will be a protocol to structure your discussion. The point of the protocol isn't to prevent people from expressing themselves; it's actually to make it easier for people to express their thoughts and feelings in a way that is positive and productive. It can be hard to give feedback—whether it's positive or negative. Giving positive feedback is sometimes hard; we'll say things like, "I like this," or, "This is really good," but we don't always get specific enough to help the person know what he or she did right so he or she can do it again in the future. Giving negative feedback is also hard when we don't want to hurt the person's feelings. Protocols create a structure for giving balanced, helpful feedback.

It can also be hard to talk about our own successes and failures. When we describe our successes, we sometimes feel like we're showing off or worry that someone else might feel bad. And describing our failures is hard, too, because we might feel ashamed of them. We might start slinging blame at other people or making excuses for ourselves, and these moves aren't helpful if we're trying to grow in ways that matter to us. Protocols allow us to talk about our work without bragging, shaming ourselves, or making excuses.

Something else can happen when discussions are more free-flowing: certain people dominate and certain people don't contribute. Maybe they don't know what to say, maybe they're afraid, or maybe they can't get a word in. Protocols might feel a little bit unnatural, but part of the point is to interrupt these patterns of overcontributing and undercontributing.

The point of these protocols is to get groups to share stories about their schoolwork so they can help each other make school more meaningful. There are two kinds of protocols, so let's look at them both. (*Distributes the "Examining Your Work" handout [figure 4.2, page 72].*)

For this first protocol, you bring in a piece of work. First, you talk about what the assignment was, what you actually did, what the teacher was expecting, and what matters to you. Then, the group asks you questions to get more information about the work itself, about you, and about the context of the work—like the unit it was part of, how long it took you, whether it was homework or classwork, whether you've done similar assignments in the past, and other stuff like that. Then, you're silent as the group discusses how your work matches up with the teacher's expectations and your own values. You're silent during this part to allow the group to talk honestly about the work without interruption. Then, you have a chance to reflect upon what you heard, not so you can defend yourself or your work, but rather to explore how you can make your future work match up better with your values.

That first protocol starts out specific, with a particular piece of work you did for a particular assignment, and moves toward more general ideas about how you can make your work match your values. The second protocol goes from general to specific. (*Distributes the "Explore a Genuine Question" handout [figure 4.3, page 74].*)

In this one, you begin with a question you have about yourself, your work style, your learning, or your interests—any question that somehow relates to making your schoolwork meaningful.

For example, say you value challenging yourself, and your music class is boring because you've been playing piano since you were three. You might bring the group a question like, "How can I make music class more interesting and challenging for myself?" Or you might even ask more generally, "How can I make all my classes more interesting and challenging for myself?"

Your question will depend on what makes school meaningful for you. So if school is meaningful when you form relationships, then you might ask a question about how you can form relationships with your teachers, peers, or older students, or perhaps how you can improve the way you talk to your family about school. If school has value when you can use your creativity, you might ask a question about how you can be more creative in a certain class, like science, or when you're doing a certain kind of task, like note taking, or you might ask a question about how you can approach school more creatively. Sample questions at the beginning of the protocol could frame these sorts of discussions.

In the discussion, you give some background. That can include describing particular situations or showing pieces of work, assignments, or feedback you've received. What you say or show depends on the question you're asking. Then, you ask the question. Next, the group asks you questions to get more information about the situation and to help you think about it in different ways. Then the group has a discussion in front of you while you're silent. The group might come up with answers, but the goal is more to understand the situation more deeply and from different perspectives. At the end, you rejoin the discussion to share what you got out of listening to the group, and you might identify a couple of next steps you're thinking of taking based on the ideas you just heard. Notice that this protocol moves from a general question you have to specific actions you can take.

Who thinks they might be interested in trying this out?

Follow-Up

Students will probably have lots of questions about how this process works, and they'll probably ask about contingencies you haven't thought about yet. If you use an online form for sign-ups, you can leave space for them to ask questions. That way you have a chance to think through unexpected issues before responding.

One issue to think about is whether you'll allow students to form their own groups or whether you'll assign interested students into groups. These study groups require trust and vulnerability, so students might prefer to choose who they work with. On the other hand, a student who's interested in doing this work might not have three or four friends who are joining. If students have to convince their friends to participate, those who are less outgoing are at a disadvantage, and those who started groups might feel pressured to maintain the group and embarrassed if the group disbands. Those who join because others convinced them might be less committed and drop out, leaving the person who put effort into starting the group with no group at all. For all of these reasons, we recommend putting out a general call for students to express interest and then putting them into groups from that pool. You can say from the outset that when you place students into groups with those who are not necessarily their friends (or even their age-matched peers), they get the benefit of perspectives that they're not used to getting.

Since study groups involve a time commitment, you might consider offering a trial run before students decide whether to continue. Students who keep participating would ideally commit to meeting enough times that every group member has a chance to present. After that point, groups that want to keep working together can, and you can remix groups that lose members. Or, you could remix everyone to increase exposure to diverse viewpoints.

After the groups have met a few times, you can give out a questionnaire to see how they're doing. What's working? How could the groups work better?

Variations

As written, it takes about thirty to forty minutes to run through either of the protocols. You can adjust the time limits for each step. You could even have the students adjust the times for themselves, perhaps spending less time when they first attempt to use these protocols and then increasing the time as they get better at describing their own situations in depth, considering different aspects of their peers' work and questions, and giving detailed feedback that helps the presenter make school meaningful.

Challenges

How many students would spend extra time examining their work in a way that makes them vulnerable? Even if you know one or two such students, do you know four or five who would all be willing to work together and commit to that work so that each person has one turn to present? Quite possibly, the students who participate in a study group will be the ones who need it least. Still, we think it's worthwhile to make these groups an option.

There's also the problem of time. When in their busy schedules will students meet? You might be able to make time for these groups—and add to their appeal—by making them a study hall alternative. While some schools successfully make study hall a time when students work productively and efficiently, we've seen a lot of students staring into space, goofing off, passing notes, stealth texting and game playing, and engaging in a variety of other avoidance behaviors. You could hold out these study groups as a more fun, meaningful alternative.

A great, if time-intensive, way to show students the value of this activity is to create a study group for yourself. You and your colleagues could authentically engage in a protocol in a fishbowl format, with your group in an inner circle and the students observing from an outer circle. Not only would the students learn what this kind of conversation is like and how it helps, but they would also see you modeling vulnerability in the service of your values.

Your Openness

In Concern Cards, you're collecting and reading the students' concerns without sharing one of your own. In Help Seeking, you do share instances when you've asked for help, but not all of these instances will have high stakes. In fact, we recommend beginning with examples when the stakes are low, so students can see a variety of situations in which help seeking is beneficial, and so those who feel more hesitant can start small. In Investigating Your Study Practices, you're facilitating the formation of study groups rather than participating yourself.

During all of these activities, you can still share times when you've opened up about your concerns and how that felt, times you've asked for help with things that mattered to you, and times you sought critical feedback. But as much as we encourage being an equal participant in the activities in this book, the activities in this chapter are about opening up to people who have as much as or more power than the one doing the sharing. Because you're the teacher and the adult, your opening up to the students doesn't invoke the same sort of vulnerability as when they open up to each other or to you.

But your colleagues and supervisors have at least as much power as you do. What if you were to use Concern Cards at a department meeting, ask a supervisor for help with something important, or start your own study group with your colleagues? What would these kinds of openness be like?

From Openness to Willingness

The activities in this chapter are about sharing concerns, difficulties, and dilemmas that matter. That's hard for a lot of people, and the physical and emotional changes of adolescence don't make it any easier. But values aren't just hard to talk about; they're hard to act on. Doing anything worthwhile usually entails some frustration, tedium, and heartbreak. Playing football means risking miserable losses, enduring grueling practices, and maybe tearing a ligament. Becoming an engineer means doing endless problem sets and spending hours making things that never work. Having a best friend means inviting the possibility of losing a best friend. Although no one wants these kinds of pain, avoiding pain also means avoiding what's meaningful in life. The next chapter's activities help students develop the willingness to struggle so they're empowered to act in accordance with their values.

Chapter 5

• • • • •

WILLINGNESS

Empower Students to Serve Their Values Even When It's Hard

If values are so great, why is it so hard to live by them? According to authors JoAnne Dahl, Jennifer Plumb, Ian Stewart, and Tobias Lundgren (2009), some of the traps that make it difficult for people to live in accordance with their values are:

- Sticking with a pattern of behavior that has worked in the past, even if it doesn't work in the present ("I've never had to study for French tests before" or "I've always teased Makaela about her weight; that's just how we *are* with each other")

- Wanting to feel good in the short term while ignoring long-term consequences ("I don't know why we were throwing the football in the hall" or "Forget French class; it's a nice day, and I'm going outside" or "I'm not homophobic or anything; it was just a joke")

- Avoiding unwanted feelings like shame, fear, frustration, and boredom ("I can't ask for help with my essay because it's too embarrassing" or "When I start to feel more confident, I'll start raising my hand in math" or "Studying without Ritalin is impossibly boring")

- Getting stuck in a particular image of themselves ("I'm a private person, so I don't share details of my life with my teachers" or "If I want to get into Middlebury, I need to get straight As, whatever that takes" or "Serious dancers don't really have time to hang out with their friends")

- Going along with social expectations ("Everybody says *retarded*" or "I have to take these classes if I want my transcript to look good")

- Rigidly pursuing a particular outcome instead of flexibly pursuing values (popularity at the expense of friendship, grades at the expense of learning, having a boyfriend at the expense of relating)

Notice that a particular form of behavior might serve any, or several, of these functions. Imagine that Bryce starts skipping gym class. Maybe he's doing it because his friends say gym is pointless and they're skipping too. Maybe he doesn't think of himself as the kind of student who needs to be in gym because he plays a lot of basketball after school. Maybe he hates getting sweaty and smelly without enough time to shower afterward. Maybe he's failing history and wants to use the time to study. Maybe he's staying up late to study and is using gym time to rest. If you were Bryce's teacher and wanted to help him live in accordance with his values, you'd need to learn what his values are, why he's behaving inconsistently with them (maybe he isn't), and how he can get out of some of the traps he might have set for himself.

These traps might not feel like traps in the moment. Skipping class, getting attention, throwing a football around, feeling powerful, not feeling embarrassed—all of these behaviors might feel great! Asking students to accept painful thoughts and feelings might sound sadistic to teachers who entered the profession because they want students to be happy and successful, but as author Mark Manson (2014) puts it:

> Nothing is pleasurable or uplifting all of the time. So the question becomes: what struggle or sacrifice are you willing to tolerate? Ultimately, what determines our ability to stick with something we care about is our ability to handle the rough patches and ride out the inevitable rotten days.

Psychology professor and author Steven Hayes (2005) distinguishes between wanting and being willing. When we want something, we seek it out, enjoy having it, and miss it if it goes away. Maybe your students want longer vacations, candy in the cafeteria, and spa treatments in the bathrooms. Willingness is different. If Bryce says he's *willing* to stay after school on Thursday afternoons to meet with his history teacher for extra help, he might not mean he *wants* to stay after school. He'd probably rather go home, play basketball, and maybe get in a nap before dinner. Despite that, Bryce might be willing to stay late because learning history thoroughly is something he values, and the extra help serves that value.

Becoming more aware of their values allows students to make a meaningful choice: stopping, saying no, going home—or willingly doing the work that matters to them. This chapter's activities help students develop that willingness to work for their values.

Singing Your Shoulds

Some students get so attached to unhelpful images of what they think they should be—wealthy, attractive, smart, popular, or cool—that they act against their values. For example, while it's healthy to want to achieve academically, some students get so attached to the thought that they should be getting an A that they study all night, pay a tutor, plagiarize, avoid challenging classes, cry over an A–, or give up after a C–. But students can learn to *have* thoughts like, "I should be getting an A" without letting those thoughts control them.

One way to decrease the power of unhelpful thoughts is to sing them (Blackledge, 2015; Harris, 2009; Luoma, Hayes, & Walser, 2007; Turrell & Bell, 2016). Singing *should* messages makes them sound a little silly and allows us to examine them without taking them too seriously. After singing, students can have a conversation about how they want to behave in the context of their shoulds *and* their values.

The sample script here uses messages about grades, but you can use it with any unhelpful message about what students are told they should be. Try this activity once students have developed some comfort with each other, and repeat it as often as you see fit.

Materials for Each Student

Students need no materials for this activity.

Sample Script

The following sample script gives an idea of how this activity might work in your classroom.

Today we're going to talk about grades. What kinds of thoughts go through your head when you get a really high grade? (*Listens for language that indicates positive or negative self-judgments or judgments of others and writes these thoughts on the board. For example, students might say a high grade makes them think that their parents will be happy, they're smart, they're proud of their hard work, the assignment was easy, or they want to tell their friends.*)

How about a really low grade, whatever a low grade is for you? (*Listens for any kind of judgment and writes the thoughts on the board. Students might say a low grade makes them think that their parents will be angry, the assignment was unfair, they should have studied harder, they want to find out what everyone else got, or they're embarrassed.*)

It seems like grades are measuring a lot more than how much you learned. Who sometimes gets caught up in these kinds of judgments? Who has friends who get caught up in these judgments? What do you notice yourself thinking you should be?

What happens when we get caught up in these shoulds? (*Leads a discussion about the effects of getting caught up in judgments, positive or negative; these may include missing opportunities to learn, taking few creative risks, ignoring other responsibilities and relationships, cheating, losing sleep, taking stimulants, or deliberately harming themselves.*)

It sounds like these judgments aren't necessarily helpful. But it's also normal to have these judgments about the grades we think we should get, and to get stuck in those judgments. Is there anything we can do with those judgmental thoughts besides get stuck in them?

Today we're going to try something a little weird. Who's up for something a little weird? Are you sure? Because this will be incredibly embarrassing if I have to do it all by myself. You'll join me? Okay, here we go. (*Sings to the tune of "Row, Row, Row Your Boat."*)

A, A, A, A plus.
B, B minus, B.
C, C minus, C, C minus.
D, D, D, D, D.

(Sings one line at a time so students can repeat and learn; continues until the group learns the song and everyone is singing together.)

Shall we try it in a round? *(Divides the students into two groups. Starts the first group off, and when the first group gets to "B, B minus, B," the second group begins the song. Continues encouraging the singing until the group has overcome the awkwardness and starts laughing, getting loud, swaying, dancing, doing the wave—or has been singing for long enough that the lyrics have become just words.)*

What did you notice as you were singing? *(Draws attention to changes in affect, such as a feeling of lightness or a sense of silliness.)* What happened to your shoulds about grades as you were singing the song?

Would you be willing to try singing the song—in your head or even aloud—the next time you get a grade?

What do grades mean? What *else* can a grade mean? Who decides what grades will mean for you?

Follow-Up

The point of this activity isn't to change students' thoughts about grades; it's to take away some of the power of those thoughts so students have more power to choose their actions. Students can think, "I should have gotten a better grade!" and decide to keep trying new things, making mistakes, taking care of themselves, balancing their schoolwork with their family and social lives, and showing honesty and integrity when it comes to their academics.

The best way to follow up on this activity is simply to repeat it as often as seems necessary. Have your students sing about grades just before getting back any test or quiz or a report card. Make singing a tradition, but vary it a little. Change the style. Use exaggeratedly low or high voices. Add hand motions, dance steps, or props. The silliness is what makes this activity work, so keep changing the style so it stays weird.

Variations

This activity doesn't have to be about grades. What messages are your students getting—from you, from the school, from each other, or from wider society—about what they should have or be? You can do the singing activity with anything: colleges they think they should get into, brands they think they should buy, sizes they think they should fit into, teams they think they should make—whatever achievements your students fixate on that keep them from acting in accordance with their values.

You can use a melody the students like, perhaps from a popular song. But since the point of this activity isn't the singing itself but rather taking away some of the power of judgmental messages, another way to do it would be to have students say should messages in the voice of a cartoon character or celebrity that they don't take too seriously. Again, when students start to laugh or get silly in the presence of what was previously a serious thought, they've expanded what that thought means and can respond to it in a wider variety of ways (Wilson & Murrell, 2004). The thought *I should be getting better grades* becomes less domineering, and the student doesn't have to obey it. Instead, the student can choose what would be most important for him or her to do.

Yet another way to take away the power of judgments is to bring the students' mental images of what they should be into the physical world by drawing them. Who is this *A student* they think they should be? What is *A student* wearing, carrying, and saying? What about *B student* or *C student*? Creating a cartoon panel—complete with speech bubbles, thought bubbles, and labels for every object—allows students to distance themselves from these images. They can still work hard and get good grades, but they don't have to be *A student*. Drawings can be posted in lockers, taped into notebooks, folded into wallets, and in other ways saved so students have a reminder of the person they don't have to choose to be.

Challenges

Sometimes this activity offends people; they think it makes fun of their hard work and pain. If students expresses offense, we recommend apologizing and explaining that the purpose of the activity is not to belittle their experiences but to take away some of the power of their shoulds so they have more room to notice everything *else* in their lives and respond in a values-consistent way. They can still work hard, set goals, and aim high—but flexibly and in the service of their values instead of rigidly serving a should.

Passengers on the Bus

It's normal and natural to have *I can't because* thoughts—beliefs about ourselves and the world that hold us back from doing what we value. We have names for some of these struggles, such as *math anxiety*, *writer's block*, *stage fright*, and the *bystander effect*. These are all moments when our thoughts interfere with our behaviors. Learning to accept these thoughts helps students choose values-consistent actions and take responsibility for their choices (Luciano, Salas, Martinez, Ruiz, & Blarrina, 2009).

Passengers on the Bus (originated by Hayes, Strosahl, & Wilson, 1999) is an activity for overcoming these barriers. We adapted this version to use in classrooms and to give students a visual tool to help them accept unpleasant thoughts and feelings that can get in their way. The sample script uses Passengers on the Bus to address a bullying problem, but you can use it to address any situation where students are avoiding values-consistent action.

Materials for Each Student

For this activity, each student will need a pen, notebook, tape, the "I Can't Because" handout (figure 5.1, page 86) or something similar, and the "Passengers on the Bus" handout (figure 5.2, page 86).

1. **Beliefs about myself:**
   - I can't because . . . I'm too shy.
   - I can't because . . . I'm not smart enough.
   - I can't because . . . I'm just not the kind of person who does that kind of thing.
   - I can't because . . . it's not my business.
   - I can't because . . . I'm already under too much stress.

2. **Beliefs about what others might think, say, or do:**
   - I can't because . . . people will think I'm annoying.
   - I can't because . . . people will laugh at me.
   - I can't because . . . someone will get back at me.
   - I can't because . . . my parents will be disappointed.
   - I can't because . . . I'll get in trouble.

3. **Beliefs about the situation:**
   - I can't because . . . no one will listen to me.
   - I can't because . . . things will just go back to the way they were.
   - I can't because . . . I'll just make it worse.
   - I can't because . . . it'll take way too long.
   - I can't because . . . it'll cost too much money.

Figure 5.1: "I Can't Because" handout.

*Visit **go.SolutionTree.com/instruction** for a free reproducible version of this figure.*

Figure 5.2: "Passengers on the Bus" handout.

*Visit **go.SolutionTree.com/instruction** for a free reproducible version of this figure.*

Sample Script

The following sample script gives an idea of how this activity might work in your classroom.

Today I'm going to ask you to think about something that might make you a little uncomfortable. I'm going to ask you to remember the last time you saw someone bothering someone else—maybe making the person feel bad, giving unwanted attention, or even intimidating someone—and you could have done something to stop it, but you didn't do anything. Just to be clear, there might have been times when you've seen things you *couldn't* have done anything about because you would have put your physical safety at risk. That's not what I'm asking about. I'm asking you to think of a time when you saw something you *could* have done something to stop, but you didn't do anything. (*Checks for understanding and gives an example if necessary.*)

Once you think of the last time that happened, take a few minutes to relive the situation. I won't ask you to share, but try to picture it. Where were you? Who were you with? What happened?

Now I'm going to ask you to list all the reasons you didn't do anything in that moment. Just write them in your notebook. I'll write my reasons on the board, but yours will be totally private. I'm not going to ask you to share, and in fact, I'm going to ask you to *not* share because this is personal. (*Silently writes reasons on the board to serve as a model while students privately write their own reasons.*)

It turns out that there are several kinds of barriers to action. (*Shows or distributes the "I Can't Because" handout [figure 5.1] and reviews the barriers. If possible, explains how some of the reasons on the board fit into the categories. For example, "I was scared I'd get made fun of" would fit into "Beliefs about what others might think, say, or do." Students can discuss the barrier types, analyze the teacher's barriers, and ask questions, but should be reminded not to share their own.*)

We sometimes see our reasons for avoiding action as external. We say we don't have the time, resources, or support. We don't always realize how many of these barriers are inside us. When we really think about it, though, some of the barriers we call external are internal. Sometimes, the things we see as impossible are just hard or unfamiliar. As you continue to think about the reasons you didn't take action in that moment, go through these different kinds of barriers. Maybe they'll help you think of more reasons you didn't take action. (*Continues to list reasons on the board to serve as a model for students.*)

As I said, I'm not going to ask you to share your list. But I am going to ask if anyone wants to share how it felt to make this list. (*Validates all feelings, which often include guilt, shame, and self-doubt, and sometimes include relief because listing barriers can make them feel more surmountable.*)

Sometimes, listing all these barriers can make people feel stuck. Would anyone like to learn a way to overcome internal barriers? (*Waits for students to give assent, and then hands out the "Passengers on the Bus" handout in figure 5.2.*)

Imagine that this bus represents your life. First, draw yourself in the driver's seat because you decide where the bus of your life goes.

The person who sits in that front seat next to the driver is sometimes responsible for helping the driver figure out where to go. You might think of that seat as the navigator's seat. In life, the navigators that help us figure out where we want to go are our values. So in that navigator's seat, write some of the values that lead you to care about the fact that a person was threatened. *(If necessary, provides "Examples of Values" handout [page 214] to help students remember words for their values.)*

Now, imagine that all of the *I can't because* statements that you listed are noisy passengers on the bus of your life. They're shouting at you, trying to keep you from driving where you truly want to go. Mine are saying things like, "Everyone will make fun of you!" and "Nothing you say is going to make a difference!" *(Gives more personal examples based on what's written on the board.)* In the windows of your bus, draw these passengers. Make speech bubbles to show what they're saying to you. And again, please keep your buses private.

The next time you encounter a situation where you have the power and ability to do something, and you begin to hear your *I can't because* statements, try thinking of them as passengers on your bus. Are noisy passengers annoying? Is it fun to drive a bus with a bunch of screaming passengers on it? But what happens if you listen to the passengers and believe what they're telling you? Do you hit the brakes? Steer off course? Turn the bus around or head a different way? Who's the driver?

What would it mean to just notice the passengers—to wave in the rearview mirror and keep driving in the direction of your values?

Take a few pieces of tape *(distributes tape)*, and tape your bus into your notebook, or your locker, or wherever you might want a reminder that you don't have to obey your passengers.

Follow-Up

You can show your class the animated version of Passengers on a Bus that psychologist Joe Oliver (2013) created. We recommend doing the activity first and then reinforcing the message with the video in order to give students an opportunity to notice their own barriers and visualize them as passengers.

Since some barriers are truly external, you might follow Passengers on the Bus with a discussion of how students can overcome external barriers by growing their support networks. They can list family members, friends, and allies who can help them find creative solutions, provide resources (time, money, or knowledge), or just listen with compassion. Recruiting support is a strength; people who make positive changes in themselves and the world do not act alone.

Variations

This particular script involves bullying situations, but Passengers on the Bus works in any situation where students avoid values-consistent action because they're letting their thoughts boss them around.

If you find that students aren't doing their homework, studying for tests, revising their writing, asking for help, or avoiding some other behavior that might feel uncomfortable but would serve their values, Passengers on the Bus could work. It could also help them manage any performance anxiety they might feel in your class: "I can't play goalie because . . ." or "I can't take this test because . . ." or "I can't read Shakespeare because . . . ."

The examples in figure 5.1 (page 86) won't work in every context. Few students would say, "I can't practice my instrument because my parents will be disappointed," and saying, "I can't take this test because no one will listen to me" makes no sense! We encourage you to write internal barrier examples that fit the situation you're asking your students to think about.

You could also incorporate this activity into your curriculum. For example, a history teacher could ask students to imagine the passengers that historical figures like Chief Joseph, Ida B. Wells, and César Chávez carried on their buses—and notice where these men and women drove anyway. A health and human development teacher could do Passengers on the Bus to help students think about the kinds of temptations they will encounter from peers. An English teacher could ask students to find passages in novels where characters faced different kinds of barriers and discuss whether the characters heeded their passengers or their values at different points in the story. Students could imagine the passengers on the buses of famous scientists and mathematicians who struggled and sometimes failed in their work.

In mental health settings, therapists sometimes have groups act out Passengers on the Bus. One person plays the part of the driver while the other group members play the passengers, shouting thoughts from their seats. While pretending to be passengers can be powerful in therapy, we advise against having students do this at school because of privacy issues. However, if you're asking students to imagine the passengers that a book character or historical figure carries, they might enjoy acting out the passengers and then find it easier to imagine and acknowledge their own passengers—and keep driving in a valued direction.

Challenges

A student might ask, "Can't you just kick the passengers off the bus?" In real life, a driver certainly can ask unruly passengers to get off the bus, but these metaphorical passengers are our own thoughts. Research on thought suppression tells us that the more we try to get rid of a thought, the more the thought persists (Hooper, Saunders, & McHugh, 2010; Najmi & Wegner, 2008; Wegner & Erber, 1992; Wegner, Schneider, Carter, & White, 1987). You can explain to your students that it's impossible to kick our own thoughts out of our heads, but it is possible to accept them as part of us without letting them control our actions.

Students might resist the idea that their thoughts don't control them. If that happens, try asking them questions: "Is it possible to think *I must eat that ice cream* and not eat it? Can you let yourself have the thought that the ice cream would be so cool, sweet, and chocolatey and still not eat it? If you try to distract yourself, does that make the ice cream less delicious? So when distraction doesn't work, what can you do? 'Hello, passenger on the bus! Nice to see you! Thanks for the reminder of how delicious the ice cream is! Yes, it sure is sweet and chocolatey!' Do you have to eat it?"

Finally, Passengers on the Bus is designed to help people develop the willingness to accept uncomfortable thoughts in the service of their values—not to accept pain for its own sake, not to accept oppressive circumstances, and not to risk their health or safety. Some students might need reminders that the activity's purpose is noticing whether their thoughts are useful. A thought like *I might get beaten up* is extremely useful. Just as many passengers are courteous to bus drivers, many of our thoughts help us. Seeing thoughts as passengers on the buses of their lives reminds students who's driving and helps them choose how they want to behave when these thoughts come up.

On Your Plate

This activity helps students link their struggles to their values and decide how they want to relate to the people, tasks, and events that are stressing them out. Use it at the end of a term, right before a holiday, when applications are due, during tryout season, before a high-stakes test, or any other busy time of year.

Materials for Each Student

For this activity, each student will need a paper plate, black marker or pen, and markers or pens in other colors.

Sample Script

The following sample script gives an idea of how this activity might work in your classroom.

> This time of year, there's a lot on our plates. Let's think about what our plates actually look like. (*Distributes paper plates and black markers.*)
>
> I'd like you to think about some of the things you're struggling with this week. They could be school related, like tests or projects or teachers or classes in general. They could be social dynamics with certain friends or groups, or people you like. Or hate. You might be struggling with certain situations at home, maybe involving certain family members and their issues. Some of us struggle with issues related to our health, with drugs and alcohol, with different kinds of pressures on us. Some of us are struggling with feelings of loss, grief, and isolation. So think about the things you're struggling with and write them on your plate. And kind of spread them out so there's space around each one.
>
> Now we're going to do something a little weird. I'd like you to imagine that each of your struggles is an actual food on your plate. If it were a food, what food would it be? You might think of certain struggles as connected to each other, and if they are, you might choose foods

that go together in some way. Some struggles might take up a giant portion of your plate. Some might not take up a lot of space but are really intense. Write what food each struggle is. You could even draw the food, so you can see the size and shape of it on your plate. (*Circulates as students write their foods and helps students think of foods as necessary.*)

So, this is the meal that life has served you this week. What are you planning on eating? Who has something on your plate that you plan on just leaving there? (*Pauses for students to raise their hands.*) Anyone want to share what you plan to leave on your plate? What is something in your life that you'll just let be? (*Waits a moment so students can share but doesn't urge them to.*)

Also, even if something isn't your favorite food, you can still eat it, right? Who has a food on your plate that you wouldn't look forward to eating? (*Pauses for students to raise their hands.*) But could you still eat it? Anyone want to share why you'd eat a food on your plate, even if you don't like it? And what about the struggle it represents? Can you share why you think it's worthwhile to engage with this struggle, even if you don't enjoy it?

Who has a food on your plate that you just want to wolf down, so it's not on your plate anymore? (*Pauses for students to raise their hands.*) Focus on that food for a moment. What would it be like if instead of wolfing this food down, you savored it? Imagine yourself eating this food slowly, as if you're really curious about it. Imagine the flavor. The texture. The temperature. And now, what could happen if you were to slow down and savor the thing this food represents? What might you learn?

And now, who has a food on your plate that you wish tasted better? (*Pauses for students to raise their hands.*) If we get served something and we're not excited about the taste, we can make it taste better by adding things, like soy sauce or hot sauce or jam. Take a different color pen (*distributes pens*) and, next to the foods on your plate that you don't like, write what you would add to that food to make it taste even a little bit better. Maybe it's parmesan cheese or syrup. Depends on your personal taste and on the food, right?

Let's do some sharing. Tell us about the actual foods and what you'd add. If I had to eat burnt toast, I would add strawberry jam. What about you? (*Students share what they wrote.*)

Now comes the hard part. If my burnt toast represents having to take my car in for repairs, what in life is the jam I can put on that toast? Well, maybe I can strike up a conversation with the mechanic and get to know her a little better. Maybe while I wait for my car to get fixed, I can read an article I've been meaning to read. Maybe I can ask to watch my car get fixed and learn something about how my car works. That'd be sort of interesting. See if you can think creatively about what you can do to add the jam to your burnt toast or put hot sauce on your soggy eggs, or whatever it is you would add to the foods you don't like. And if you think of something, write it on your plate in that colored pen.

Would anyone like to share a struggle and what you could add to make it better? (*See figure 5.3 [page 92].*)

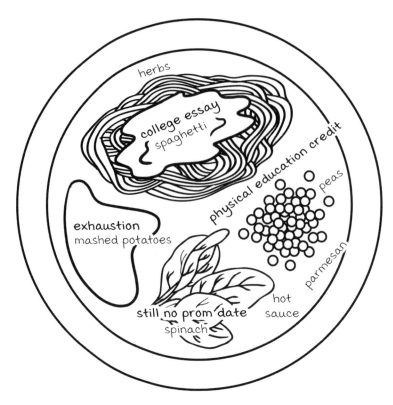

Figure 5.3: Example plate.

Follow-Up

We've found the plate metaphor to be highly extendable. If you want to help students notice the power and responsibility inherent in committing to their actions, you can ask, "Who's doing the eating?" If you want them to notice patterns in their struggles, you can ask, "What did you eat last week? What's on the menu this week? Are you facing the same kinds of struggles over and over, or is there always something new for you to deal with?" Some students might identify a pattern, like being unable to manage long-term projects or constantly attending to a friend who's seeking attention. Of those who identify patterns, you can ask, "What did you do the last time you were served this food?" and then ask more questions to help them assess the workability of their behavior and try new behaviors that might better serve their values. For example, you might say, "It sounds like you're pushing that asparagus around your plate every time. What if you gobbled it up this time?" Or, "That mushroom your friend keeps putting on your plate—what would happen if you left it there?" If you want to bring in the idea that they can choose their qualities of action, you can ask, "*How* do you want to eat these foods?" If they ask what you mean, you can give examples such as appreciatively, carefully, or inventively and then ask, "What would be an inventive way to eat boiled carrots? And if the boiled carrots represent your science homework, what would be an inventive way to do that homework?"

Writing and drawing on paper plates is intentionally playful; turning their struggles into physical objects allows students to step back from them, notice their features, relate to them in new and interesting ways, and make decisions about them. The decisions themselves will be hard. Students can discuss, as a whole class or in pairs, how their struggles are connected to their values and how much energy they're willing to put into difficult, frustrating, and otherwise unpleasant tasks. They can make and share commitments to values-consistent behaviors, and they can use each other as a support system to solve problems or cheer each other on.

You can also follow up with individual students about their struggles. Simply asking questions like, "What happened to that overcooked broccoli that was on your plate?" or, "Did you end up sprinkling some oregano on that cold pizza?" reminds your students that you care about them and provides them with more opportunities to notice their behaviors, make values-consistent decisions, and develop greater willingness to struggle.

Variations

Food on a plate is a metaphor that pretty much everyone can understand, and the expression *on my plate* is already a metaphor for the obligations in our lives. Still, lots of other metaphors would help students relate differently to their struggles, and maybe you can think of metaphors specific to your population or even your curriculum: animals in a forest, players on a basketball court, or even features of a geometry diagram. (That last one might be a stretch, but maybe not.)

You could do On Your Plate with struggles that specifically relate to your class. For example, in a mathematics class, what concepts or algorithms are students struggling with? If those concepts or algorithms were foods, what foods would they be?

Sharing allows classmates to hear each other's struggles and get support as they face their own, but you might not think your students are ready for these discussions. In that case, you can have them write responses to some of the prompts on the backs of their plates.

Challenges

While food works as a metaphor because everyone understands it, food is also a source of enormous stress for some students. Those dealing with food insecurity might become angry or upset at the suggestion that they don't have to eat everything on their plates. Those who have been taught that it's morally wrong or disrespectful to leave food over might resist the idea that eating a particular food is a choice. Those with eating disorders, obesity, or allergies might find this activity painful. Those whose cultural or religious traditions make their diets different from their friends' might find that this exercise magnifies those differences.

The issues students have with food are themselves struggles—ones they must learn to accommodate in order to survive. While you might be tempted to avoid the food metaphor because you don't want to bring up all the stress that comes along with thinking about food, the ways students manage their food issues might illuminate how they can deal with other struggles in their lives. If a student needs help addressing food-related struggles, this activity could reveal that need, and if a student is struggling in other ways, the underlying cause could be a food-related struggle. This activity creates an opportunity for you to learn about these struggles and to connect the student with sources of help.

Some students might resist the idea that they can do anything to make a difficult struggle manageable. It's important to validate the fact that, for example, the toast is still burnt. The struggle isn't going to be fun. But is there anything that makes it even a little bit more manageable? And even if there's nothing that can make the struggle more palatable—no metaphorical jam to put on the metaphorical toast—you can still ask, "Why is this struggle worthwhile?"

Accepting struggle, sacrifice, and pain is *not* the same as accepting injustice in schools. Bullying, underfunding, high-stakes testing, opportunity gaps, discrimination, harassment, violence—we are not suggesting that students should accept whatever they encounter. Rather, we are suggesting that students can increase their willingness to experience thoughts and feelings that might not feel pleasant but that go along with values-consistent action.

For example, Jamie is a ninth grader who loves to share her creative ideas, but some of her peers respond by rolling their eyes or snickering. When she posts her poems and artwork to her social media pages, these too get sarcastic comments. At this point, not only has Jamie stopped posting her poems and artwork; she's writing and drawing less often. She's also participating much less in class. Jamie has a few friends, but they're not in any of her classes and all have busy schedules after school, so they don't always get back to her when she reaches out. She cares about them and wants to be close to them, but she's begun to wonder if they even like her or if they're making mean comments behind her back. She still sits with them at lunch but doesn't talk much. Jamie has actually counted school days until graduation even though it's three years away, and she often tells her mother that she can't go to school because of the anxiety she feels every time she walks into the building.

Clearly, Jamie should be able to come to school without the threat of getting eye rolls and snickers. The trouble is, she's associated her anxious feelings not only with the students who are mocking her but also with making art, writing poetry, participating in class, spending time with her friends, and generally being at school. Her strategy of avoiding anything that might make her feel anxious is leading her to avoid doing things that matter to her. Terminating her social media accounts and reporting bullying behaviors seem like healthy avoidance moves. But if she avoids every activity in which she starts to feel anxious— if she refuses all the food on her plate—she starts to sacrifice the meaning and vitality she gets from art, poetry, friendship, and school.

As teachers, we can help our students decide whether avoiding certain people and situations is worthwhile or whether that avoidance would interfere with valued living.

Your Willingness

Modeling willingness for our students means telling them what's important to us and then talking about how our own *shoulds, can'ts,* and *don't want tos* stop us from doing what matters. It's hard to share our pain and acknowledge struggle even when we do so in private, and in these activities, we're talking to a room full of people who see us as experts and authority figures. Leading a willingness activity is itself an act of willingness! We can express, for ourselves and our students, the difficulty of relating differently to our thoughts—even our thoughts about the activity itself—and that we ourselves get stuck in unhelpful thoughts and don't always choose values-consistent behaviors. Despite that, we persist and learn from the results of our efforts, and our students need to see what that looks like if they're going to do it too. Sure, it's hard. If we wanted easy, would we have become teachers?

From Willingness to Empathy

This chapter is about helping students willingly accept the struggles that come along with valued living. The playful activities "disrupt ordinary meaning functions of language" (Hayes, Strosahl, & Wilson, 1999, p. 74): *I should be getting better grades* is just a song lyric, *I can't try out for the play* is just a noisy passenger on a bus, and an *impossible science project* is just food on a plate. The thoughts themselves don't change, but the way students relate to their thoughts—what the thoughts *mean*—does change. When they can learn to relate differently to their thoughts and feelings, students have more choices about how to respond. They can obey the thoughts, which might or might not help them. They can avoid doing things that bring up these thoughts and feelings, which often means avoiding their values too, or more positively, they can willingly accept *shoulds*, *can'ts*, *don't want tos*, and other unpleasant thoughts and feelings as normal parts of committing to values-consistent action.

One important way students can use their willingness to have difficult thoughts and emotions is in the context of their relationships with each other. The next chapter is about how students can notice and overcome judgmental thoughts about each other, imagine each other's perspectives, and treat each other with kindness—not simply because these are school rules but because behaving kindly and compassionately is part of living in accordance with their values.

EMPOW**E**R

Chapter 6

● ● ● ● ●

EMPATHY

Empower Students to Treat Each Other According to Their Values

As much as we want our schools to be oases of caring and compassion, our students' behavior stems from a larger social context that includes judging and labeling, which over time can culminate in prejudice, discrimination, bullying, and outright violence. These behaviors are pervasive in our culture and require very little training to learn (Hayes, Barnes-Holmes, & Roche, 2001). Meanwhile, students learn how to be nice and polite without confronting their feelings and biases, understanding one another, or deciding how they want to treat each other.

Character education programs are useful, especially when they train specific prosocial behaviors using positive reinforcement (Berkowitz & Bier, 2005, for example) and include system-level approaches (Sugai et al., 2000). We might hope that treating each other with kindness and understanding would become enough of a reward for students to sustain these behaviors without needing contrived reinforcers like praise, awards, class parties, special privileges, and higher grades. The problem with rewards like these is that the behaviors might stop as soon as the rewards do. We see this from time to time. Students are perfectly pleasant in the classroom when they think it counts, and then they make mean or offensive comments in the hallways, on the bus, and online.

This chapter's activities are not necessarily to increase or reduce any particular set of behaviors, or even to make students change their behavior at all; it's to help them discover why they might *want* to behave kindly to their classmates and how they might do that.

Shifting Your Judgments

This activity helps students notice judgmental thoughts and still act with kindness and understanding. It involves students writing (but not sharing) negative judgments about their peers. Some groups will find this activity powerful, and other groups won't be able to handle keeping their judgments secret after they leave the room. We recommend doing this activity late in the year, after you've established trust and respect in the classroom, so that it doesn't turn into an opportunity for relational aggression and instead becomes an opportunity for students to notice their own judgments of others and choose behaviors that reflect their values.

Materials for Each Student

For this activity, each student will need a pen, the "Sentence Building" handout (figure 6.1), and the "Examples of Values" handout (page 214).

1	2	3	4	5	6	7
		annoying				
		mean				
		pathetic				
		stupid				
		creepy				

Figure 6.1: "Sentence Building" handout.

Visit go.SolutionTree.com/instruction for a free reproducible version of this figure.

Sample Script

The following sample script gives an idea of how this activity might work in your classroom.

When you were younger, did you ever do one of those sentence-building exercises? Maybe it started with "The cat slept" and you expanded it into "The orange cat slept" and then "The orange cat slept peacefully"? And you eventually had something like "The enormous orange cat slept peacefully on the soft, fluffy bed while I had to clean up the milk it knocked over." Today's activity is sort of like that. (*Distributes the "Sentence Building" handout [figure 6.1] and draws the first row of the chart on the board to use as a model.*)

Before we begin, I need to stress the importance of being totally silent and not sharing what you write on your sheet. You probably noticed that column three of your chart has some adjectives: *annoying*, *mean*, *pathetic*, *stupid*, and *creepy*. This might feel a little strange for some of you, because adults have probably told you at some point in your life not to use words like these to describe people. And I'm going to ask you to use these words to describe people. But absolutely not out loud. Does everyone think they have the self-control to do that? (*Waits for students to assent and stops the activity if anyone says no.*)

In each of the boxes in column three, above each word, you're going to write the name of a person who you would describe with that word, and you're also going to write *is*. For example, if I think my cousin Lia is annoying, then I would write the words *Lia is* in the box with the word *annoying* (*demonstrates on the board*), and I end up with *Lia is annoying* in that box. Again, please do not share the names you write. (*Students fill in their boxes. They don't have to fill in a box if they feel like it's wrong to do so or can't think of anyone they'd describe with the word in it.*)

Without sharing what you wrote, does anyone want to share how it felt to write it? (*Students might share feelings of guilt, satisfaction, relief, or other emotions. Validates as normal any student feelings.*)

Now, in each box in column two, you're going to write the words *I'm making the judgment that*. I know it might seem a little tedious to write these same words over and over, and some of you might want to take a shortcut by just writing it in the top box and then drawing an arrow. I'm going to ask you not to do that, and actually write out *I'm making the judgment that* each time. (*Waits until students have started to write in their charts, and then adds to the sentence on the board so it now says, for example,* I'm making the judgment that Lia is annoying. *Waiting to write the example sentence allows the students to discover for themselves that they're making judgments.*)

What happens when you add the words *I'm making the judgment that* to your sentences? (*Validates all feelings and reminds students not to share the sentence itself.*)

In each box in column one, I'm going to ask you to write the words *I notice*. Again, I know it's a little tedious to write the same words over and over, but please do it. (*Waits until students are writing and then adds to the sentence on the board so it now says, for example,* I notice I'm making the judgment that Lia is annoying.)

What happens when you add the words *I notice*?

When you notice something happening in your mind, you're not on autopilot. You might agree with the thought, or you might not, but the thought isn't controlling you anymore. Instead of your thought being in charge, you are. You can still make choices based on your judgments, but you've opened up new possibilities, too. In each box of that skinny middle column, you're going to write the word *and*. That *and* means there can be more to the story than your judgments. It shows what the new possibilities can be.

In each box in column five, write *I can approach her*, *I can approach him*, or *I can approach them*. (*Demonstrates and then provides the "Examples of Values" handout [page 214] as students are writing.*)

I've just given you a list of adverbs that describe qualities of action that some people think are important. Look them over carefully. Circle ones that are most important to you when you think about how you want to act toward others. You can also add your own.

Put at least one of the adverbs you just circled, or one you think of yourself, into each box in column six. For Lia, I'm going to write *kindly*. (*Demonstrates on the board.*) You can use the same adverb more than once, and you can put more than one adverb in the same box. (*Checks to make sure students understand how to fill in their boxes correctly.*)

How did that feel?

Take a few silent moments to think about the people whose names you've written on your paper. What are their lives like? Do you really know? Can you imagine how each of them might be struggling? Can you imagine what they might need? (*Pauses between questions to give students time to think about each one.*)

Without sharing who the person is, and without giving clues that will make it obvious who you're talking about, does anyone want to share what you think one of the people on your paper might need?

What's it like to think about that?

I've said I can approach Lia kindly, but what exactly can I do to approach her kindly? How might she need me to treat her kindly today or this week? Well, she just started a new job in a new city, and maybe she'd want to talk about that. So maybe I can approach her kindly (*writes on the board*) *by calling to ask how her new job is going*. In each box in column seven, write the word *by* and then add a single, specific action you can take today or in the near future to behave in the way you value. (*Coaches students who need help and answers questions.*)

You've finally finished building your sentences. My first one says *I notice I'm making the judgment that Lia is annoying, and I can approach her kindly by calling to ask how her new job is going*. Read each of yours silently to yourself. How did that feel? (*Validates all responses; see figure 6.2.*)

1	2	3	4	5	6	7
I notice	I'm making the judgment that	Lia is annoying	and	I can approach her	kindly	by calling to ask how her new job is going.

Figure 6.2: Sample completed sentence.

One more step. Fold your paper in half, right through that skinny middle column four, and so the words are on the outside. (*Demonstrates.*) Now open the paper up again. Look at how everything on the left half involves thoughts inside your head. Those thoughts are invisible unless you decide to say them out loud or act on them. (*Pauses.*) And look at how everything on the right half involves actions in the world. The *and* in the middle shows that you can *have* the thoughts without necessarily *acting* on them. I can have the thought that Lia is annoying without avoiding her, making fun of her, or complaining about her. You can have your thoughts and act on your values.

> To symbolize this idea that our thoughts are invisible and our actions are visible, fold the paper back in half. (*Demonstrates.*) Put it down so you only see the right side. All I see is *I can approach her kindly by calling her to ask how her new job is going*. And I can!
>
> Would anyone like to share just your right-side sentence? How did it feel to say it out loud?
>
> How did it feel to hear your classmates' sentences?
>
> One last thing. Carefully tear the paper in half along the fold you made. Hand me the left side so I can shred it for you, and feel free to keep the right side as a reminder of what you want to do.

Follow-Up

After the activity, collect the left sides of students' papers, making sure you have them all, and either shred or recycle them in a bin that no student has access to. It would be incredibly painful for a student to have his or her paper discovered, or to find his or her name written on someone else's paper.

After a few days, you can ask your students if they tried any of the behaviors they put in column seven of their charts. What was it like? In many cases, the behaviors will not be all that rewarding in the short term. If I call up someone I find annoying, I'll probably get off the phone feeling annoyed, wondering why I bothered and resolving not to bother in the future. Students might say they felt frustrated, afraid, or angry. You can ask, "How do you feel about yourself after acting on your values? How do you think the other person felt, even if he or she didn't show it? What did that person possibly need that you gave him or her?"

Other students might say they didn't try their behaviors and don't plan to. You can continue to validate the students' feelings. Of course it's unpleasant to interact with people we find annoying or mean. What was *not* doing the behavior like? Was it a choice? Or was the judgmental thought in charge? What kind of life do we build for ourselves if we act only on our judgmental thoughts? What kind of life do we build when we act on our values? What happens when we think about the other person's needs? Helping students keep connecting their actions back to their values can provide the source of reinforcement they need to continue these behaviors even if they're aversive in the short term.

Variations

Instead of the adjectives on the chart, you can use those you hear students using to describe each other, or let students come up with their own. Their language might be offensive to you or to other students in the classroom, so we recommend providing parameters.

You can use a chart with fewer rows if time is a concern or if you want your students to focus on one or two particular labels you've heard them give each other.

Challenges

When you ask students to notice their judgments, some will think you're questioning those judgments and become defensive. A student might insist that the other person really *is* mean, that she doesn't care what the other person needs, or that she doesn't want to approach the person differently (or at all). But in this activity, you're not telling students that their judgments are wrong, nor are you telling them what to do. Rather, you're helping them notice that they have a choice. They can choose to act upon judgments that turn out to be helpful, or they can choose other actions that might be more consistent with their values.

If students become upset or defensive, you can validate their feelings and ask questions to help them decide if their judgments are useful. For example, if they say they can't imagine the other person's experience, you can say, "It's normal to have trouble imagining why people do things we never would. What if *they* tried to imagine *our* lives? What might change? Who's going to take the first step toward that change?" Or if they say they don't want to behave kindly toward someone who's been mean, you can say, "That's understandable. This person hasn't earned your kindness, right? But when you say you *can* do something, you're saying you have a choice. What will you choose?" More generally, you can ask, "What is that thought telling you to do? If you listen to that thought, will it move you toward the life you want?" Questions like these can help students notice that they're not beholden to their judgments. They can *have* their judgments and still behave in accordance with their values.

If students do try the behaviors they wrote, they might end up feeling like they're the better person. If you hear bragging or gloating, ask questions about the other person: "If I asked Leon what it was like for him, what do you think he'd say? What might he need now? What did you learn about him?"

Finally, during this activity, a student might identify a dangerous situation, such as bullying or abuse. Of course, you should contact the school psychologist and follow all school policies and laws related to mandatory reporting; and, of course, that student should not write a sentence about how he or she would approach someone dangerous. Instead, you can ask that student to write *I will approach myself* in column five and then choose self-care values and behaviors.

Taking Perspectives

Being able to take someone else's perspective means understanding that each of us experiences the world differently, based on the thoughts, emotions, perceptions, memories, and expectations we bring to our encounters (McHugh & Stewart, 2012). In schools, students find themselves in various groups, such as classes, teams, clubs, locker blocks, lunch tables, and buses—and they sometimes move from group to group all day long. This constant reshuffling requires a certain amount of flexibility in how students behave, but it doesn't necessarily mean they can flexibly consider another person's perspective, especially when they feel threatened. Although many students value behaving kindly and compassionately, they can have trouble acting upon those values when their sense of safety or belonging is compromised. In this activity, students practice noticing how perspectives can shape an encounter, imagining another person's perspective, and behaving in a values-consistent way even under threat.

Materials for Each Student

For this activity, each student will need a pen, paper, the "Different Perspectives Scenario" handout (figure 6.3) or something similar, and the "Examples of Values" handout (page 214).

The teacher has just recapped that during the civil rights movement when Rosa Parks refused to give up her seat on the bus, it was not because she was tired that day or because she felt like it but because she was taking a stand against an injustice. The teacher asks what the injustice was.

Marcus: The injustice was that black people were slaves.

Terry (*laughing*): What? Dude, slavery was abolished, like, a hundred years before that.

Marcus: I know. But they were still sort of slaves. And Rosa Parks sat on the bus even though the black slaves were required to give up their seats.

Terry (*still laughing*): Did you even do last night's reading? Or, like, the reading from the last month? Are you completely stupid? Or just completely racist?

Discussion Questions

1. How are Terry and Marcus likely to interact in the future?
2. How might this scene play out differently if Terry knew that Marcus is recovering from a concussion that's made it hard for him to concentrate?
3. How might this scene play out differently if Marcus knew that Terry has been called *slave* as a racial slur?

Figure 6.3: "Different Perspectives Scenario" handout.

Sample Script

The following sample script gives an idea of how this activity might work in your classroom.

> Today I'm going to ask you to think about a time when you suffered because another person said or did something mean, excluded or embarrassed you, destroyed something you care about, or hurt you in any other way. I'm going to ask you to begin with the words *One time* so you can focus on one specific incident, although I recognize that it might be part of a pattern. Take a few minutes and write what happened. This will be totally private writing; I won't ask you to share. (*Students write about their experiences.*)
>
> We all act on limited information based on our own perspectives. Here's an example. Did you play with alphabet blocks when you were little? They're building blocks with different letters on the different sides. So if two of you were looking at different sides, one of you might call a block *the A block* and the other might call it *the J block*. Even though you're looking at the exact same block, you're looking at it from two different perspectives, and based on what you see, you're calling it by different names. Make sense so far?
>
> Now suppose you're in preschool, and you're trying to make a word with the letter *J*. You ask your friend, "Have you seen the J block?" Your friend says no. Then you find the block you want in a tower your friend is building. Maybe you get angry. Your friend had the block you wanted

all along, and then *lied* about it. And maybe in your anger, you knock down your friend's tower. Now your friend is angry too, because you knocked down his tower, and you're shouting at him about the J block, and he's thinking, *I never had the stupid J block*. He decides you're a little unstable and would be better off avoiding you in the future.

I know we're talking about preschoolers playing with blocks, but look what just happened: a friendship ends because two children didn't understand each other's perspectives. And not understanding someone's perspective can cause confusion, conflict, and pain, no matter how old you are. Let's look at another example. Can I have two volunteers willing to perform a very short scenario? (*Students perform a scene of a brief conflict [as in figure 6.3, page 103] and the class has a discussion in response to the follow-up questions.*)

In the scenario we just discussed, we had information about each person's life. In reality, we don't know the details of each other's lives, and it isn't always appropriate or kind to ask each other personal questions. But if we can't always know each other's perspectives and we can't always ask, what can we do in those tense moments? Well, we can notice that everyone *has* a perspective: a set of experiences that impacts how they see the situation and respond to it.

We're going to do something now that might be hard. Go back to what you wrote earlier about your own painful interaction. And below it, make a list of possible reasons for the other person's behavior. What might have happened to this person over the last several years to prompt him or her to act like that? What might have happened over the last few weeks or days to prompt the person to do that to you? What might have been going on that morning that led this person to behave that way? What might be going on for this person physically? Emotionally? In his or her family? (*Writes these questions on the board as students make their lists.*)

I'm not going to ask you to share these lists, but would anyone like to share how it felt to make the list?

It's not that this person had no choice but to treat you badly. This person could have been suffering and not made *you* suffer. They're still responsible for their actions. But when someone treats me badly, I sometimes say I hate them, or that they're a horrible person, or that they're not worth my time. But every time I decide that another human being is horrible or worthless, I've lost sight of how I want to live.

What about you? How do you want to live? (*Distributes "Examples of Values" handout [page 214].*)

Sometimes, it's very appropriate to fight back or run away. I'm not suggesting that if someone pulls a knife that you should ask them about their feelings. But if they pull a verbal knife, do you have to pull out your own? How else could you respond in a way that connects back to your values? (*Takes responses.*)

In moments when we feel relaxed and we're not in the middle of a conflict, we can imagine that other person's perspective. That's what we just did. Even if we're wrong about the details, we're right that the person *has* a perspective. Everyone has a history of suffering, just like we do. It doesn't excuse the other person's actions, but it does remind us of our shared humanity and help us choose who we want to be.

We can also practice noticing—kind of like how a soccer player practices dribbling and passing so she's better able to dribble and pass the ball during a game when things are more stressful. If we build our capacity for noticing, then in those moments of conflict when we're focused on our own perspective, we can notice that the other person has a perspective too.

Follow-Up

You could add a brief mindfulness exercise. It could be something as simple as taking ten mindful breaths, or it could be more involved, like students standing with their arms above their heads and noticing the ache. Mindfulness activities don't just promote relaxation; they can also help students practice the noticing skills necessary for perspective-taking and values-consistent action in challenging situations (Wilson, Sandoz, Flynn, Slater, & DuFrene, 2010).

You can also reference this activity when conflict inevitably arises. Better than stating that there are multiple perspectives in the room is to ask questions: "How could she be seeing the situation differently? What might have happened in her distant and recent past to lead her to think this way? What else might be going on for her right now? How do you want to respond? Is that the kind of life you want to create for yourself?"

Variations

Instead of using the scenario in figure 6.3 (page 103), you can write your own to reflect what conflict looks and sounds like at your school. Often, the biggest conflicts don't occur in class but rather on the bus, in the cafeteria, in locker rooms and hallways, at events and parties, or on social media. As problems come up, you can use perspective-taking scenarios as a way for students to develop empathy for everyone involved, look for solutions, and hold themselves accountable to their values.

You can also have your students rewrite their own stories as dialogues, changing the names and any identifying details. You could choose a few of these dialogues to have students perform, analyze, and reimagine for the class. How could this story end differently?

Another option is to use a conflict from a work of literature, a current or historical event, or a scientific debate. Not only would this connect the activity to your course content, but it would give students some practice with the concept of perspective taking before they try to take the perspective of someone who hurt them.

Challenges

As they discuss the scenario and their own conflicts, some students will say what they think will be socially acceptable or funny. Some will insist that the person who hurt them is just evil, and some will chafe at the idea of inventing someone else's backstory. These are all ways of avoiding the vulnerability this activity provokes. You can say that your agenda isn't to get them to behave in a particular way; it's to help them be the people they want to be. You might also remind students that the writing is private and if they opt out of doing it you wouldn't know. That way, if they do participate, it's by choice.

Undermining Prejudicial Thoughts

Categorization is a normal, natural human process (Allport, 1954). Through multiple-exemplar training, we learn to label the giant brown and green thing in the backyard, the smaller brown and green thing in the front yard, and the brown and green thing in a storybook *tree*. When our son, at one year old, pointed to one and said, "Tree," we said in overly excited and high-pitched voices, "Tree! That's a tree!" and probably kissed him and danced around and got a cake or something.

Categorization and labeling are highly reinforced in childhood and continue to help us throughout life, such as when we decide to see a movie because it has a great director or avoid taking a road that tends to have traffic. We usually don't spend much time noticing this kind of thinking, which frees up our headspace to think about what matters.

But sometimes categorization interferes with values-consistent action. Prejudices on the basis of social categories can lead us to insult and demean each other in subtle everyday acts known as *microaggressions* (Sue, 2010). Imagine that a white girl asks a black girl if she wants to go out for pizza after school and the black girl says she can't. The white girl says, "My treat." The white girl might want to get to know the black girl better but may also convey the assumption that the black girl doesn't have the money. Someone who values behaving respectfully, compassionately, and open-mindedly might do unintended harm by acting in a biased way.

People who have prejudiced thoughts about one group tend to have prejudiced thoughts about other groups, too (Allport, 1954). Michael Levin and his colleagues (2016) found that this *generalized prejudice* comes from psychological rigidity. Some people take their prejudices as absolute truths ("But girls really *shouldn't* wear short skirts unless they want sex"), rather than understanding their prejudices as thoughts they don't have to act upon ("I'm having the thought that girls shouldn't wear short skirts unless they want sex, *and* I'm going to treat girls respectfully no matter what they wear").

Many activities in which students notice their own prejudices teach them to question, replace, or suppress their own thoughts. This activity is different. Students learn how to take away the power of prejudiced thoughts to influence their actions so they can instead act on their values. We based the script on the work of Jason Lillis and Steven Hayes (2007) and use adapted versions of Hands as Thoughts (Harris, 2009) and the Eye Contact Exercise (Hayes, Strosahl, et al., 1999).

Do this activity late in the year, after you've created a trusting community in your classroom, and be prepared for lots of avoidance anyway. You can respond to any avoidance moves with compassion ("It's understandable to want to stay out of this conversation") and questions about how their avoidance works out for them ("Where could this conversation take you? What happens if you stay out of it?").

Materials for Each Student

For this activity, each student will need a pen, a notebook, two highlighters in different colors, and the "What Comes to Mind?" handout (figure 6.4) or something similar.

For each word or phrase, write whatever words, images, or ideas first come into your head. Try your best not to fight the thought or write something different from whatever comes to mind. No one but you will see what you write.

Teenage girls	
Asian kids	
Black men	
Latinos	
Muslims	
Jewish people	
White women	
Native Americans	
Europeans	
Africans	
Gay men	
Southerners	
Elderly people	
Overweight people	
People with disabilities	

Figure 6.4: "What Comes to Mind?" handout.

Visit go.SolutionTree.com/instruction for a free reproducible version of this figure.

Sample Script

The following sample script gives an idea of how this activity might work in your classroom.

Today we're going to think about prejudices. You're going to get a series of words and phrases, and I'm going to ask you to notice and write down the very first thing that comes to mind—words, images, ideas, or whatever else pops into your head. See if you can do this without fighting the thought or writing something different. This will be totally private writing. (*Distributes the "What Comes to Mind?" handout [figure 6.4, page 107] or something similar, and students complete it.*)

How did that feel? Did anyone find themselves having a thought and immediately thinking of a different thought you liked better? Or trying to cancel out a thought? Or pretending a thought didn't come up? (*Pauses between questions for students who respond.*)

Let's try this: everyone raise your hand. Now keep your hand up if you *want* to have all of the thoughts you just wrote down. (*Gives students a moment to drop their hands.*) Look around the room. How many people are raising their hands?

So most, if not all, of us have thoughts we wish we didn't have. Here's the thing, though. We live in a society where we're bombarded by images of black men committing crimes, Latinos in poverty, women as sex objects, and families consisting of a father and a mother and their biological children. And all of that is flowing from a history of oppression that is hundreds, even thousands, of years old. None of us created racism, sexism, or homophobia, but our culture is polluted by them. That pollution gets into us, as thoughts in our minds.

But there's something we can do to deal with those thoughts. We're going to try an activity, and anything you write will still be totally private. Take two different colored highlighters (*Distributes them.*), and in one color, highlight all the thoughts you wrote down that you think are sort of true. In the other color, highlight thoughts you're pretty sure aren't true.

Now, pick a thought you believe is true. What happens if you let it guide your actions? Take a moment and write in your notebook about what your life would be like if you always acted on this belief.

What problems would there be if you acted on every thought you wrote down? (*Students discuss the costs of acting on prejudicial thoughts, including that it prevents people from being their full selves, it can cause isolation, and it shuts down opportunities for communication and friendship.*)

Now pick a thought you know isn't true. Maybe it's a thought you wish you didn't have. What happens if, whenever the thought comes up, you put your energy into pushing it away? Let's say you have one of the thoughts you wrote down about a person you're just meeting. You immediately think you're a horrible person for thinking that. You try to think about other things. Or maybe you try to be extra nice to this person to make up for the thought you had. Take a moment and write in your notebook about what would happen if you put all your energy into pushing this thought away.

What problems happen if we put all our energy into pushing away these thoughts? (*Students discuss the costs of trying to suppress prejudicial thoughts, including that it uses up a lot of energy, distracts from other pursuits, and prevents an authentic relationship from forming.*)

So it doesn't work to act on prejudiced thoughts, and it doesn't work to try to get rid of these thoughts. Would you like to try a different way to deal with these thoughts? (*Waits for students to give their consent.*)

You'll need to sit so you're facing a partner. While you're moving your chairs to face your partners, I'm going to come around and collect the papers you were writing on so I can shred them for you. Fold them over so I won't be able to see what you wrote. (*Collects papers while students move to face their partners.*)

Ready? This might feel a little weird. Imagine that your left hand represents a prejudice you really believe is true. It's like you're looking at the world through it. Put your left hand over your eyes, and keep your eyes open so it's like you're looking at the world through this thought. Notice what happens. Look at your partner. Can you see this person fully? Would you be able to have a real conversation this way? Can you live the way you want to live when you're doing this?

Next, put your left hand down and imagine that your right hand represents a prejudice you wish you didn't have. One you'd really rather get rid of. Try to make it go away, or at least keep it out of sight. How could you do that? You could put it behind your back, but then the people behind you would see it. You could try sitting on it or hiding it in your sleeve. Hide your right hand and really make sure no part of it is visible. Notice how this feels. Is it actually gone?

Now try this: with your hand still hidden from view, don't feel it. Whatever you do, don't feel your right hand. Don't feel the thumb, or the fingers, or the palm. Don't feel your knuckles. Don't feel your wrist either, because that's dangerously close to your hand. Can you make yourself not feel your hand? Look at your partner. Would you be able to have a deep conversation while you're concentrating on hiding and not feeling your hand? How well can you focus on living the life you want?

Now do both at once. Put your left hand over your eyes while also making yourself not feel your right hand. Kind of ridiculous, right? But this is what we do all the time; we look at the world through our prejudices and unintentionally act upon them, and we also try to not think our prejudiced thoughts. How likely are we to live meaningful lives while we're busy doing all that?

So here's a different option. Put your hands in your lap. Let them just be there. Let your prejudiced thoughts just rest in your lap. You don't have to like them. You don't have to want them. You're just not acting on them or trying to not have them. They're just there. Look at your partner. Can you have a conversation now?

Now I'm going to ask you to look in your partner's eyes. Really look. Allow yourself to be seen. Notice how you experience another person seeing you as *you*, here, in this moment. Whatever thoughts come up, let them just be there like your hands in your lap.

And notice how while you're letting this person see you, you're also seeing another human being who is allowing you to see him or her. Again, notice how you experience seeing this person, as you are being seen here right now. If any thoughts come up, just let those thoughts be there. Keep looking. (*Pauses between prompts so students are making eye contact for at least a minute; some might laugh, look away, or interrupt.*)

What was that like? (*Students share their reactions.*)

If we let our thoughts be there, like our hands resting in our laps, without their controlling our actions or making us hide from them, how does that change the way we can interact with other people?

The next time you discover you're thinking a prejudiced thought, you can just notice it and let it be there. And that gives you room to really see other people, and to choose to behave toward them in a way that matches the life you want to live.

Follow-Up

After the activity, make sure you have all the students' papers and either shred or recycle them in a bin that no student has access to. These precautions might sound extreme, but revealing prejudices makes students especially vulnerable, and seeing the papers could be painful or traumatic for students.

Accepting prejudiced thoughts is not the same as accepting prejudice in the world. If you have students who are troubled by the effects of prejudice, you could add to the network of images portraying a particular group and thus take away the saliency of prejudicial thoughts, like how a bead is less eye-catching when it's part of a necklace than on its own. For example, if you think of world leaders as white, you can post images of world leaders who are people of color. Or if you associate femininity with weakness, you can share videos of women showing strength.

You can also develop a more inclusive curriculum. For example, a history teacher who has students compare 19th century captains of industry to today's business leaders could make sure the list features business leaders of color. A science teacher could emphasize the contributions of women to the knowledge students are learning. An English teacher could incorporate the work of LGBTQ writers into the book list. These simple shifts aren't enough to undo centuries of messaging about these groups, but they're a start.

Variations

When the students write down prejudiced thoughts about different groups, you can focus on just a few groups (boys and girls, for example) or replace the list from figure 6.4 (page 107) with your own list of targeted and dominant groups at your school.

Challenges

Confronting prejudiced thoughts dredges up a long history of oppression that continues today. This activity might be very painful for some students, particularly if they've been targets of microaggressions, discrimination, or violence on the basis of their social identifiers. As students share their reactions, they might make efforts to suppress or avoid thoughts, or express stereotypes they believe really are true. Listen for these kinds of statements and ask questions to help the students explore whether the thoughts are useful: "What happens if you act on that belief?" or "What happens when you try to make that thought go away or keep it from coming up in the first place?"

Your Empathy

Shifting our own judgments about people is hard when we're so sure we're right about them. Taking another perspective is hard when we're so attached to our own, and undermining prejudiced thoughts is especially hard when we're living in a stew of them every day. In our experience, students *and* teachers want to avoid confronting their own beliefs and biases.

If you find yourself avoiding this work, you can practice noticing your own thoughts about people. What comes up when you do? Do you beat yourself up when you have these thoughts? Do you try to make them go away or avoid situations where you might have them? Do you sometimes act on them? How is that working out? Can you let that thought be there and still act in accordance with your values? These struggles aren't only our students'.

We can also deliberately choose contexts in which empathy is a challenge. Are you a sixth-generation liberal? Go for a walk with a conservative, bring up a political issue, ask lots of questions, and really listen to the answers. Are you an enthusiastic carnivore? Invite a vegan over for dinner. Jewish? Visit a mosque. New to teaching and excited about the latest trends in education? Ask your seasoned colleagues why they do what they do. Nearing retirement and feeling that if your curriculum isn't broken you're not going to fix it after all these years? Ask your junior colleagues why they do what they do. If we enter into these situations as tourists, treating people as exotic or wrongheaded, or as if it's their responsibility to educate and enlighten us, we won't build much capacity for empathy. If we approach intending to build an authentic relationship, we just might.

In addition, we can seek out friends and colleagues who support us in this area—co-explorers who are open and interested in our efforts to learn and grow, and who treat us with kindness and curiosity and the courage to be authentic, especially when we fail.

If all of this sounds challenging and uncomfortable, then you're succeeding. Pushing your boundaries and exceeding your comfort level is leadership by example and an opportunity to improve your own flexibility with social categories.

From Empathy to Resilience

This chapter is about how students can develop the capacity to understand each other, instead of wallowing in perceptions, judgments, and prejudices that don't help them behave in a values-consistent way. These activities won't turn your school into a giant love fest; they're a tentative beginning, not an endpoint. You can repeat all the activities in this chapter throughout the year to help students notice their unhelpful thoughts about each other and become aware of their values. Whether they choose their values as their guide is always up to them.

While this chapter's activities focus on how students can overcome judgments about each other, the next chapter's activities focus on how students can overcome judgments about themselves and treat themselves in ways that match their values.

EMPOWE**R**

● ● ● ● ●

Chapter 7

RESILIENCE

Empower Students to Treat Themselves According to Their Values

As teachers, we're accustomed to telling students to do things that they might find painful in the short term, but we don't always teach them how to confront their disappointments, failures, and difficult choices. We might tell them, "That's life" or, "This too shall pass," but telling students that life is sometimes painful and that they'll be fine doesn't teach them how to accept the pain inherent in living a meaningful life. Statements like these can even make students more likely to avoid their own feelings ("I don't care about this stupid test!") or increase feelings of shame ("Why can't I just shake it off? What's wrong with me?"). Sometimes we try to counteract the pain, like when we bring in candy on test days. But then, students learn that the best way to respond to short-term pain is to give themselves short-term pleasure, rather than how to take care of themselves in the long term.

Researcher and author Kristin Neff (2011) says the core components of self-compassion are being warm and caring to ourselves rather than self-critical, accepting imperfection as part of our shared human experience, and seeing our problems as they are instead of playing them up or down. These activities are designed to help students persist, not by telling them to buck up or by indulging them with treats but by teaching them to be kind to themselves, normalizing their suffering, and linking their renewed efforts to their values.

Regenerating Possibilities

A self-compassionate attitude helps students cope with the disappointment of failure, continue to see themselves as competent, and refocus on learning (Neff, Hsieh, & Dejitterat, 2005). In this activity, students identify the larger values underneath their disappointments and think of other ways to serve those values, as well as ways to increase the possibility of future successes in areas where they previously failed.

Materials for Each Student

For this activity, each student will need a pen, paper, the "Four More Arms" handout (figure 7.1), and the "Examples of Values" handout (page 214).

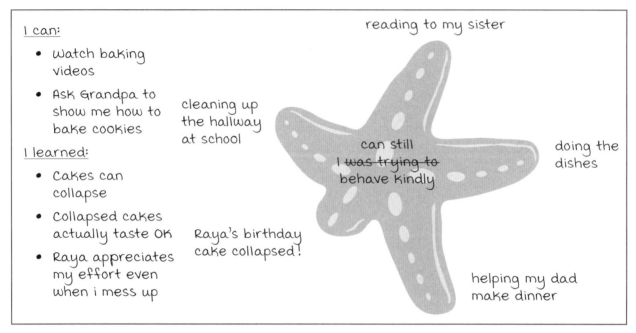

Figure 7.1: "Four More Arms" handout.

Visit go.SolutionTree.com/instruction for a free reproducible version of this figure.

Sample Script

The following sample script gives an idea of how this activity might work in your classroom.

> Today I'm going to ask you to think about a recent time when you tried to accomplish a goal and fell short. Maybe you spent an hour following a recipe for a cake to give your friend on her birthday, and when you took the cake out of the oven, it collapsed. Maybe you practiced hours for an audition and you got the part of tree number two, or you studied really hard for a test and you got a 57 percent. Or you got an 87 percent but were hoping for something higher. This isn't about how well you did according to someone else's definition of success; it's about falling short of your own.
>
> This could be an academic, athletic, or social disappointment. Maybe you tried out a new outfit that didn't work. Maybe you tried out for the basketball team and got cut. Maybe you raised your hand in class because you were sure you knew the answer, and what came out

of your mouth was totally wrong. Try to think of something pretty recent and meaningful. Jot it down somewhere so you don't forget it.

Okay. How many of you know what a starfish looks like?

For those of you who don't know everything there is to know about starfish, they are not fish but a type of animal called an *echinoderm*. One thing that makes starfish and other echinoderms so interesting is they have the ability to regrow their arms. If something comes along and tries to eat the starfish, the starfish can lose its arm and then grow it back. It takes them about a year, but they can do it. And in the meantime, the starfish still has other arms to do things like move and grab onto clams.

While it's waiting for its arm to grow back, it looks sort of like this. (*Distributes the "Four More Arms" handout [figure 7.1].*)

Imagine that your recent meaningful disappointment is like the starfish's missing arm. Write it next to that little nub where it looks like an arm used to be. It's a failed attempt. It's gone now. (*Pauses so students can write.*)

But before you had this disappointment, you tried. There was some effort involved. Why was that effort worth it? For example, when I was baking my cake, I might have been working toward being kind to my friend on her birthday. What were you working toward? What quality of action were you attempting to demonstrate in that moment? Please write the words *I was trying to behave* in the middle of the starfish. Then add an adverb to the end of that sentence that says how you were trying to behave. Mine would be *kindly*. If you can't think of one, I can give you a list of adverbs. (*Distributes the "Examples of Values" handout [page 214]. Students write their value statements.*)

Now notice that the starfish still has four more arms. See if you can think of four other ways you could behave that way. For example, if the reason I was trying to make the basketball team is that I was trying to behave athletically, actively, or collaboratively, what are some other ways I can behave athletically, actively, or collaboratively that have nothing to do with the basketball team? If I were trying to behave kindly by baking a cake for my friend, what are four other ways I can behave kindly that have nothing to do with cake? (*Helps any students who are struggling as they write.*)

Anyone want to share any part of what you wrote? (*Students can share just their value statement and their four other ways of working toward it. They can also share their disappointments if they want to.*)

Look at that. You can cross out the words *was trying to* and replace them with the words *can still*. As in, *I can still behave athletically*. (*Students write.*)

Now remember, the great thing about starfish is that they can regrow their arms. But it takes time. What can you do to regenerate the possibility of success in the area where you failed? Like, if you failed to bake a cake, you can try again, and maybe you'll make a good cake this time, but maybe you won't. So if baking a cake is important to you, what can you do to help yourself learn how to do it? Can you read a book about baking? Can you watch a show about baking? Can you invite someone over who's great at baking to bake a cake with you? If you didn't make the basketball team, you could try out again next year. But in the meantime, what can you do to increase your chances? Practice more? Find somebody to coach you? Or perhaps try a different sport more suited to your abilities and try to make that team?

By the little arm bud, write one or more things you could do to regrow the possibility of success in the area where you were disappointed. (*Takes any questions and encourages students as they write.*)

Did anyone write something that would be worthwhile even if they didn't end up succeeding at the goal? Like, if I said I'm going to ask my grandfather to teach me how to bake, I might really enjoy that time with him even if I don't end up making a better cake. Or if I practice basketball every day I might really enjoy playing even if I still don't end up making next year's team. Does anyone have an action that would be worthwhile regardless of the outcome? (*Students share.*)

Now at the bottom of your sheet, or on the back, I'm going to ask you to write some of the things you learned from your failed attempt. For example, I learned that cakes can collapse into themselves. I didn't know that, but now I do. (*Students write.*) Anyone want to share a lesson you learned?

Of course it would've been nice to have known that before, but are you glad you know now? What will you do now that you know? Let's close by writing what we've learned from our disappointments and how that might help us as we continue to live by our values.

Follow-Up

You can collect the starfish sheets and, after a period of time, return them and ask students if they tried any of their ideas. You can ask those who tried something new to describe what it was like and share how they feel about themselves as a result of exploring new behaviors (or renewing their commitments to old ones). For those who didn't do any of the actions they wrote on their sheets, did they do something else in the service of the value in the middle? How did that go? If they did nothing, what's getting in the way? Can the group help imagine even more alternatives?

Some students might compare the area in which they found disappointment to the new attempt: "Yeah, I hung out with these two girls who are in my English class, and they're super nice, but I miss my old friend group." Continued feelings of sadness and anger are normal when we lose something important. Or you might hear something like, "I've been hanging out with these two girls who are in my English class, and we've been having so much fun! Why was I wasting my time with that other group?" Of course it's great to discover a new friendship or interest, but the point isn't to replace valued relationships or actions—it's to notice new possibilities.

Variations

Rather than asking students to come up with alternative behaviors themselves, you could have them look at the value statements on their classmates' starfish and make behavior suggestions for each other. This might help students discover ways to serve their values that they wouldn't have thought of and perhaps haven't even heard of. For example, if Janayah says she wants to behave actively and she's a soccer kid, she might not think to try musical theater, roller derby, parkour, or orienteering. Maybe none of these will appeal to her, but getting her classmates' perspectives might open up her thinking about behaving actively so she can later discover new possibilities on her own.

If you decide to do a group brainstorm, we recommend having the students cover up the corner of the sheet where they've written their disappointments so they can keep these private. They might choose to share them later, with the whole class or just with you, but even if they don't, they'll still get the benefit of their classmates' ideas.

The starfish works as a metaphor because of its ability to regenerate arms and the fact that it can continue to function well with the four arms it has left, but you could use something else that can regrow but carry on in the meantime. Spiders can regrow legs (but might freak out some students), newts can regrow legs (but some students might not know what newts are), and sharks lose and regrow thousands of teeth in their lifetimes (but not because of struggle, so the metaphor doesn't work as well). If you can think of your own metaphor that will work better for your students, then by all means use it.

Challenges

Students might have trouble with this activity if their disappointment is about lack of recognition and status. If Janayah wants to be recognized as a strong soccer player and to gain the status of being on the varsity team, she won't find any consolation in joining the junior varsity team, a local league, or a pick-up match in the park. And if she gets a part in *Cats*, she might enjoy the recognition and status that brings but not get a sense of meaning and vitality from acting and singing. If you see signs that students are focusing on recognition and status, you can help them distinguish between what they're *getting* and what they're *doing*. If Janayah were to get sick the night of the show and couldn't be in the performance, what would still be worthwhile about the experience?

Similarly, some students might say that trying something new didn't make them feel any better, but alternative ways to pursue values aren't escapes from the pain of disappointment. Say Janayah has been playing soccer since she was very little and worked hard to make her school's varsity team, but then she got cut. Joining her school's production of *Cats* will not take away the frustration, anger, and self-doubt she might be feeling, but she can feel disappointed and continue to live actively. The point of this activity is not to take away disappointment; it's to live a meaningful life *with* disappointment.

Hanging My Failures Out to Dry

Part of what it means to develop self-compassion is learning to "forgive personal failings and recognize the failings as normal" (Marshall et al., 2015, p. 119). In this activity, students learn to see their failures not only as normal and forgivable but also as opportunities to show kindness to themselves, see what's truly important to them, and find new ways to do what matters.

Materials for Each Student

For this activity, each student will need a pen, paper, and the "Failure Clothesline" handout (figure 7.2).

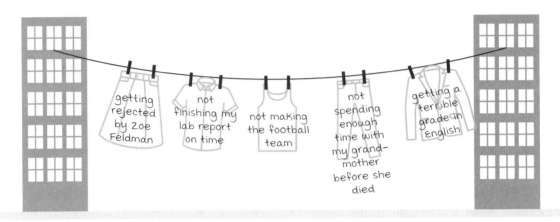

Figure 7.2: "Failure Clothesline" handout.

Visit **go.SolutionTree.com/instruction** *for a free reproducible version of this figure.*

Sample Script

The following sample script gives an idea of how this activity might work in your classroom.

> Today I'm going to ask you to make a list of times in your life when you've failed. I'm going to do it too. Your list will be private. Mine won't. (*Begins writing a list on the board.*)
>
> They could be big failures or small but significant failures. They could be public failures or failures that only you saw or knew about. They could be academic, athletic, or artistic failures. Maybe you were in a gymnastics meet and failed to stick the landing, or you were in a play and forgot some of your lines. Maybe the failure is that you didn't make the team or get the part in the first place. (*Pauses to list more failures and give the students an opportunity to list theirs.*)
>
> They could be social failures—times when you failed to make friends or keep friends. They could be romantic failures, whether that means you failed to attract someone's interest or the relationship started and then failed. They could be times when your family relationships were failing or when your health was failing. (*Pauses and writes more.*)
>
> Maybe you have a cooking failure, an organizational failure, or a failure to take a chance you now wish you'd taken. (*Continues to list failures on the board while students make their lists privately. Distributes the "Failure Clothesline" handout [figure 7.2] and draws a clothesline on the board.*)
>
> I've just given you a sheet with a clothesline on it. For those of you who have never seen one of these things, a clothesline is a long rope where people hang wet clothes to dry in the sun. I'm going to ask you to imagine that each of your failures is an article of clothing. If my failure to make the football team is an article of clothing, maybe it's a football jersey. (*Draws a football jersey on the board and labels it "not making the football team."*) There it is, all sopping

wet, hanging out to dry on my failure clothesline. What could my failure to get a good grade in English be? What about my failure to finish my lab report on time? What about my failure to ask out Zoe Feldman? What about my failure to spend more time with my grandmother before she died? (*Draws and labels.*)

Thank you for helping me come up with articles of clothing to represent my failures. Now, in the privacy of your handout, which you will not share with your classmates, see if you can come up with an article of clothing to represent each of your failures. Just like I did, draw the articles of clothing on your clothesline and label them. (*Continues to draw and label clothing while the students draw and label theirs.*)

Notice that everyone has a failure clothesline. You are not the only one with a whole history of failures. Failing is normal. All humans fail. How does it feel to notice that failure is something we all share?

Now focus on each article of clothing hanging on your clothesline. Really imagine how cold and wet and heavy and soggy they all are. How would it feel to put these clothes on? (*Lets students react.*)

If you get caught in a cold, heavy rainstorm of failure, what are some of the things you need? Some people eat a lot of junk food or drink alcohol or use drugs to make themselves feel better after they fail. Is that what their bodies need? How can you take care of yourself physically after a failure? (*Students might suggest eating a healthy meal, taking a warm bath, getting exercise, sleeping, or other self-care routines. They might also suggest doing these things to excess, which would be a way to avoid the pain associated with the failure. If avoidance behaviors come up, ask students, "Would that be the best way to take care of yourself? Is that what your body needs most?"*)

And what about your emotional needs? How can you take care of yourself psychologically after a failure? (*Students might suggest activities like spending time in nature, seeing friends, listening to favorite songs, exercising to relieve stress, praying, meditating, or just getting a hug. Again, they might also suggest self-indulgences that function as avoidance moves. Ask, "Is that a want or a need?"*)

And now, think about the sun coming out and a gentle breeze picking up. The clothes get nice and soft in the breeze, and warm and dry in the sun. What would it mean for your failures to dry in the sun and soften in the breeze? (*Gives examples if necessary, such as the failure to make the football team might eventually feel okay and the failure to attract someone's interest might still be embarrassing but feel less important over time.*)

How about this: does any one of these failures define you? Does this entire clothesline define you? What other clothes are in your wardrobe, and not on the clothesline? Jot down some of the other clothes in your wardrobe and what they represent.

And what could it mean for you to put some of these failures back on again? Why would you want to? (*Gives examples if necessary. "Putting the football jersey back on" might mean trying out for football again or spending time playing football with a younger sibling. "Putting on the failure-to-attract-someone jeans" might not mean asking out that same person again; it might instead mean expressing interest in someone else.*)

So this week, I'm going to give us all a challenge—and when I say "us all," I include myself in this. Let's each pick one article of clothing on our failure clothesline, and let's put that clothing back on. Maybe you're just putting on one sleeve of your flunked-the-math-test jacket. What would that mean? Or maybe you're throwing on that I-disappointed-my-dad sweater and seeing what happens.

On the back of your paper, write what you'll try putting on. What will that mean? How will you take care of yourself as you prepare for this attempt, as you make it, and afterward?

How does it feel to explore the possibility of putting your failures back on?

How does it feel to think about taking care of yourself?

Follow-Up

After a few days, you could ask your students if they wore their failures. How did it feel? Why was it worthwhile? You can also reference the failure clothesline when students fail in the future, such as when a class is having trouble with an assignment, or when someone does poorly on a test. You can ask what article of clothing this new failure is. What would it mean to let it dry out and also to put it back on? Can the students identify their own needs in this moment of failure? How can they take care of themselves?

You could keep extending the clothing metaphor to help students explore new possibilities in their lives. What kinds of clothing do you imagine yourself wearing in the future? What new clothes do you want to try on now? What's a piece of clothing you'd just want to borrow? What's an article of clothing that's been sitting in your dresser for a while that you'd like to put on again? What piece of clothing is worn out? What piece of clothing have you outgrown but can hand down to someone else?

Variations

Hanging My Failures Out to Dry is intentionally a little bit funny, and while some failures are funny, some are not. The clothing metaphor allows students to personalize their failures, react physically to the idea of returning to a meaningful but painful experience, and imagine possible valued outcomes of that return, all in a whimsical way. Feel free to come up with your own metaphors for your students.

Challenges

Naming our failures can bring up fear, embarrassment, guilt, shame, regret, sadness, anger, and other not-so-fun emotions. Students might avoid these emotions by sticking with low-stakes failures that don't really matter to them. They might also make jokes, tease each other, blame people for their failures, or get very quiet. Your own willingness to be vulnerable, and your responses to any avoidant behaviors, will set a tone for your students.

Alternatively, some students might overshare their stories or get visibly or vocally upset. If these students make themselves the center of attention, their problems begin to look bigger than everyone else's, diminishing the idea that failure is part of our shared human experience. If you ignore the behavior, or if you send distressed students out of the room to calm themselves down, your students learn that emotional reactions are disruptive and unacceptable. You also miss an opportunity to normalize failure and the pain that comes with it.

If a student has a strong emotional reaction, we recommend bringing the focus back to the group. You can say something like, "We're seeing that people react in all kinds of ways to the pain of failure. Failing at something that matters *is* painful, and all of us fail. So what do we need in those inevitable moments when we fail? How can we give ourselves and each other what we need?" If students want to help their classmate who's upset, you can affirm their move toward compassion and ask how they plan to show themselves compassion, too.

Self-Kindness Gift Cards

Adolescents' ability to be kind to themselves in the face of struggle is linked to overall well-being (Neff & McGehee, 2010). In this activity, students discuss the difference between self-kindness and self-indulgence, brainstorm ways they can be kind to themselves, and make themselves gift cards to represent a particular kindness they want to give themselves.

Materials for Each Student

For this activity, each student will need a skinny marker, a pen, a notebook, and a wallet-sized card. (A 3 × 5–inch index card cut in half will work; you can also get blank business cards or loyalty cards.)

You'll need at least nine sheets of paper, each with a different category of self-kindness behaviors, such as *Exercise* or *Visiting friends*, written at the top. See figure 7.3 (page 122) for self-kindness categories, and feel free to add more.

Sample Script

The following sample script gives an idea of how this activity might work in your classroom.

> Have any of you seen those gift cards that are sometimes sold in the front of stores? Or maybe you've bought one for someone, or gotten one yourself?
>
> Those gift cards are usually to indulge someone so they can get something they wouldn't have bought for themselves, like twenty-five songs or some giant, expensive, sugary, caffeinated beverage. Other people buy those cards for us as gifts because they think maybe we wouldn't treat ourselves to those things. And the things we buy with gift cards aren't always necessary. Sometimes they're not even so healthy. But they're fun!
>
> Today, instead of thinking about ways that we can indulge ourselves, we're going to think about ways we can be kind to ourselves. What do you think the difference is between self-indulgence and self-kindness?

Self-indulgence is giving yourself something you enjoy in the short term but that might be harmful to you in the long term if you do it too much, like a brownie sundae or a couple of hours in front of the television. Self-kindness is giving yourself something that's helpful to you, like a fresh apple or a walk on the beach or a couple of hours in the gym. These *might* be pleasant in the moment, or they might be things you don't necessarily enjoy in the moment, but either way they help you over time.

Let's look at some of the ways people can be kind to themselves. (*Posts and, as needed, explains papers that have different categories of self-kindnesses [see figure 7.3].*)

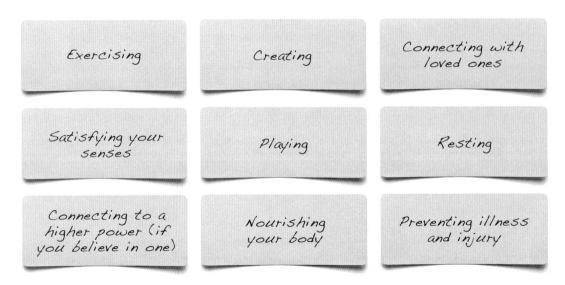

Figure 7.3: Categories of self-kindness.

I'm going to give each of you a marker. You'll have about five minutes to walk around the room and, on some of these papers, write things you can do that would fit into that category. (*Gives examples of specific activities that would fit into some of the categories, such as biking or swimming for exercising, or going to an art museum or listening to late 1980s heavy metal for satisfying your senses.*)

Before we get started, this absolutely must be a safe space. We're not going to write anything disrespectful, offensive, or private. (*Checks for understanding.*) Also, there are *many* ways to be kind to ourselves, and someone might write something that seems surprising or different to you. You might see a word and not know what it means. It's great to show curiosity, but let's do it in a way that doesn't make someone else feel judged. Are we all okay with that? (*Checks for understanding and gives examples if necessary.*)

Let's try this. (*Students and the teacher circulate and write under the headings.*)

What did you notice as you wrote on these, or what are you noticing now as you're looking at them?

Those of you who shop online may have seen sites that have a wish list feature, where you can create a list of items that you share with people who you think might buy some of the items for you. Nice, right? Well, now I'm going to ask you to grab your notebook and walk around the room again, and make yourself a wish list of ways you can be kind to yourself. If you think of new self-kindnesses, you can still add them to your wish list.

A wish list has things you want but don't already have, so don't write things you're already doing. Your list can be as long or as short as you want it to be, but the stuff you're putting on it should be things you genuinely want to do. Sometimes people put stuff on a wish list that they don't really want, and then they're kind of disappointed when they get it! (*Students and the teacher circulate and make wish lists of self-kindness behaviors.*)

OK, have a seat so we can do our last step. (*Distributes the cards.*) Imagine that this is a gift card. On it, write one behavior from your wish list that you will give yourself in an act of self-kindness. Just like if you were to give other people gift cards because you want them to enjoy something they wouldn't buy for themselves, give yourself the gift of a behavior you're not already doing. But unlike gift cards, which are usually indulgences, you'll give yourself something that's a genuine kindness. If you're feeling artistic, you can even draw a little icon to represent the behavior. (*Students make their gift cards.*)

If you have your wallet with you, stick your gift card in where you'll see it. Unlike actual gift cards that eventually run out of money, this one is unlimited. So use it as many times as you want!

Follow-Up

Some people get gift cards, stick them in their wallets, and forget they're there. A week or so after doing this activity, you might ask your students if they've used their gift cards yet—that is, if they've done the behaviors—and then either set themselves reminders to use them or make new gift cards they think they'll actually use.

You could also repeat this activity whenever it seems like stress is high. Since there are so many types of self-kindness, you could feature a particular type each time.

You could also do the activity at gift-giving times during the year, as a reminder that self-kindness matters too. How can students gift themselves with kindness during the December holiday season, when the short days tend to make people feel like staying inside and indulging themselves? How can students be kind to their bodies around Halloween, when people eat too much sugar or go to parties where they might be offered drugs and alcohol? How can students be kind to themselves by building connections with loved ones in mid-February, a time that has traditionally been about celebrating heterosexual romantic relationships, often by spending money on indulgences?

Variations

Your students can create check boxes on their cards and make a mark every time they do the behavior. This would be more like a loyalty card than a gift card, but it would allow students to keep track of their self-kindness behaviors. You can even get a hole puncher and have the students punch their cards when they do their behaviors. With loyalty cards, customers usually get a free gift when they've accrued a certain number of punches, but the free gift here can be another self-kindness.

This activity includes several discussion parts, but you can have your students respond in writing to some of the prompts and then share, or they could share with a partner instead of with the whole group. If your group tends to be very quiet, or if you have some students who dominate discussions, these more intimate ways of sharing might help more students say what they want to say.

You could also ask your students to connect the concept of self-kindness to the content of your course. For example, students in an English or history class could discuss a book character's or historical actor's needs and self-kindness behaviors. Students in a geography or language class might examine some of the ways self-kindness behaviors differ across cultures, as well as self-kindnesses all humans need. Science, health, and physical education students might focus on a particular aspect of self-kindness (such as exercise or rest), but then contextualize that aspect within a broader picture of what self-kindness means. Not only would these curricular connections strengthen students' understanding of self-kindness *and* of topics under study, but they might also be entry points for students to share what they need and how they want to take care of themselves.

Challenges

Some students might chafe at the idea of discussing personal business like self-kindness behaviors. If this happens, you can explain that they shouldn't reveal anything that feels too private. You can also acknowledge that many self-kindness behaviors *do* occur outside of school, but that they can affect students in school. For example, how do sleep, nutrition, and exercise impact students' ability to learn? How do acts of creativity, connection, and appreciation outside of school impact students' ability to create work, connect with each other, and appreciate discoveries in school? How do rest, play, and spirituality (if they practice it) restore them so they can bring their whole selves to school?

Students might say they don't have time to take care of themselves in the ways they'd like to, or that they can't do some behavior or other. Instead of arguing the point, try asking questions: "Are there ways of being kind to yourself that feel important, but that you feel like you're not doing as much as you'd like? What's it like to notice that? Are there things or people that demand a lot of your attention, and you'd like to save some energy to take care of yourself? How could you set limits in those situations?"

Another challenge lies in the guilt and shame that this activity can stir up. Students might say things like, "If connecting to my family is so important to me, why was I so nasty to my mom this morning?" or, "Ugh! I need to get off my fat butt and exercise." Or they might not say anything if feelings of guilt and shame shut them down. Again, instead of trying to persuade them that they shouldn't feel that way, try asking questions: "Do you feel pressured to do some of these behaviors? Where's that pressure coming from? How is that type of self-kindness important to *you*?"

Your Resilience

Teachers are supposed to be the authority figures, the ones qualified to answer students' questions and assess their performance. Won't we look weak if we share stories of our failures and flaws? Can't we just show them the excellent speech J.K. Rowling (2008) gave, "The Fringe Benefits of Failure," about the struggles she not only overcame but learned from in the process of writing *Harry Potter*? Or tell them about how Albert Einstein failed in school, Steve Jobs failed in business, and Oprah Winfrey was told she didn't have the talent to do television?

Sure, we can share other people's stories. But if we also share our own, then our students will know that the human who's standing before them is not above the difficult work they're being asked to do. They'll also know that when we fail, we don't have to vindicate ourselves with fame or wealth or any other traditional measure of success. We can instead define success as the act of continuing to pursue meaningful lives. Telling your students about your struggles also shows them that imperfection is normal. Feeling frustrated, embarrassed, and hurt is also normal. Being kind to ourselves can be normal too.

From Students to Teachers

The activities in this chapter help students overcome feelings of disappointment and doubt and treat themselves with compassion and care. This seemed like a fitting way to conclude part I of this book. How can anyone feel empowered to choose values-consistent action and accept struggle if they're not taking care of themselves? Since self-care is always a challenge and always important—not just in school but throughout life—you might repeat these activities as needed.

While part I contains activities that empower students to transform school into a context for values-consistent behavior, part II describes how teachers can put student values at the center of their work in ways that ultimately lead to empowerment.

PART II
Strategies That Empower Students

This part of the book contains strategies teachers can use to empower students through various aspects of their work.

- **Chapter 8**—"Empowering Dialogue: How to Activate Student Values Through One-on-One Conversations"
- **Chapter 9**—"Empowering Partnerships: How to Involve Parents in Helping Students Enact Their Values"
- **Chapter 10**—"Empowering Collaborations: How to Center Student Values in Discussions with Colleagues"
- **Chapter 11**—"Empowering Curriculum: How to Incorporate Student Values Into Your Course Content"
- **Chapter 12**—"Empowering Inquiry: How to Assess the Impact of Helping Students Pursue Their Values"
- **Chapter 13**—"Empowering Yourself: How to Bring Your Own Values to Your Work"

As you read these chapters, you might recognize the EMPOWER processes—exploration, motivation, participation, openness, willingness, empathy, and resilience—woven throughout.

We don't want to give the impression that we think you need to change how you do your work. We proceed from the assumption that you care about your students and are already working to create a learning environment in which they all can thrive. But if you'd like to do more to empower your students, these chapters offer ways you can use student values as a lens through which you consider various aspects of your work at school. Because we intend these chapters to offer possibilities, not mandates, we use language like *you can* and *you might* as opposed to *you should* and *you must*. We offer tools, but you're the expert on whether, when, where, and how to use them.

We also assume that you don't have a whole lot more control over the elements of your students' context than they do. You didn't design the school building. You didn't design the school schedule. You didn't decide which students would be in your class. You probably don't determine much of what will be in the curriculum—if you have any say at all. And maybe you're getting pressure from an administrator to teach in a way you don't think is best, or pressure from colleagues to teach the way they do, or pressure from parents to give more or less or different work and to give their children more attention and higher grades. That's not accounting for stressors in your out-of-school life that might impact your ability to make changes in the classroom, or institutional barriers to your success such as racism, sexism, and homophobia.

We've tried to focus on the places where you do have control: *your* interactions, *your* work products, and *your*self. Even in situations where you have little freedom or control, there will be ways you can choose the qualities of your actions—*how* you approach these aspects of your work.

• • • • •

Chapter 8

EMPOWERING DIALOGUE

How to Activate Student Values Through One-on-One Conversations

With your whole class, you can help students become more aware of their values, commit to behaviors that are consistent with their values, and develop the willingness to struggle with any thoughts and feelings that might get in the way. But in the privacy of one-on-one interactions, you can help students examine their behaviors more closely.

Imagine that Marla and Ned are lab partners in biology class. Marla raises her hand frequently and often receives praise for going above and beyond. Even though she has lots of friends, she won't talk about her feelings when she doesn't get perfect grades; she just stays up later and works harder the next time. Meanwhile, Ned has trouble listening in class, and he finds that even when he tries his best, he still gets low grades. Explaining his thinking is particularly effortful for him, and most assignments involve explaining his thinking. After school, he's so tired that usually he flops onto the couch to watch cartoons with his little sister, or sometimes he makes up funny songs on his guitar. His parents work late and get angry when he hasn't completed his homework by the time they get home.

Marla and Ned have extracted DNA from bananas and are expected to turn in a lab report. Ned doesn't fully understand the process, though he made up funny lyrics about bananas to sing to Marla while she spooled the DNA around the glass rod. Marla writes her part of the report that night. A few days later, she asks Ned to email her his part. He'd forgotten about the assignment, and he lies that his computer crashed. Marla tells her friends that Ned "screwed her over" and ends up crying in the bathroom after staying up late to write Ned's half of the report. She asks her teacher if she can switch lab partners, and when her teacher obliges, Ned is relieved that he won't have to deal with Marla anymore.

Even though Ned and Marla have very different forms of behaviors, the functions of their behaviors are actually quite similar. Both are acting to avoid feelings of inadequacy and embarrassment, leading both of them to sacrifice important aspects of their lives (self-care and authentic friendships for Marla; academic achievement for Ned). Their behaviors aren't working.

Kirk Strosahl and his colleagues say that conversations about whether a behavior is working boil down to three simple questions: "What have you tried? . . . How has it worked? . . . What has it cost you?" (Strosahl, Gustavsson, & Robinson, 2012, pp. 70–79). When students notice that the consequences of their behaviors don't move them toward the lives they want for themselves, they can begin exploring other possible behaviors. Let's see how to start conversations with students about whether their behaviors serve their values.

[handwritten margin note: Nice technique]

Shifting Conversations With Students

When students approach you, they're probably *not* looking for help examining how their behaviors relate to their values. What are they looking for? Sometimes, students come to us because their basic needs are not being met. Students need safety; freedom from harassment and violence; and proper rest, nourishment, and hydration. They need access to friends and mentors, to resources and feedback, and to time for inquiry and reflection. They need challenges that stimulate their curiosity and creativity, and they need standards of excellence they can aspire to meet. They need compassion, care, and love. They need people to treat them equitably. Of course teachers, administrators, and staff have a responsibility to create environments that meet students' needs so they can learn.

[handwritten margin note: Looking beneath the surface of student motivation]

But sometimes, students want us to do something for the sake of their academic or social status, or their happiness or comfort. "Is there extra credit?" means "Will you give me a higher grade than I've earned?" "Can I change my seat?" means "Will you rearrange the class so I can feel comfortable?" "I couldn't finish this homework last night because of a family event" is code for "Will you keep my grade as it is even though I didn't do the work?"

Perhaps you're the one who reached out to a student because of some behavior that goes against school expectations. When students misbehave, you might find yourself in the role of judge. You see or hear about a student who didn't meet behavior expectations, you ask questions to make sure you have the correct details, and you deliver some sort of verdict and punishment, even if that punishment is a verbal warning or a look.

Perhaps you've also found yourself in the role of savior. You see or hear about a misbehaving student, and when you investigate, you discover some horrible situation in the student's life. (The dad left, the mom works all the time, and the grandfather is dying of cancer. The student stays up late taking care of the grandfather and a new baby sister.) You start looking for things you can do to save the student, either by trying to mitigate the situation itself (enroll the student in an after-school homework help program, give his mother the number of a free elder-care service) or ease school-related burdens to make the student feel better (excuse the student from minor assignments, inflate his grades, group him with students who pick up his slack on projects).

[handwritten margin note: What can you do to ameliorate the situation from. Find out the source of behavior.]

You already know that you can't punish every student who misbehaves, and you can't save every student who's suffering. Even if you could, punishments often carry unwanted side effects, and favors to students that remove their burdens can do more harm than good. Perhaps most importantly, taking on the role of judge or savior positions *you* as the actor and the student as the passive recipient. Instead, you can help students take charge of their own education by assessing whether their behaviors *work*—that is, whether their behaviors move them toward the lives they want for themselves. When we use the term *workability*, we mean how well the student's behavior works in terms of his or her own values. Conversations about workability ultimately empower students to hold themselves accountable to their values.

[handwritten margin note: Put the student in control — sense of empowerment]

Having a Conversation About Workability

The quarter is ending, and Marla has an A– average in science. She goes to see her teacher to ask about extra credit. A judging response would be something like, "In this class, grades don't measure who you are as a person or even a scientist. They measure how you did on these particular assignments. And by the way, an A– is an excellent grade!" A savior response would be something along the lines of, "Marla, I know you've had a tough time this quarter. I'll tell you what. I don't give extra credit, but your grade is right on the line between an A– and an A. You've worked hard on every assignment and give such insightful responses in class, so I'm going to bump you up to an A." Neither judging nor saving engenders much conversation. The teacher has spoken and that's that.

Helping Marla assess the workability of her behaviors requires a significantly longer conversation in a tone that's authentic, warm, and genuinely interested in what the student wants his or her life to be about. That conversation might sound something like this.

[handwritten margin note: I just had this conversation w/ a student! (89.31%)]

Teacher: I'm hearing you say you're unhappy with any grade below an A. What have you done this quarter to work for that A?

Marla: A lot. I highlight and then I take notes in my own words so I can make sure I understand. If I don't understand, I go back and reread or I look it up online.

Teacher: Sometimes you email me to ask questions.

Marla: Yeah, sometimes. I make study guides for all the tests, and my dad quizzes me after dinner.

Teacher: I've seen your study guides. They're works of art.

Marla: I color-code by topic.

[handwritten margin note: self-reflection]

Teacher: And what about labs?

Marla: You have no idea. I'm super careful in the lab so I don't make any mistakes.

Teacher: I've seen that. You also follow all the safety procedures so no one gets hurt. What else?

Marla: I spend a lot of time on the write-ups, because those are most of our grade. That banana lab report was a fluke.

[handwritten margin note: I have lots of these convos w/ AP kids]

In asking about her work, the teacher gives Marla an opportunity to describe her study behaviors. He makes a few observations of his own, but mostly he asks questions. That way, Marla can describe her behaviors in her own words.

Teacher: What do you mean? You did well.

Marla: Getting a B+ is not "doing well" for me.

Teacher: Fair enough. So what happened?

[handwritten margin note: Considering how they learn, what their strengths are.]

The teacher and Marla have different ideas about what it means to do well. As soon as he sees that, he validates her idea rather than trying to convince her of his own beliefs. Then he goes back to asking questions so she can continue to describe her behaviors and identify their consequences.

Marla: I didn't want to say anything, but Ned didn't do his share of the work.

Teacher: That sounds unpleasant.

Marla: So unpleasant!

Teacher: What did you do?

[handwritten margin note: → very mature qualities – critical of own behaviors]

Marla: I tried to get him to do the lab report. I kept texting him to remind him, and he totally said he would, but then he didn't. So I had to do it.

Teacher: So first your partner didn't come through on doing work that was important to you—

Marla: I mean, not earth-shatteringly important, but yeah. This class matters to me.

Teacher: That's nice to hear. It matters to me too! So Ned didn't come through on his promise to do the work.

Marla: Yeah, he lied.

Teacher: So you're angry at him and disappointed about how this assignment turned out.

Marla: Yes! I had to do all the work myself. I had to stay up late. I wish I hadn't waited so long for Ned to give me his part. Then I could've done the work earlier and done a better job.

The teacher has built some rapport with Marla by validating her feelings. He doesn't try to convince Marla that she's wrong to feel angry and disappointed, and he gives her some language to name those feelings. If she'd said something like, "Well, maybe I'm not angry, but I'm definitely annoyed," then the teacher could correct himself by saying something like, "Okay, annoyed." In these conversations, the students choose how to characterize their own experiences.

Teacher: So it sounds like for you, working for an A means taking notes, making color-coded study guides, and writing thoughtful lab reports, and it also means taking someone else's responsibilities on yourself and staying up late.

Marla: Kinda, yeah.

Teacher: What else?

Marla: Nothing really.

Teacher: How's your relationship with Ned?

Marla: I don't really have a relationship with Ned. We're not friends.

Teacher: You two are classmates and lab partners. How did that go?

Marla: Bad. He lied. And he didn't do his work, so I had to do it.

Teacher: And how did you treat him?

Marla: Really well! I sent him reminders. I gave him so many chances. And during the lab, I did all the work while he was singing. I mean, really? Who sings when they're supposed to be doing a lab? I could not have been more generous toward Ned.

Only after they've established the benefits of her study behaviors does the teacher move into asking questions to help Marla assess the costs.

Teacher: So, all this generous stuff you do—giving reminders and chances and doing someone else's work and staying up late—has all of that gotten you the A?

Marla: It will if you give me the extra credit. Please? I can do another lab and write a report. Or I can do some extra reading and write an essay or something.

Teacher: What you're doing right now—coming to me to ask for extra credit—is that also part of working for an A?

Marla: I guess.

Teacher: How do you think this conversation is going?

Marla: I don't know. I was hoping you'd let me do an extra credit assignment.

Teacher: What kinds of conversations do you want to have with your teachers?

Marla: I don't know.

Don't want to seam like we're lecturing

Notice that Marla has started to say, "I don't know" and, "I guess." She was speaking pretty confidently at the beginning, but then she became less sure of herself. Moments of uncertainty can become opportunities to play with new possibilities. You can make suggestions for what the student could do, but if *you* sound too certain, you take away the student's power to discover a different course of action and evaluate whether it will serve his or her values. In other words, suggesting what students *could* do is different from telling them what they *should* do. If you make a suggestion, try using a genuinely curious tone, as if to ask, "What would happen if . . . ?" You become a fellow explorer, standing beside the student as you figure out possibilities together. Too much certainty on your part puts you back into the position of authority figure and puts your values ahead of the student's.

The teacher now offers more support by giving an example of the kind of relational behavior he thinks Marla might be after.

Teacher: Well, last week you were asking me about protein structures. We ended up talking all through study hall. That was a pretty fun conversation.

Marla: It was pretty dorky.

Teacher: Is "dorky" good or bad?

Marla: I don't know. I guess it can be good.

Teacher: So is that the kind of conversation you want to have with teachers?

Marla: I guess, yeah.

Teacher: And what about your classmates? What kind of relationships do you want to have with them? What kind of a relationship do you want to have with Ned?

Marla: I don't know. I have to think about that.

As this conversation progresses, the teacher shifts Marla from trying to avoid the fear and potential shame of getting an A− toward noticing how her behaviors serve her values. While Marla will likely leave upset if she doesn't get to do extra credit work and raise her grade, she might also start thinking about some of her behavior patterns. Perhaps she'll question herself the next time she's studying after midnight, or maybe she'll treat Ned a little more like an equal. Even if she doesn't, her focus in the conversation shifted from the outcome (her grade) to her genuine academic interests and relationships. The teacher can watch Marla for signs of values-consistent behavior and point out those moments so she's aware of them.

Empowering students to assess whether their behaviors are working does not mean encouraging them to change or deciding for them if their behaviors are positive. Instead, you're asking questions to help them describe behaviors they've tried and discover for themselves any mismatch between their behaviors and their values. Once they see for themselves that their behaviors aren't moving them toward the lives they genuinely want, they become more willing to explore other behaviors that could work better (Hayes, Strosahl, & Wilson, 1999).

Helping Students Notice Values-Inconsistent Behaviors

Can you think of a recent time when you and a student discussed a problem? How did you respond? How could you have shifted the conversation to an assessment of the long-term workability of the student's behavior, in terms of the student's own values?

Because of the great diversity among students, teachers, problems, and communication styles, you'll have your own way of holding these sorts of conversations with students. Figure 8.1 includes general questions designed to help students understand their behaviors in light of their values. How would you adapt these questions to the specific problem you discussed with your student? How would you change the wording to reach your student? How do you think your student would respond? You might even try role-playing the conversation with a colleague or writing it out as a script.

[handwritten margin notes: "Students become so blinded by the grade, they lost sight." ; "Importance of follow up" ; "Purposeful, meaningful conversations."]

Use these kinds of questions to help students figure out whether their behaviors are consistent with their values in the long term.

What have you tried?

- What's the situation that you don't like?
- What have you done to change this situation?
- What have you done to make the problem go away?

How has it worked?

- How have your actions changed the situation in the short term?
- How have your actions changed the situation in the long term?
- What kind of life do you want at school?
- Did your actions enrich your life?
- Did your actions lead to the education you want?
- Did your actions lead to the relationships you want?

What has it cost?

- How have your actions affected your education?
- How have your actions impacted your relationships?
- How have your actions impacted your health?
- If you could get back the time you spent doing this, how would you use it?
- If you could get back the energy you put into this, how would you use it?
- How do you feel about yourself after doing this?

Figure 8.1: Questions that help students assess behavior workability.

*Visit **go.SolutionTree.com/instruction** for a free reproducible version of this figure.*

When asked to describe behaviors and their consequences, some students might claim they don't remember or that they didn't mean to do what they did. They might try to skip the discussion altogether by offering apologies and self-evaluations: "I'm sorry. It was stupid." Statements like these sometimes indicate fear, embarrassment, or shame, which are powerful emotions that people will go to great lengths to avoid. *Be careful of avoidance.*

Psychologists Jason Luoma and Melissa Platt (2015) suggest getting through fear and shame using perspective taking and self-compassion. You can ask, "How would an observer describe what you did?" (If you can, use the name of someone who was involved in or observed the incident.) Then you can ask, "What would one of your best friends think of that version of the story?" (Again, try to use the name of one of the student's friends.) Taking the perspective of a close friend will allow the student to notice any harsh criticisms and to express more warmth, forgiveness, and compassion. From there, you can ask, "What's your version of the story? What do you wish you could change about what happened? What changes can you make now?"

Looking inward

Questions to help

Moving from Workability to Change

According to psychologists William Miller and Stephen Rollnick (2013), most people know when their behavior is a problem, and they're already having an internal debate about it. Although we, as teachers, might instinctively give students advice on why and how they should change, that makes us the voice of *one* side of their internal debate, which prompts the student to voice the *other* side—if not directly to you, then internally.

[handwritten margin note: AVOID]

A more effective way to motivate students to act in accordance with their values is to get them to do less of what Miller and Rollnick (2013) call *sustain talk* and more of what they call *change talk*. In simple terms, sustain talk is giving reasons for why things are the way they are, such as pleading innocent ("I didn't realize it was plagiarism because I made some changes") or defending an action ("I just got desperate because I didn't know what to write").

[handwritten margin note: Go from being defensive, to working toward change]

While sustain talk is defensive and critical, change talk is exploratory and creative. It involves imagining new possibilities ("I guess I could read more articles before I start writing so I don't accidentally copy one") and making a plan of action ("Next time I'm stuck, I'll ask for help"). Encouraging students to talk about change means you, the teacher, don't have to do any convincing and thus don't invoke the student's natural resistance. Instead, your open-ended questions get the *student* to describe why a new behavior might be desirable. Once the student has articulated those reasons, you say those reasons back and then ask more open-ended questions to get the student to describe what specific actions he or she will take (Miller & Rollnick, 2013). Let's see what that kind of conversation might sound like.

[handwritten margin note: Change is hard for students ... but a noble goal.]

Having a Conversation About Change

Our friend the science teacher is grading research papers and is working on Ned's. The vocabulary and style sound much more sophisticated than Ned's usual prose. The teacher feels a little sick. Ned might be a little flaky about assignments, but he's honest, and he tries his best in class. He wouldn't plagiarize. Would he? The teacher types a sentence from Ned's paper into a search engine, hoping that nothing will come up. But something does.

It would be easy and normal to play judge by reminding Ned of the school's strict academic honesty policy: "Copying and pasting from a website into a report constitutes plagiarism, and the consequence of plagiarism is an automatic zero." It would also be easy and normal to play savior with a response like, "Ned, I know you've been struggling with expository writing, and this was a very challenging assignment. I'd like to help you practice your science writing strategies. Let's meet outside of class to work on a rewrite."

The judge and savior responses don't help Ned understand how plagiarism might conflict with his values. In fact, as a method of avoiding uncomfortable emotions, plagiarism works. In the moment he plagiarized, Ned probably felt less shame, because he was able to finish his paper, and less fear, because he wouldn't disappoint his teacher by turning in a poorly written report. But once he finds out his teacher

Some teacher will be resistant b/c this takes time and they don't want to know baggage.

Empowering Dialogue | 137

is aware of the plagiarism, Ned probably feels a new layer of shame, along with fear of the consequences. He needs strategies to help him manage his academic struggles in a way that matches his values.

Imagine that when Ned's teacher sits him down to discuss the plagiarism incident, he learns that Ned often feels stuck because he doesn't know what to write. He sits at his computer, playing a game or going online while he waits for an idea to come to him, or else he gives up on homework in favor of television or his guitar. When his dad gets home, Ned asks him for help. His dad prompts Ned through the whole assignment. Ned has admitted to the fact that Marla wrote the banana lab report and that he copied parts of his research paper off the web. As the conversation continues, the teacher helps him explore the costs of his behaviors in terms of his values.

Ned: I'm so pathetic.

Teacher: I don't know about that, but it sounds like the writing process you've been using is making you feel pretty disappointed in yourself.

Ned: That's putting it mildly.

Teacher: You feel pretty bad. And it probably wasn't so fun to get caught plagiarizing. Has your writing process had other costs?

Ned: I don't know. What do you mean?

Teacher: Well, has your writing process cost you in terms of your time? Or maybe your relationships?

Ned: I honestly don't know.

"I don't know" often indicates that a student is feeling vulnerable. Sometimes, "I don't know" is code for "I don't want to think about it" or "I don't want to tell you." Sometimes students genuinely don't know why they do what they do. Either way, students often need more values clarification to discover what's important to them. Ned mentioned earlier that he usually works with his dad, so the teacher decides to explore that relationship as a possible source of meaning in Ned's life.

Teacher: How much do you enjoy the time you spend with your dad working on science writing?

Ned: Oh, it's my all-time favorite thing to do with my dad.

Teacher: What else do you like to do with your dad?

Ned: Watch hockey. Sometimes cook.

Teacher: Cook?

Ned: Yeah.

Teacher: What do you like to make?

Ned: Eggplant parmesan. Pasta with broccoli. It depends when he gets home.

> **Teacher:** And my guess is that you were being sarcastic before and that you wouldn't actually rather do science writing with your dad than make eggplant parmesan or watch hockey.
>
> **Ned:** Yeah.

Now that he's gotten Ned talking a little bit more, the teacher decides to venture into Ned's values with respect to other relationships.

> **Teacher:** What about your other relationships? Your relationship with Marla, for example?
>
> **Ned:** Oh, she hates me.
>
> **Teacher:** So your strategies for doing science writing have cost you in terms of your opinion of yourself, the time you could be spending doing other things with your dad, and your relationship with Marla.
>
> **Ned:** She really hates me.

Notice that the teacher is mostly asking open-ended questions and summarizing what Ned has said. Next, still using lots of open-ended questions and summary statements, the teacher asks Ned to describe possible changes to his behavior.

> **Teacher:** How could you change the way you approach science writing?
>
> **Ned:** I don't know.
>
> **Teacher:** Do you remember any of my suggestions from your last report card?
>
> **Ned:** Not really. I'm sorry.
>
> **Teacher:** That's okay. You get a lot of suggestions from teachers! I don't know how anyone would remember them all.
>
> **Ned:** Wait. You said to make a list of questions after every class. I tried that a couple of times, but I couldn't think of what to write.
>
> **Teacher:** Well, that was one suggestion. I'm glad you tried it, but it sounds like it didn't really work.
>
> **Ned:** Sorry.
>
> **Teacher:** Not your fault. Not every suggestion works for every student. That must be why teachers suggest so many options. Let's see what other great words of wisdom I had. (*Pulls up the report.*) I said, "Ned can try drawing his ideas and reading popular nonfiction books and magazines about science so he gets a better sense of what science writing sounds like. He might also try connecting what he learns in science to his outside interests, such as music." Now I'm wondering if cooking and hockey could connect to science too. There's a great book about the chemistry of cooking that I can lend you.
>
> **Ned:** That actually sounds kind of cool.
>
> **Teacher:** The chemistry of cooking book?
>
> **Ned:** Yeah. And I guess the drawing idea sounds kind of fun.

Notice that while the teacher referenced an old report card and offered a book for Ned to read, these gestures were less to advocate for a particular solution than to make the student aware of his options. Next, he asks questions to help Ned explore the possible consequences of these new behaviors.

Teacher: If you start drawing and reading good science writing to help you figure out what to say in your writing assignments, what would be different?

Ned: I don't know. I might actually get a half-decent grade in science?

Teacher: You might. What else?

Ned: I don't know.

Teacher: What about your dad?

Ned: He's going to be so mad.

Teacher: I meant, would anything change with him if you try the reading and drawing ideas?

Ned: Maybe. I might not have to bug him as much.

Teacher: It sounds like you're worried about how he'll react to the plagiarism.

The teacher wants to connect the science strategies to Ned's relationship with his dad, since that's something he clearly already values. But since Ned brought up how his dad would feel about the plagiarism, the teacher moves back to that topic. He's taking his cues from Ned.

Ned: Yeah. My dad's big on integrity.

Teacher: How will he feel when he sees you trying these new ways to approach science writing?

Ned: Good, I guess. He's always lecturing me about hard work.

Teacher: Hard work and integrity.

Ned: Yeah.

Teacher: How important are hard work and integrity to you?

Ned: I don't know. Important, I guess.

Teacher: I get that you're disappointed in yourself about the plagiarism, but how do you feel about yourself now that you're exploring ways to change your approach to science writing?

Ned: Good.

Teacher: Oh, good!

The teacher makes no attempt to play savior by prioritizing possible behaviors or convincing the student that behavior changes are necessary or even important. Ned does that himself! The teacher also makes no attempt to play judge and instead moves the student toward talking about behavior that would bring satisfaction, pride, and vitality. At the end of the conversation, the teacher asks questions that get Ned to commit to a first small step toward change.

Teacher: So, reading about science and drawing to help you think are things you can do while you're waiting for your dad to come home.

Ned: Maybe.

Teacher: Well, if you were going to do those things, what would be your first step?

Ned: I don't know. I guess I could borrow that chemistry of cooking book.

Teacher: You can totally borrow this chemistry of cooking book.

Ned: Thanks.

Teacher: When do you plan to start reading it?

Ned: I don't know. Tonight?

Teacher: Great! How much of it?

Ned: The first chapter?

Teacher: Sounds good! And if by some chance you don't read the first chapter tonight, or you end up not liking this book, is there something else you could do that would help you work on science writing?

Ned: I could read a different book?

Teacher: Okay, Ned. Tomorrow, I'll ask you about the chemistry of cooking book. If you like it, we can talk about it. If not, I'll find you another book. How does that sound?

[handwritten margin note: Turn over change control to student.]

Asking open-ended questions, validating all feelings and experiences, and putting the student in control might feel unnatural and even unnerving when we're used to being in charge in class. But in one-on-one interactions, we have more flexibility to explore possibilities *with* students and leave them in charge of changing.

Helping Students Choose Values-Consistent Behaviors

Since you'll have your own way of encouraging students to talk about change, figure 8.2 has generic questions that can elicit change talk. How would you adapt these questions to help a particular student change? How do you think your student would respond? How would you create opportunities for the student to say more? Again, try writing or role-playing a conversation that would encourage a student to explore possible new behaviors in terms of his or her values and to specify a first step. Naming a first step gives the student an attainable goal to focus on, and succeeding at that goal feels good, which increases the likelihood of the student taking the next step (Nevin, 1992).

Use these kinds of questions to help students experiment with the possibility of values-consistent behavior change.

How does the change match your values?

- Why make changes now?
- What is important to you about making this change?
- How would your life be different if this changed?
- What else in your life could this change affect?
- What will happen if you don't make this change?
- What will happen if you do?
- How important is this outcome to you?
- What kind of life would this change contribute to?

What behaviors would match your values?

- What are some of your options to move toward this change?
- Which options are you considering?
- What would someone who's important to you (a close friend, family member, coach, or mentor) think of these options?
- How do you feel about yourself as a result of exploring the possibility of change?

What happens now?

- What's your first step?
- When do you plan to start?
- How confident are you that you can make this change?
- If this doesn't work out, what else could you do?
- If this does work out, what could you do next?
- How can I support you?
- Who else can support you? How?

Figure 8.2: Questions to encourage change talk.

Visit go.SolutionTree.com/instruction for a free reproducible version of this figure.

Open-ended questions invite students to develop their own ideas and choose what they want to do, but some students might be afraid you're probing for some secret right answer, or they might not know what to say and get flustered. If you're getting a lot of shrugs and *I don't knows* in response to your open-ended questions, offer a few suggestions—preferably ones that reflect the student's interests and values. We recommend giving just a few suggestions so the student has a meaningful choice but isn't overwhelmed by too many possibilities. If the student doesn't seem interested in any of your suggestions, you can offer more. You can think of suggestions ahead of time, maybe in collaboration with your colleagues. But even if you think your own idea is brilliant, if a student comes up with his or her own, honor the idea. You can always revisit your ideas if that of the student doesn't work.

Think of some of the difficult conversations you've had with students. If you could redo one of these conversations, how would you help the student assess behaviors and make changes? How would those changes make school more meaningful and vital for that student?

From Dialogue With Students to Partnerships With Parents

In one-on-one conversations with students, we can help them assess the workability of their behaviors in light of their values and explore the possibility of values-consistent behavior change. We might be tempted to just tell students which behaviors are and aren't working, and what they should and shouldn't do. The problem is that telling them what to do isn't particularly helpful. They might not listen. Even if they do listen, they might be complying just to please us or get us off their backs—not because they're noticing all the different factors that might influence behavior and choosing for themselves what best serves their values. But when we ask them open-ended questions, we're not telling them what to do; we're getting *them* to tell *us*. The next chapter is about how to get parents involved in these conversations too.

We must come to our conclusions on our own.
Can't force change on someone.

Chapter 9

• • • • •

EMPOWERING PARTNERSHIPS

How to Involve Parents in Helping Students Enact Their Values

Usually parents give kids more independence in 11/12th grade.

Middle and high school teachers might not communicate with parents all that often—at least, not as often as our colleagues in elementary schools. We communicate directly with our students and expect them to communicate with us. But we do sometimes get in touch with parents, perhaps through welcome letters, open-school-night presentations, report cards, parent-teacher conferences, and emails. We might maintain websites that parents can access or send newsletters we hope parents will read. We notify parents when a student is not doing well academically, socially, or emotionally. And parents sometimes get in touch with us, usually when they think something is going wrong.

Maybe you love to connect with parents, and maybe you wish you didn't have to interact with them so you could focus on the parts of your job that directly involve students. Maybe your feelings depend on the parent. Regardless of how much (or how little) you enjoy contact with parents, what if you could make this contact more meaningful? What if all the different contexts in which we communicate with parents could become opportunities to empower students?

This chapter gives you tools for framing all communication with parents or guardians in terms that empower students, explaining what EMPOWER work is and how parents can continue it at home, and responding when parents show inflexibility.

Framing School-to-Home Communications

School-to-home communications tend to share information about a student, a class, a program, or a transition. Some go on to suggest (or demand) some sort of response from the parents: "The Thanksgiving food drive begins this Monday. Please send boxed stuffing and canned cranberries." Or, "Conferences are December 9. Please sign up using the parent portal on the school website." Or, "Clara has accrued three tardies and will serve an after-school detention. Please make arrangements to pick her up from the school office at 5:00 p.m."

When you share information with parents or make requests of them, you can frame these communications in terms of helping students make school meaningful. The next three figures are various types of letters home. Despite the fact that they're different kinds of communications, they all do the following.

[handwritten margin note: Important elements in parent contact.]

- Describe what's happening at school, whether it's a program, unit, project, assessment, event, or set of behaviors

- Explain how students can make what's happening meaningful

- Invite parents, as experts on their children, to participate in a collaborative process of empowering the student

- Coach parents on how to empower the student in this context

- Ask for feedback, concerns, and questions

- Provide a variety of methods for further communication, including phone, email, text, and face-to-face meetings

Figure 9.1 is a sample letter that discusses a recent assessment task.

Dear parents and guardians,

In English 8, each writing assignment is an opportunity for students to develop long-term skills and to do personally meaningful work. Our emphasis is on learning effective writing processes, not on creating perfect products. When students do a writing project, they get the following.

- A description of what they'll be creating
- A list of expectations so they know what excellence means
- Model texts so they can see what excellence looks like
- Strategies for writing and revising
- Work time in class and at home

After the due date, I assess the extent to which students met each expectation using the following scale.

- Developing: The student has not yet met expectations in this area. In the future, this student should spend more time using strategies to improve in this area.

- Proficient: The student has met expectations in this area. In the future, this student should keep using the strategies he or she used.

- Exemplary: In this area, the student's writing could serve as an example of excellence. In the future, this student should keep using the strategy he or she used and consider showing it to peers.

You can help by asking your child to describe his or her process and figuring out what worked and what didn't. You could ask questions like these:

- What did you do to write this?
- What did you do to revise?
- What strategies did you use?
- Which strategies were helpful?
- What do you think you'll do next time?

Questions like these empower students to notice what works, make decisions, and grow. Please let me know what thoughts and concerns you have.

All best,

Mr. Solomon
555-555-1263
p.solomon@medianmiddleschool.edu
Open hours 2:00–3:00 p.m.

Figure 9.1: An empowering letter about assessment.

When students can observe and describe their experiences and keep track of which behaviors serve their values, they're empowered to make choices guided by what works for them in different contexts (Villatte et al., 2015). Figure 9.2 is another example of an empowering school-to-home communication. This one helps parents talk with their children about a field experience.

Dear Mathematics 9 parents and guardians,

As part of our study of geometry, our class will be visiting a local architectural firm. Students have heard that mathematics is everywhere, but this is an opportunity for them to see how geometry is used in the real world. We will tour the firm, see the processes of building design, and meet with one of the architects.

Besides signing the attached permission slip and making sure your child returns it by Friday, you can support the work we're doing by asking your child questions about the trip after he or she has returned.

You can try asking, "What did you notice? How do architects use geometry? What communication and collaboration skills do they need? Do you think you'd enjoy a job where you used these kinds of skills? What did you think of the architect you met today? What do you think he or she was like when he or she was in ninth grade?"

A few questions like these can help your child connect his or her experiences on this trip to his or her own values and goals.

If you have any questions or concerns about this trip or about this class, please feel free to contact me.

All best,

Ms. Duncan
555-555-3765
w.duncan@medianhighschool.edu
Open hours 9:00–9:45 a.m.

Figure 9.2: An empowering letter about a field experience.

Figure 9.3 is a letter about a tough but not uncommon issue—classroom behavior that needs addressing. Rather than only describing the behavior and its consequences, the letter discusses how the teacher is helping a student assess whether her behavior is consistent with her own values and invites the parents' participation in that work.

Dear Mr. Carson and Mr. Baker,

Jacqueline is doing well in school overall. I'm writing to let you know that she asks to leave the room quite often—usually once per class—whether it's to get materials she left in her locker, use the bathroom, get a drink, or see the nurse. I've heard from her Spanish and English teachers that she does the same thing in their classes, and they no longer allow her to leave the room.

I know from talking to Jacqueline and seeing her in class that she gets excited about new knowledge—she was particularly passionate during our recent unit on the suffrage movement—and she loves to debate ideas. Jacqueline and I talked about how she's making it harder for herself to learn and debate. Even if she's only gone for a few minutes, it takes her a while to reorient herself and become fully engaged again. I asked why she's leaving class so often, and it sounds like she gets overwhelmed and needs breaks. We discussed ways she can take brain and body breaks, such as stretching in her seat, that will meet her needs without disrupting the learning that matters to her.

I was hoping you might be willing to follow up at home by asking Jacqueline what she finds meaningful in my class and in her other classes. When she leaves class, what is she missing? What can she do in her classes when she needs a break so she doesn't miss out on learning that matters to her?

If you want to talk about this further, please let me know. Let's work together to help Jacqueline make the most of her learning time.

All best to you,

Ms. Topial
555-555-2974
i.topial@medianhighschool.edu
Open hours 9:45–10:45 a.m.

Figure 9.3: An empowering letter about inappropriate behavior.

All of these communications contain questions that parents can ask to help the students talk about their lives: what happened, how they responded, how their response worked out in terms of their own values, and what they might want to do next. We can't have a deep one-on-one conversation with every student after every learning experience, but parents can have those conversations at home with their children.

Soliciting help from parents who see them more often

Describing EMPOWER Work to Parents

We've explained how to frame school-to-home communications about typical school experiences, such as field trips and problem behaviors, in terms of how parents can empower their children to make the experiences meaningful. If you're doing a lot of values activities in your classroom, you might want to send a separate communication about them.

EMPOWER work is probably quite different from what students and their parents would expect of a class. For example, science students expect to read science articles, discuss science concepts, do labs, write reports, take tests, and practice scientific thinking. They probably *don't* expect their classwork to include exploring their values as scientists, using those values as the motivation to do science, participating in making science class personally meaningful, opening up about their values as scientists, developing the willingness to struggle with difficult scientific concepts, learning to treat fellow scientists with empathy, and showing resilience when their scientific endeavors fail. A letter home about these values activities will prevent parents from being surprised or confused by them.

More important, any values activity will have greater impact if students revisit and renew their commitments. What did they try? How did it work out? How did it feel? How did it match up with their values? If they failed, would they like to try again? Is there a different way to accomplish the same goal? Most importantly, what pattern are they building? Psychologist Steven Hayes (2005) explains the importance of noticing patterns in our behavior:

> There is no "time out" from life; no dress rehearsal. This means that every single moment you are building a behavioral pattern. It helps to build larger patterns that serve your interests by acknowledging the patterns that are being constructed as they occur. (p. 187)

Our students might not notice their own patterns, and they might have trouble changing their patterns to serve their values. As their teacher, you haven't necessarily known them long enough or well enough to see their patterns, but their parents have. You also won't necessarily be with your students over years as they continue developing behavioral patterns, but their parents will. For values activities to empower students, even in the short term and especially in the long term, parent involvement can make a big difference.

Both to ensure that parents understand and support EMPOWER work and to invite their help in making it stick, you can send a letter home. If you anticipate doing values activities throughout the year, you might send a letter early on. Visit **go.SolutionTree.com/instruction** to download a free reproducible letter you can use or adapt.

If you send a letter before doing EMPOWER work, know that the word *values* can distract some parents. It's not a bad word (look how many times we've used it in this book), but when hearing or reading *values*, parents sometimes assume you're teaching students what to value, as opposed to helping students see school as a context for enacting values they choose. No matter how well you describe this distinction, some parents might still say it's *their* job to teach their children values and the school's job to teach academic content. One way around this problem is to say *making school feel more meaningful* instead of using the word *values*. You can also use the words in the EMPOWER acronym: exploration, motivation, participation, openness, willingness, empathy, and resilience.

Another way to communicate with parents about EMPOWER work is to send letters home after each activity instead of giving an overview ahead of time. Follow-up letters can give more specific details about the activity and its purpose, thus helping parents continue conversations with their children at home and reinforce the work.

Figure 9.4 has an example of a follow-up letter that a teacher might send after doing the Focus Stickers activity (chapter 2, page 37). Like the earlier letters in this chapter, it describes the activity, explains how the work will help students make the class meaningful, invites parents to participate, explains what they can do, and welcomes further dialogue.

(*) These types of suggestions are helpful — Kids don't always talk to parents, but parents want to be kept in loop

Dear parents and guardians,

In chemistry class, we have recently completed our study of atomic structure and begun a new unit on how atoms bond to form compounds. This unit will take us to winter break.

Now that we've settled into the routines and expectations of this class, and given the excitement of upcoming breaks and events, it seems like an important time for students to think about who they want to be as learners. Today, we did an activity in which we considered past learning experiences that were particularly meaningful. Students wrote about science classes in middle or elementary school, learning from nature or at home, and learning beyond science. Each student listed things he or she was doing during the learning experience, such as asking questions or imagining possible outcomes, and chose one behavior that would make chemistry class (and perhaps other classes) more meaningful. Finally, each student created an icon to represent his or her chosen behavior and drew the icon on dot stickers. They put these stickers on their lab notebooks, chemistry textbooks, calculators, laptops, and other personal belongings to remind them to try the behaviors.

You might see the stickers on your child's materials. You can ask what the icon represents and whether your child has tried that behavior in chemistry class or elsewhere. You can ask questions like, "What did you do? What happened next? How did it feel? What if you tried this more often or in other contexts?"

If you're interested, you could even try this activity yourself! What learning experience was particularly meaningful to you? What were you doing during that experience? Which of those behaviors could you do in other contexts as a way of making them more meaningful? What icon could represent that behavior? Where could you put it to remind yourself to do what you want to do?

As always, please be in touch if you have questions about this or any work we do in chemistry class, or with any other concern.

Be well,

Dr. Sosa
555-555-1384
r.sosa@medianhighschool.edu
Open hours 2:30–3:15 p.m.

Figure 9.4: A letter to parents following a values activity.

As parents learn about how you're empowering students in your class, some might want to keep building their capacity to have related conversations at home. Figure 9.5 has a list of more general questions you can give parents to ask their children. Send it along with the "Examples of Values" handout in the appendix (page 214).

At school, the students have been working to connect their assignments and interactions to their values. Some of you have expressed interest in continuing this work at home. Attached is a list of common values, which we are defining as *qualities of action that make life meaningful*. Ask your child to choose one that feels particularly important. Then ask one of the following questions, filling in the blank with the value. You might even try doing this yourself, with the same value your child chose or with a different one.

- When did you act _____ today?
- When can you act _____ tomorrow?
- When is it hard to act _____?
- When you have trouble acting _____, what do you do?
- If you could, how would you create an opportunity to live more _____ at school?
- Who can help you create an opportunity to live more _____ at school?
- How can I help you live more _____?
- How could learning about [a topic] help you live _____?
- How could practicing [a skill] help you live _____?
- How could reading [a book] help you live _____?
- How could going to [a place] help you live _____?
- How could doing [an extracurricular activity] help you live _____?
- Who is one of your classmates who supports you when you try to act _____?
- Who is one of your classmates who pushes you to act _____?
- Who is one of your classmates who inspires you to act _____ by setting an example?
- How can you support other people who act _____?
- How can you push other people to act more _____?
- How can you inspire other people to act _____ by setting an example?

Figure 9.5: Asking questions about values.

Visit go.SolutionTree.com/instruction for a free reproducible version of this figure.

Gets students to think outside the box of all that matters is grades rather than character + values.

If you want to get parents even more involved in EMPOWER work, try adapting one of the activities from part I to do with them. You could try a quick one on open-school night and introduce it by saying, "This is the sort of work we'll be doing this year." Or, you could organize a parent event specifically to do these activities. Better still, ask some of your students to lead them.

So far, we've seen how you can communicate with parents when you're the one reaching out to them. What about when they reach out to you? Often, parents reach out because their children are upset about something at school or aren't getting grades the parents like. Sometimes parents' agendas can actually frustrate students' efforts to live by their values. In the next sections, we'll see how that works and what you can do about it.

Parent Behaviors That Interfere With Student Empowerment

Some parents might seek your help so their children behave in values-consistent ways, but often they're looking for something else. Let's look at two common agendas—happiness and achievement—that parents have when they contact teachers.

The Happiness Agenda

Sometimes parents are upset because their children are upset. They're looking for the quickest way to make them happy again. Imagine that a history teacher paired Lanny and Rachel together for a project. Rachel works hard and gets decent grades, mostly upper Bs, and she's very vocal during class discussions. She has lots of friends, goes to parties, and is out as bisexual. Lanny also works hard and has always been a top performer, but she's quiet in class so no one realizes how smart she is. She spends her free time making art and doing imaginative play with her younger siblings. Lanny understands the causes of the French Revolution better than Rachel does, but she doesn't want to contradict anything Rachel says. The girls end up getting a B– on their project. Rachel is annoyed that Lanny didn't speak up during the assignment and tells her friends that Lanny is probably homophobic. Lanny's parents call to complain and ask to have her moved into a different history class.

Of course parents want their children to be happy. No parent in his or her right mind wants to see a child suffer, whether it's because of a conflict with a peer or a teacher, a challenging assignment, a heavy workload, a distracting noise, or anything else at school that's unpleasant. As always, the basic response to an aversive is to get away from it (Sidman, 1989). The easiest way for the parents to escape their own distress is for their child to be happy, and the easiest way to make the student happy is to get her away from the aversive.

While removing a student from a context that makes her unhappy might resolve the problems initially, this would be a missed opportunity to understand something important about the student's school experience. Pain can teach us about the students involved in such situations; often, their pain means something important is at stake. Instead of removing the child from the aversive context, we can try to understand the context better. What's important to the student? How is that important thing at stake? What can the student do to work toward what's important? Who else is involved, and what are their responsibilities?

Sure, Lanny will be happier if she's not in class with Rachel. But learning, using her imagination, and nurturing others (like her younger siblings) seem like they're important values for her. Maybe instead of switching her history class, she could learn some communication skills that will help her assert herself at school and some willingness skills that will help her accept uncomfortable thoughts and feelings that show up when she's partnered with a student who has more social power. What if Lanny's parents and teacher all worked together to help her understand her values, commit to them, and accept the struggles that come along with that commitment?

The Achievement Agenda

Another common reason parents get upset is that they have higher expectations for their child's academic achievement than what the student actually achieves. Imagine that Rachel's parents are also upset. Sure, Bs are great, but their daughter is capable of getting As. Why isn't she? They call her history teacher to argue about the B– on the project. She worked so hard on it, they say, and they complain it's not fair that her semester grade will get pulled down because "that girl, who we're sure is very nice," didn't pull her weight. They tell the teacher that they're getting Rachel a tutor who will work with her on all projects in the future.

Again, most parents want their kids to have every possible chance at a good life, so of course they care about grades, scores, and other achievement indicators. But parents can get attached to images of what they think their children should get at school—the grades they should get in class, the scores they should get on tests, the parts they should get in plays, the positions they should play on teams. And like any other time someone gets caught up in an image of how he or she thinks things should be, parents can lose sight of their own values, as well as those of their children (Dahl et al., 2009). Without an understanding of the student's values, any attempts to raise achievement will be unlikely to result in meaningful learning and might even subvert it. Focusing on getting better grades can mean avoiding challenges, risks, and imaginative leaps that lead to learning.

Instead of treating the situation (and the student) like a problem to fix, we can attempt to understand why the student is having difficulty achieving parent-determined criteria of success. Again, we can ask what's important to the student, not only in terms of outcome (because most students want good grades) but also in terms of process. What makes learning meaningful for this student? What can the student do to make her experiences at school more meaningful? Who can help, and how?

Rachel will probably get better grades with the help of a tutor, but working hard, speaking her mind, and having authentic relationships seem like they're important values for her. Maybe instead of getting a tutor, which she might not even want, she could learn some study skills so her hard work gets her where she wants to go, and some empathy skills that will help her engage in deeper dialogues in class and while working on projects. What if Rachel's parents and teacher all worked together to help her gain greater awareness of her values, commit to them, and develop the willingness to struggle?

Parents Moving Toward an Empowerment Agenda

The happiness agenda and achievement agenda aren't things. They're convenient labels for common influences on parent behaviors. Often, you'll see both agendas operating at once. Rachel's parents want her to get good grades so she'll eventually have access to a life that will make her happy, and Lanny's parents want to remove the source of her unhappiness so she can focus on her work and get better grades.

When parents ask you to make changes in the service of their children's happiness, achievement, or both, you can reframe the conversation in terms of the students' values. Just as you would with a student,

They want you or them to be the saviors for the student

you can ask open-ended questions: "What's going on? What's important to the student? How have the student's behaviors worked out in terms of those values? What else could the student try? How can we all help?" You can validate parents' feelings and experiences, *and* you can keep turning the conversations back to the students' values. *(handwritten: (x) We often take the child out of the equation — disservice to student for parent to swoop in.)*

Here's what an empowering conversation with Lanny's mom might sound like. Notice how the parent immediately expresses her happiness and achievement agendas, and how the teacher shifts her toward empowering the student to serve her own values.

Mom: Thanks for meeting with me. I just want to start by saying Lanny loves your class and loves you. Her favorite subject was always art, but now it's art and history. She likes school, and she's always been a strong student.

Teacher: Still is.

Mom: Exactly. That's why she needs to move into a different class, or at least have her seat changed so she doesn't have to work with Rachel anymore.

Teacher: Well, before we discuss possible solutions, help me understand more about what you're seeing. What did Lanny do for this project?

The parent comes in with a pretty clear position: she wants her daughter moved. Instead of offering a quick solution, the teacher asks questions to explore more of the context.

Mom: If anything, she worked harder than ever. She was talking about the French Revolution all last week, and then she was texting back and forth with Rachel all weekend. At around eleven on Sunday night, right when I was about to go to bed, of course, Lanny was in tears trying to edit the document Rachel sent her. She wanted me to help her make some of the arguments clearer and add more evidence, but every time I made a suggestion, she got very anxious and said Rachel wouldn't like it. I really hate to say anything negative about another child, but I don't think it's right that Lanny had a partner who intimidated her and dragged her down academically. Can she redo the assignment?

Teacher: Hold on. Lanny said Rachel intimidated her?

Mom: She didn't use those words, but it was very clear to me that she was worried about what Rachel would think, and that she understood the material better but didn't want to rewrite Rachel's parts.

Teacher: And you're concerned that Lanny will struggle in history class this year because most of her assignments involve group work.

Mom: I'm concerned that she's going to stop loving history and that she won't learn how to assert herself because she's afraid her partner will say something mean to her.

Teacher: It sounds like it's important to you that Lanny develops her passions and learns how to assert herself.

Mom: Yes.

The teacher is giving the parent a chance to express her concerns and saying back what the parent seems to value. Once the parent's values are clear, the teacher asks a question to get the student's values into the conversation, too.

Probing conversations to get at the root of problems.

Teacher: Would you say those things are important to Lanny?

Mom: Definitely. Well, learning about history is important to her. I'm not sure about asserting herself. She's the oldest, but she's not a typical firstborn. She's not bossy at all. My younger two are always bossing her around. They roll right over her.

Teacher: Yeah?

Mom: Oh yeah. Always asking her to make them a snack or read to them or help with their homework. Sunday night, while Lanny was supposed to be working on her paper for your class, her brother got her to help him build a fort and make him popcorn to eat in it. And I was like, "Are you kidding me?"

Teacher: Sounds like Lanny's got a lot going on.

Mom: She does. But she never slacks on her schoolwork, no matter how crazy it gets at home.

Teacher: She's never missed an assignment in my class.

Mom: Oh no, that wouldn't be Lanny. She'd get up in the dark before she came to school without her homework.

Now that the parent has more fully described the student's context—her values, feelings, and actions at home and at school—the teacher summarizes what the parent has said so far.

Teacher: I think we agree that the issue isn't a lack of effort or an inability to do well in history. It's more that she's so concerned about other people's needs that she doesn't always assert her own.

Mom: Yes. That's exactly right.

Teacher: And even if she's not necessarily interested in becoming more assertive, the fact that she's always putting other people's needs ahead of hers sometimes gets in her way.

Mom: I mean, she's good at keeping up with her responsibilities.

Teacher: Sure.

Mom: But maybe it's hard on her.

Teacher: Especially if she's staying up late to do her work because she was busy helping her brother. And she wasn't even pleased with the result of all that work. How can we support Lanny in becoming more assertive?

The teacher has continued to summarize and validate the parent's concerns, so that now the teacher and parent are telling the same story and are ready to work toward the same goal, together.

Mom: What do you think?

Teacher: I think she might need some practice saying what she needs.

Mom: That she does. Well, what if I talk to her about it? I could help her practice telling her siblings what she needs. And telling me.

Teacher: I think I can help with her assertiveness the next time there's a group project by asking her and her partner about their vision for the assignment. That way I'll be able to ask questions to help Lanny say what she thinks. I can also watch for signs that her partner is taking over and coach her on how to respond.

Mom: That sounds like it could work. I hope Lanny is willing to give it a try.

Teacher: Me too! How should we talk to her about it?

Mom: Let me raise it with her at home and then we'll go from there.

Teacher: Okay, let me know how it goes. I'm excited to give this a try.

Mom: Me too.

Since you'll have your own way of talking to parents about their children's behaviors, figure 9.6 has general questions that can help move parents toward an empowerment agenda. How would you adapt these questions when talking to a particular parent who has a strong happiness or achievement agenda? How do you think that parent would respond?

Use these kinds of questions to help parents assess how well their children's behaviors serve their values, imagine new possibilities for their children, and discover how they can help.

Questions about the situation

- What do you see from your end?
- What is your perspective on your child's experience at school?
- How is this situation affecting your child?
- Has this kind of situation happened before?
- How is this time different?

Questions about workability

- When does your child avoid some aspect of school (such as doing a task, taking on a challenge, making decisions, or working with another student)?
- What does your child do to avoid this aspect of school?
- What do you do when you see your child avoiding this aspect of school?
- What have you tried at home to address the situation?
- What strategies seem to help?

Questions about the student's values

- What does your child spend his or her free time doing?
- What is your child good at?
- When does your child seem to care the most about something at school?
- When does your child try his or her hardest at school?
- Has there ever been a topic, project, or assignment your child continued to learn about or work on after he or she no longer needed to for school?

Questions about alternative behaviors

- What strategies haven't you tried?
- What's stopping you from trying these strategies?
- Why try something new?
- What will happen if you don't try this?
- What will happen if you do?
- How important is this outcome to you?
- What would help you try this?

Questions about supporting the student

- When your child is struggling with some aspect of school, what does he or she need from you?
- How can other members of your family support your child with something he or she is struggling with?
- Do peers play a role in supporting your child?
- Which adults at school does your child talk the most about?
- What role can adults at school have in supporting your child?

Figure 9.6: Questions to encourage an empowerment agenda.

*Visit **go.SolutionTree.com/instruction** for a free reproducible version of this figure.*

Dealing With Parent Inflexibility

Some parents are so stuck in their happiness and achievement agendas that they'll resist your efforts to empower their kids. Perhaps you've met these parents. Parents who minimize their children's misbehavior: "He studied really hard and only *one* answer was copied. It's not fair that he should get a zero on the test." Parents who deflect responsibility and blame others: "Of course she's getting bad grades. She hasn't learned a thing in that class." Parents who negate other people's experiences: "I understand that touching in school is inappropriate, but she's his friend. It was just a joke. Don't you think a suspension is a little harsh?" Parents might try to intimidate us into giving them what they want, or they might feign warmth in an attempt to manipulate us. These are all strategies for avoiding the pain of seeing their children suffer.

In situations when parents avoid their pain by attacking us, we sometimes go on the defensive. We refer the parents to a supervisor who will back us up, or we invoke the authority of a school policy. Maybe we avoid a face-to-face confrontation and use email instead, or we give difficult parents what they want because the conflict doesn't feel like it's worth our energy. We don't need difficult parents to make our jobs harder, but are students empowered when their parents and teachers are at odds?

Professor and author Paul Gilbert (2010) explains that when we feel threatened or goal driven, we tend to focus all of our attention on whatever moves us away from the threat or toward the goal, and our thoughts and behaviors become very rigid. We see no perspective but our own and no course of action but the one we've already decided is right. This makes sense from an evolutionary perspective; when our ancestors on the savanna saw an animal they could eat or that could eat them, they would have been mauled or starved to death if they'd sat around exploring their thoughts and feelings. Now our context is very different, but it's as if our brains never got that memo. Only when we feel safe and content do we become more flexible. It's then we can look around, consider other perspectives, develop creative solutions, and work together (Gilbert, 2010). When we represent the institution that's making their children suffer, how can we get parents to feel safe and content around us so that we can have a conversation that empowers their children?

One way to increase feelings of safety and connection is to use compassion (Gilbert, 2010; Kolts & Chodron, 2015). Compassion means noticing that a person is suffering and finding the motivation to respond in a way that's helpful. As teachers, we can develop compassion for parents—even and perhaps especially for inflexible parents. Rather than labeling them as obnoxious jerks (which might feel accurate but doesn't particularly help us or the student), we can attempt to notice how they're suffering, find the motivation to respond, and respond in a way that will help the parent—and ultimately empower the student. We can also develop compassion for ourselves, since our jobs are tough. Self-compassion is when we notice how *we're* suffering, find the motivation to respond, and respond in a way that will help *ourselves*, and again ultimately empower the student (Neff, 2011).

Figure 9.7 helps you explore compassionate responses when you encounter a difficult situation with a parent. In the first row, you're noticing the parent's suffering, finding the motivation to respond, and figuring out how to respond in a way that's helpful to the parent and ultimately empowering to the student. In the second row, the person whose suffering you're noticing and responding to is *you*.

	How is this person suffering right now?	Why would I want to help this person?	What can I do that will be helpful?
Compassion for the parent			

Compassion for yourself			

Figure 9.7: Exploring compassionate responses.

*Visit **go.SolutionTree.com/instruction** for a free reproducible version of this figure.*

[handwritten: Suppress ego, need for control]

Instead of responding to parents' rigid behaviors with our own rigid behaviors—labeling them as difficult, judging their parenting abilities, invoking authority, arguing back, letting them roll us over—we can respond with compassion. We can ask about the parent's experience: "What has this been like for you?" Asking about the parents' perspective will make them feel like you hear and support them rather than that you are ignoring or judging them. They might even return the compassion and ask what your experience has been like. From there, you can move the conversation back toward exploring the student's values, possible behaviors, and ways you and the parents can work together to support the student. Even if you don't come up with a plan that satisfies everyone, you can say something like, "I might not know exactly what to do here, but I'm in this with you. Let me think about this more. I might come up with some new suggestions of things to try, but I want to hear from you if you think they'll work."

From Partnerships With Parents to Collaborations With Colleagues

[handwritten: Similar experiences like these.]

Communications with parents—from course information to emails to family conferences—can become contexts for empowering students. We can coach parents to ask questions that get their children talking about how their experiences at school match up with their values. When parents come to us with their own agendas, we can try to shift those conversations so they become about student values. Even if the parents stay attached to their agendas, we can show compassion and build the kind of partnership that enables us to work with them in the future. In these ways, student values can frame all communications with parents so that we're collaborating with them to empower their children. In the next chapter, we'll see how student values can frame collaborations with our colleagues too.

Chapter 10

• • • • •

EMPOWERING COLLABORATIONS
How to Center Student Values in Discussions With Colleagues

[handwritten margin note: → This actually backefires. We have a preconceived notion that limits the student]

At many schools, teacher teams meet regularly to discuss students they have in common. When we talk about achievement, we're asking if the student is meeting someone's benchmark of success in an area someone defined as important. What constitutes success and whether an area is important depends on values. When we discuss discipline, we're asking if the student is complying with a rule someone thought was necessary for ensuring a good learning community. Whether a rule is necessary and what makes a learning community good also depend on values. Any time we discuss whether a student is following rules or meeting standards, we're making determinations based on values, but not necessarily the *student's* values.

We're not saying that rules and standards are bad. They're important for creating a safe, healthy, and respectful environment where all students can learn and grow and become their best selves. But when we're discussing an underachieving or misbehaving student in a team meeting, we don't necessarily ask questions like, "What makes school meaningful *for this student*? What kinds of behaviors would empower him or her? What contextual factors would help this student notice and choose more values-consistent behaviors?" The approach to faculty-team discussions in this chapter doesn't ignore rules and standards; it just makes room for student values too.

To *center* student values in discussions with colleagues means making those values the focus. In this chapter, we'll explain how focusing on student values can encourage productive, positive conversations

[handwritten margin note: ↓ This is lacking]

about students. We'll then offer tools to help you understand the contextual influences on student behavior and work with your team to support students, including those who underachieve or misbehave and those who are successful.

Having Productive Conversations

Yes.

If your school has team meetings, what happens in them? Do people sometimes complain about students? That's understandable. Whatever the student under discussion does probably frustrates and exhausts a fair number of the people in the room. The students don't do their work. They don't pay attention. They misunderstand even the simplest of directions. They waste time disputing the merits of the assignment instead of actually completing it. They don't ask for the help they need, or they ask for help they don't need. They show up for class without the most basic supplies, they talk when they're supposed to listen, and they don't talk when they're supposed to contribute.

Sums it up. Can't stand these convos. (Unproductive)

When we can't get a student to follow rules or meet standards, complaining to our colleagues and hearing their similar complaints might help us feel better. We find we're not alone, the situation isn't our fault, we did our best, and we're still good teachers. But complaining often serves as an avoidance move that ultimately doesn't help our students or ourselves. After a meeting, we might feel like we've done something about the problem, because we have: we've talked about it. At that point, we feel a sense of satisfaction, and that good feeling reduces our motivation to make changes that actually would help the student (Villatte et al., 2015). And if we don't change what we do, the student continues to misbehave or underachieve, we continue to feel stressed out, we complain some more, we feel better, and we don't take further action. All of this is understandable, and none of it works.

Interest- ing point.

More useful team meetings involve identifying specific actions that will help solve the problem, and then deciding who will take each action and when. Say Silas gets back a quiz with a low score, and as soon as class ends he runs into the hallway and shouts, "Ms. Hernandez is a . . ." (you can make up your own ending to that sentence). Silas's teachers meet and create a set of action steps. They'll have him do some reflective writing on why using foul language is wrong, make sure he apologizes to Ms. Hernandez and does some work in her classroom, provide him with extra help so he doesn't do poorly on future quizzes, and call home to inform his family.

While this team undoubtedly intends to support Silas, in all likelihood, he sees these supports as punishments. They don't address whatever was happening in his life that prompted him to make the nasty comment. Also, the teachers proceeded from the assumption that Silas's comment is bad. *They* surely experience it as offensive; most teachers would. But how is it bad *for Silas*? What makes school meaningful for him, and how does making offensive comments about teachers get in the way of his making school meaningful?

Beyond complaining and before taking action to support students who break school rules, we can focus on understanding the behavior. How are these students benefiting from what they do? There must be

Getting at the root of the behavior.

some benefit to what they do, or they wouldn't do it (Chance, 1998; Skinner, 1981). What are the costs to them in terms of their own values? What might they want to try doing instead? When collaborative teams ask questions like these, they set themselves up to help students notice how their behaviors interfere with enacting their own values.

Understanding Behavior in Context

Goal is to better understand the context of the behavior.

Imagine that Silas gets home and discovers a plate of freshly baked oatmeal cookies in the kitchen. Whether he eats one will depend on all kinds of factors. How hungry is he? How soon is dinner? Is he aware of the benefits of eating whole oats? Is he sensitive to the gluten or worried about the fat? Who made the cookies? Was it his brother, who needs them for tomorrow's bake sale, or his ninety-year-old grandfather, who might be insulted if no one eats the cookies? The last time Silas had oatmeal cookies, were they chewy and delicious, or were they flavorless and hard as rocks? Behaviors occur in a context that includes physiological, psychological, social, cultural, historical, and environmental factors—and all of these factors will influence the form and function of the behavior.

Silas's use of foul language also happened in a context. Maybe in the past he's used foul language and his friends and even some of his teachers thought it was funny. Maybe he didn't realize how offensive the word was. Maybe he thought Ms. Hernandez deserved it. Maybe Silas is feeling particularly stressed because his mom is in the hospital recovering from surgery and the outburst made him feel better. Or maybe this is his third time yelling obscenities in the hallway and now he'll be on probation, which he secretly sort of wants because it means the school will put him into a social skills class with his favorite teacher and his best friend.

Yelling the expletive had some desirable function for Silas, or he wouldn't have done it. School officials might attach a punishing consequence, like placing Silas on probation. But punishing the behavior doesn't take away whatever reinforcing consequences he got from doing it in the first place. If Silas's outburst allows him to spend more time with his friend and his favorite teacher, probation isn't even a punishment; it actually functions as a reward!

What if Silas learns that even if he's on probation, the school won't place him into the skills class with his friend? Then the outburst doesn't have the same reinforcing consequences. And what if his friend also takes a coding class that Silas has the opportunity to take? He's always been interested in how things work, and he sort of wants to learn how to code. The coding class serves one of the same functions (giving him time with his friend) but isn't problematic and might even have other rewards. Is Silas going to be as likely to yell expletives in the hallway?

Once we discover the functions of behaviors, we can frame them as problems not because they're inherently bad or against the rules, but because they move the students away from outcomes they value. We can encourage new behaviors (like going to coding class) that will serve some of the same functions and move the students toward their values, and we can remove reinforcing consequences of problem behaviors (like when Silas learned he wouldn't take the skills class anyway). We can also try to create learning environments that don't trigger the behaviors in the first place.

The rest of the chapter offers tools you and your team can use to understand student behavior in relation to its context and help students shape their behaviors to match their values.

Working Together to Understand Student Behavior

Determining the functions of problem behaviors, encouraging students to try behaviors that make school meaningful, and creating conditions that make the problem behaviors less likely and the new behaviors more likely represent a lot of work. Not only do we make all that work easier if we share it, but the student is more likely to succeed at behavior change with assistance from multiple adults.

Figure 10.1 is a form you can use to structure discussions about student behavior.

[Handwritten margin note: Good activity! Wouldn't think you'd need this, but we do. Convos quickly devolve.]

1. What makes school meaningful for this specific student?	2. What is this student doing that's a problem in terms of his or her own values?
3. What does the student gain from behaving in these problematic ways? □ Tangible things □ Sensory stimulation □ Peer attention □ Adult attention □ Escape □ Other:	4. What behaviors could this student try in order to move toward a more meaningful school experience?
5. What conditions might support these more values-consistent behaviors?	6. What conditions tend to trigger the problem behaviors?

Figure 10.1: Understanding problem behavior.

*Visit **go.SolutionTree.com/instruction** for a free reproducible version of this figure.*

You and your colleagues identify what makes school meaningful for that student. From the beginning, you orient the discussion toward empowering students, not fixing them. It helps to have already done a values clarification activity such as Flight Plan (chapter 1, page 15) or Grading Your Classes (chapter 2, page 32). Values clarification can happen after a problem behavior has already occurred, but then you risk making the activity feel like a punishment.

Next, your team discusses the student's problem behavior, but rather than telling stories about the student's transgressions and sinking further into collective exasperation, you discuss how the behavior is inconsistent with the student's own values.

From there, your team identifies possible functions of the behavior. In general, students engage in problem behaviors because they want a tangible object or activity, some kind of sensory stimulation, attention from adults or peers, or an escape (Steege & Watson, 2009). The escape can be from a task, like when a student fakes an illness to get out of a dodgeball game or spends half her writing time getting her pencil to a perfect point. But the escape can also be from an unwanted emotion, like boredom, frustration, or shame.

Sounds like Jeff S.

You won't know just from the behavior what its function is; you have to understand the student's context. For example, if Sierra is constantly clicking her pen during independent work time, she might just like the way it sounds and feels (sensory stimulation), she might be looking for attention from the teacher who keeps shushing her and the peer who keeps elbowing her, or she might be clicking her pen to escape actually writing with it. If Benny grabs Tula's furry hat, it's probably because he wants attention from her and from the peers who egg him on, but he might want the hat itself (a tangible item), or he might like the way it feels (sensory stimulation). If Krishna jokes around during algebra lessons, it could be to escape the work or his anxiety about it, to get attention from his peers and teacher, or even to get the sensory stimulation of hearing his classmates laugh. It could be a combination.

You also won't know how any particular function will manifest as a behavior. Look at some of the ways students avoid feeling embarrassed. Sometimes they try to control people or situations so they're less likely to feel embarrassed in the first place. They might make mean comments, exclude their peers, clown around, get straight As, compete for leadership roles, or drink alcohol. Other times, students avoid embarrassment by withdrawing from people or situations. They might skip class, stay quiet, read constantly, overuse technology, hide in the bathroom, or take drugs. These behaviors don't *always* serve the function of embarrassment avoidance, but they all can.

Since you can't know just from the behavior what its function is, it helps to have a team of teachers working together to figure it out. Your colleagues see your student in different contexts and have different insights, and as a group you can see patterns that no single one of you is as likely to notice.

Once you have a hypothesis about the behavior's function, you can collaboratively generate ideas for other behaviors that would serve similar functions without getting in the way of students finding meaning at school. How can Krishna occasionally escape the pain of algebra lessons without disrupting class or missing the mathematics skills he'll need to plan environmental justice actions? How can Benny get Tula's attention in a way that feels less like harassment and more like the friendship he's seeking? How can Sierra use her creativity to get sensory stimulation that won't disturb her classmates? Maybe she could lead drumrolls when the teacher changes topics, or wear a funky necklace she can fidget with silently.

Coming up with functionally similar but formally different behaviors is often difficult, especially if you're also trying to match the new behaviors to the student's own values *and* produce several possibilities in case the student can't or won't try some of them or doesn't find the new behaviors as reinforcing as the old problematic ones. Involving more people—colleagues, the student, the family—can make a big difference.

Last, your group identifies *antecedents*, or conditions that cue the behavior. Sierra is more likely to click her pen if she has the kind of pen that clicks. Then again, if she had a different kind of pen, she might just tap it instead. It helps to look for other antecedents. Does she click her pen more when she's stressed? Tired? In history rather than French? When she's in the windowless basement classrooms? During the final minutes of each period?

Getting definitive answers to these questions just to get Sierra to stop clicking her pen is probably not worth the data-collection effort. The point is that all kinds of internal and external factors might affect the frequency, intensity, and duration of problem behaviors, such as Sierra's pen clicking. And while it might not be possible to remove these factors, her teachers and parents, in cooperation with each other and with Sierra herself, can do their best to mitigate them—or at least be more aware of how they work.

Similarly, if Sierra's new behaviors are to become successful replacements for her pen clicking, then she'll need support. Her parents can buy her a necklace to fidget with, remind her to get enough rest, and express interest when she comes up with creative ways to meet her sensory needs. Her teachers can signal moments in class when it's appropriate for everyone to tap and fiddle, since other students might need sensory stimulation, too. The teachers can also have further discussions about how to meet students' sensory needs as they get older.

To make the process of analyzing student behavior go more quickly, you could create a version of the form that includes checklists of problem behaviors and student values you commonly see at your school. Figure 10.2 (page 165) shows an example. We adapted the checklist of what makes school meaningful for students from "What Makes a Class Meaningful?" (figure 2.1, page 32; you could also use the "Examples of Values" handout in the appendix, page 214). If your school has the technology platform to support it, you can create an electronic version of the form, which would allow you and your team to track progress and share information more easily.

Another helpful resource, Administrators should have these... Especially now that restorative justice is a thing > Academy fodder ?

What makes school meaningful for this specific student?

- ☐ Learning about topics of personal importance
- ☐ Learning about topics of importance to the student's family
- ☐ Learning about topics of importance in the world
- ☐ Learning about him- or herself, identity, and place in the world
- ☐ Using his or her creativity
- ☐ Exploring, experimenting, and asking questions
- ☐ Building relationships with peers
- ☐ Building relationships with teachers
- ☐ Developing skills that help in other classes or outside school
- ☐ Developing the skills of a responsible adult
- ☐ Developing the skills to get into a good college, career, or both
- ☐ Developing the skills to make positive change in the world
- ☐ Seeing new perspectives and developing empathy
- ☐ Belonging to a community
- ☐ Showing leadership
- ☐ Doing challenging work
- ☐ Other:

What is this student doing that's a problem in terms of his or her own values?

- ☐ Dealing with irrelevant matters during class
- ☐ Using electronic devices inappropriately
- ☐ Calling out
- ☐ Chatting with peers
- ☐ Teasing or attacking classmates
- ☐ Disrespectfully arguing with the teacher
- ☐ Refusing to do academic tasks
- ☐ Leaving the classroom
- ☐ Clowning
- ☐ Constantly demanding help
- ☐ Lying
- ☐ Other:

What does the student gain from behaving in these problematic ways?

- ☐ Tangible things
- ☐ Sensory stimulation
- ☐ Peer attention
- ☐ Adult attention
- ☐ Escape
- ☐ Other:

Figure 10.2: Understanding problem behavior (with checklists and action steps). continued ⇨

*Visit **go.SolutionTree.com/instruction** for a free reproducible version of this figure.*

What behaviors could this student try in order to move toward a more meaningful experience at school?

What conditions might support these more values-consistent behaviors?

What conditions tend to trigger the problematic behaviors?

Action steps:

What?	Who?	When?

This form also has space to write action steps. Your team can use the behavior's consequences (what the student gains) to help you decide how you'll provide and withhold reinforcers. For example, if Krishna jokes during algebra class to get attention, one action step for his mathematics teacher (and maybe all of his teachers) can be to laugh at his jokes only during passing time and not during lessons.

The antecedents (conditions that cue behaviors) will also have action implications. Your team can decide whether and how to restructure the student's environment to make problem behaviors less likely and values-consistent behaviors more likely. Perhaps Krishna needs a seat near the door so he can take a water break when he gets overwhelmed. If he's concerned about environmental justice, maybe his teacher can occasionally give problems related to water access or smog-alert days to help him stay engaged in class and take his work seriously. If he shares his knowledge and concerns during these lessons, he might even get a different sort of attention from his peers and teacher.

Some antecedents and consequences might have to occur at home. For example, Krishna might need more attention from his family and help with his algebra homework so he's less likely to escape class. A helpful action step after any meeting about students is for a team member to share the functional analysis with the parents, see if it comports with their experience of their child, and enlist their help.

In the end, the students' new behaviors could simply replace problematic old ones. It's also possible that Sierra will return to her pen-clicking ways or that Krishna will find new unhelpful attention-seeking behaviors. A functional analysis of behavior is only a first step; the harder part is taking action and then monitoring the student's progress in terms of his or her own values.

Discussing Successful Students' Behaviors

Getting more perspectives on challenging students, analyzing their behaviors, and collaboratively brainstorming ways to support them seems like a useful way to spend meeting time. Behavior concerns might include scoring low on assessments, acting out in class, struggling with organization, having friendship troubles, and harming themselves. In all of these cases, the discussions are about students who are faring poorly.

What if meetings sometimes focused on students we consider successful? What criteria would we use for nominating students to discuss? What procedures would we follow at the meeting? What kinds of stories would we tell, and what would the action implications be?

Imagine a group of seventh-grade teachers who meet each week to discuss their students. A few days before the meeting, the team leader sends an email asking which students they should discuss. The English teacher nominates Freddie, who's in her study hall. The first few weeks of school, Freddie had trouble using his time productively, but this past week he stayed completely focused on his history homework. He asked questions about some of the vocabulary in the U.S. Constitution and was interested in completing the assignment thoroughly. What changed for Freddie? How can the teacher help other students change their approach to study hall?

The English teacher also nominates Zora. In the personal essay she wrote this week, Zora's language evoked images of her backyard that made it sound spooky and enchanted, something out of a modern fairy tale. The English teacher never taught a lesson on how to use imagery to create tone, so where did Zora learn? What's her writing like in other classes? Is connotative description a skill worth teaching the rest of the students? If so, what's the best way to teach it? If not, how can the English teacher, and the rest of the team, support Zora as she develops her voice?

At the meeting, the teachers talk about these two students, along with Jamal. Jamal hasn't made much of an impression on his English teacher; he's thoughtful and raises his hand occasionally, but nothing about him or his writing seems particularly strong. But the science teacher has noticed that Jamal is an exceptionally compassionate listener. She describes some of the ways Jamal asks questions to understand different perspectives, validates the person making a point even if he doesn't agree with the point itself, and in groups ensures everyone gets a chance to contribute.

Teachers already put energy toward stopping problem behaviors and supporting students who struggle. But when a parent or colleague asks about a stronger student, we might say, "Oh, Jamal is fine," or, "Zora's an awesome kid," or, "I love Freddie," and that's as far as the conversation goes. Do we want to put all of our energy into moving students from negative to neutral, or do we *also* want to put energy into moving students from neutral to positive, or positive to more positive?

By raising the names of strong students for discussion, we also might help each other notice and encourage positive behaviors. Say the English teacher pays a lot of attention to what her students say and much less attention to how they listen. If her colleague brings up Jamal for this reason, she might develop greater appreciation for Jamal and for compassionate listening behaviors, and maybe she'll even rethink what participation means in her class. The next time the English teacher notices Jamal (or any student) listening compassionately, she could ask him to describe for the class how he did it. Now everyone gets to learn something about compassionate listening and can practice the techniques they've learned from their classmate. How incredibly empowering that could be—for Jamal as resident expert and for everyone as a learner and a potential expert on something else.

Finally, when we talk about a successful student's actions, we set ourselves up to notice and name meaningful qualities of that student's actions—his or her values. If we say, for example, that Freddie asked questions and did his homework, we might add that he asked *curiously* and did his homework *thoroughly*. In discussing this student as a team, we might echo each other's comments ("Freddie's been doing his homework thoroughly in Chinese, too"), describe the same behavior in different ways ("Yeah, he made a lot of careless errors earlier this year but lately he hasn't"), or offer examples of other behaviors the student does with that quality of action ("He actually draws really thoroughly, too; he spends lots of time getting the details right"). This talk might sound repetitive, but sharing multiple examples helps the whole team practice noticing and describing that student's values-consistent behavior, as well as values-consistent behavior in general.

Different teachers will have different understandings of what a successful student is. The English teacher might notice students who approach assignments creatively or manage their time wisely. The science teacher might notice students who go out of their way to help others or take on leadership roles in groups. The art teacher might notice students who have a well-developed sense of humor or are willing to learn from failure. Being asked to identify strong students becomes an opportunity to clarify *our* values: "What do I mean by *strong*?" Listening to colleagues describe specific student behaviors *they* classify as strengths becomes an opportunity for each of us to expand our own values by asking, "What else can *strong* mean?"

[handwritten margin note, left:] Most of our convos about students are surface-level. It reduces them as complex humans.

[handwritten note, bottom:] even articulation is basic. But classes are so large that maybe it needs to be this way. Fewer students would be easier.

Figure 10.3 is a form your team can use to guide discussions about successful students. Becoming more aware of the antecedents and consequences that shape values-consistent behaviors in one student can help your team more deliberately create contexts that empower this student and other students, too.

1. What makes school meaningful for this specific student?	2. What behaviors are moving the student toward a meaningful experience at school?
3. What else does the student gain from behaving in these ways? ☐ Tangible things ☐ Sensory stimulation ☐ Peer attention ☐ Adult attention ☐ Escape ☐ Other:	4. What conditions seem to support these values-consistent behaviors for this student?
5. What conditions might support similar behaviors in other students who share this value?	6. What other behaviors could students try in order to move toward a more meaningful experience at school?

Figure 10.3: Understanding values-consistent behavior.

*Visit **go.SolutionTree.com/instruction** for a free reproducible version of this figure.*

Many school support systems are deficit-driven. We alert families when their children get low grades, don't turn in their work, come to class late or unprepared, or act inappropriately. What if we sent reports when children act conscientiously, productively, generously, or in whatever other ways they find important? We keep records of student infractions so we can track patterns of harmful behavior. What if we tracked patterns of helpful behavior? When students commit the worst violations, perhaps there's a disciplinary hearing with the student, his or her family, teachers, and administrative team members. What if students received this amount of attention for behaving creatively or kindly?

No time... But see the importance of follow-up / improvement.

Obviously, these sorts of systems won't change overnight. We still need to support students who struggle and address problems when they arise. But our various spoken and written discussions are part of a larger narrative. Maybe teacher meetings are a good place to start shifting from a problem-solving narrative ("What should we fix?") to a values narrative ("What qualities of action matter to our students?"). What kinds of narratives will empower our students most?

We can't fix the problem, the student can.

From Collaborations to Curriculum

In teams, we can learn to use principles of contextual behavioral science to help our students choose actions that will contribute to what they themselves have defined as a meaningful life. Another way we can encourage students to build meaningful lives at school is to embed opportunities for values-consistent action within the academic curriculum. The next chapter discusses how to do that.

Chapter 11

• • • • •

EMPOWERING CURRICULUM

How to Incorporate Student Values Into Your Course Content

Academic tasks can become opportunities for students to discover, develop, and act in accordance with their own values. How can your course itself empower your students to make their lives meaningful?

Consider the fact that most actions have multiple purposes. Imagine a dad making grilled chicken for his children's dinner. Maybe he wants his children to eat something rich in protein, and they like chicken. Maybe he hates shopping, and he already has chicken in the fridge. Maybe he also has summer tomatoes on hand, and they'd taste delicious with grilled chicken. Maybe he likes being outside in the warm weather, and he can grill outside. Maybe he's tired today, and grilled chicken doesn't produce a big mess to clean up. The dad might grill chicken to serve all of these purposes.

Similarly, the tasks we give our students serve multiple purposes. A Spanish teacher who has her eighth graders form pairs and discuss their plans for the upcoming weekend might have many purposes in mind. She wants her students to practice conversational Spanish. She wants to see how well they use the future tense. Some of her students will be performing in a jazz concert this weekend, and she wants to give them an opportunity to tell their peers about it. She thinks students learn best from each other and that partner work makes off-task behavior less likely. Finally, she thinks her principal will drop by her classroom today, and her principal is a big proponent of partner work.

Most classroom tasks serve purposes of instruction, like giving students practice in conversational Spanish; assessment, like seeing how well students use the future tense; or management, like keeping all students focused. Some tasks also serve purposes of pleasing our students, our administrators, or ourselves. Take a moment and think of a task you recently gave your students. What purposes did it serve?

Just as most tasks serve multiple purposes, people can fulfill most purposes in multiple ways. For example, if the dad wants his children to eat something rich in protein, he could give them roasted chicken, or stewed chicken, or stewed beef, or bean burgers. If the Spanish teacher wants to create a partner activity that ensures active participation and will impress her principal, she could have pairs create skits or study for a test together. Take another moment and think of a few other ways you could have fulfilled one of your task's purposes.

Since every task you assign *already* serves multiple purposes, you might be able to find creative ways for your students to explore what makes their lives meaningful through those tasks. For example, if your students keep journals about their learning, could they occasionally write about how their learning is meaningful to them? Or if they record their insights and questions after a lesson, could they also record why the lesson might matter to them in your class, their other classes, their lives outside school, or their futures? If they do any sort of portfolio-based assessment, can they base their selection criteria on their own values as well as the standards? *This is something I do often. Get students to look inward.*

Perhaps you're willing to be flexible about the form an assignment or lesson takes. (For help, try the Hacking the Curriculum activity in chapter 3, page 54.) You might think of even more ways to fulfill instructional, assessment, and management purposes while *also* helping students understand their values and practice engaging in values-consistent action.

The rest of this chapter discusses how to incorporate EMPOWER work into various disciplines, including the humanities, sciences, physical education, and the arts. It also offers tips for how to create curriculum that increases students' awareness of their values.

English is easy to do this.

EMPOWER Work in the Humanities

End project regarding literacy.

When Ruby first started teaching seventh-grade English, the course began with a unit on short stories, including such classics as Edgar Allan Poe's "The Cask of Amontillado," Ray Bradbury's "There Will Come Soft Rains," and Kurt Vonnegut's "Harrison Bergeron." The students read each story, discussed its themes in class and in analytical paragraphs, and then wrote their own short stories on the same themes. After assigning "The Cask of Amontillado" for homework, Ruby led a discussion about revenge and then looked forward to reading eighty paragraphs analyzing the theme of revenge in Poe and eighty Poe-like stories. Was it really a good idea to ask thirteen-year-olds to imagine revenge scenarios? Was it okay that every last author in the short story packet—Poe, Vonnegut, Thurber, Steinbeck, and Bradbury—was a white male?

vignettes / anecdotal stories

The following year, Ruby proposed replacing the short stories with Sandra Cisneros's (1991) *The House on Mango Street*, a novel that consists of a series of vignettes. The book would serve all the same purposes that the short stories served. Just as the students had analyzed themes in the stories, they could

Teachers incorporating values into curriculum.

This actually mirrors my own development in getting curriculum to become more meaningful

Love the english example w/ vignettes

analyze themes in the vignettes. The book brought some much-needed diversity into the curriculum by introducing a Latina perspective. The main character, Esperanza, was about the same age as the students and therefore more relatable than the adult protagonists of the short stories, and Cisneros's writing would help the students learn the importance of using concrete, specific imagery to bring a topic to life. Instead of writing stories modeled after Poe and Bradbury, the students wrote their own vignettes, modeled after Cisneros, but on themes they chose. For example, a student might write a series of vignettes about trust, what it means to feel at home, or people's relationships with animals.

In class, the students examined different types of vignettes in the novel. Some were brief episodes in Esperanza's life, some were character sketches of people in her neighborhood, and some were contemplations of objects or places that had symbolic significance for her. The students then wrote their own episode, character sketch, and contemplation vignettes about events, people, and things in their own lives. One girl wrote about her trip to see the orphanage in China from which she'd been adopted. Another girl wrote about how she loved trains when she was small and described how she leaned down to the grates in the street to listen for passing subway trains. A boy wrote about a tunnel near his apartment, describing how the graffiti and stink grossed him out but were also familiar and a part of his home. And predictably, several students wrote about safe topics like dogs, pizza, and summer jobs. Ruby felt satisfied overall but was a little frustrated by the fact that some students weren't fully investing themselves in their work.

One day, while talking to a colleague about *The House on Mango Street*, Ruby realizes that the book is all about values. The main character Esperanza starts out believing in the American dream but later questions its availability to those around her. She envisions a different kind of success than looking pretty, finding a husband, getting stuck with domestic duties, and repeating the cycle of poverty and violence that affects almost every woman in her neighborhood. Esperanza wants a life in which she can express herself, make her own home, and stand up for the women who don't have the opportunities she has. Success for Esperanza means living creatively, independently, and helpfully.

Ruby decides to infuse the entire unit with values exploration. Class discussions are about how the characters succeed and fail to behave in accordance with their values. The class then does a values-clarification activity, and each student chooses one value (like *live authentically* or *communicate effectively*) as the theme of his or her vignette collection. Students still write the same three kinds of vignettes, but now they're writing about episodes of living by (or struggling to live by) their values, people whose actions exemplify their values (or whose actions serve as useful counterexamples of the values the students want to live by), and objects symbolic of their values. When Ruby teaches strategies for generating imagery, she emphasizes that people can only realize their values through visible action. She asks her students to reread parts of *The House on Mango Street* and highlight images that reveal Esperanza's values (Cisneros, 1991):

> My mother says when I get older my dusty hair will settle and my blouse will
> learn to stay clean, but I have decided not to grow up tame like the others who
> lay their necks on the threshold waiting for the ball and chain. (p. 88)

Then the students list their own images that show what it looks like to live by the values that matter to them.

Although she still gets a few safe vignettes about dogs and summertime, Ruby gets more and more students like Madison, who writes about getting pressured by her cousins to jump off the garage roof even though she wants to make her own decisions; Noam, who writes about how playing baseball makes him feel connected to his birth mother in Colombia; Corinna, who writes about how she still talks to trees even though she knows she's too old; and Amir, who writes about the unkind tennis coach who picked on him.

Ruby's purposes for teaching the original short story unit were for students to analyze themes in various texts, explore a theme in their own writing, apply genre conventions to their own writing, use specific imagery to orient and engage a reader, and proofread carefully. As the unit changed over the years, it continued serving all these purposes while *also* enabling students to understand their own values, recognize specific examples of values-consistent and values-inconsistent action in their lives, notice successes so they could continue building patterns of values-consistent action, and accept their own thoughts and feelings about failures to live by values so these wouldn't hinder future action.

Here are more ways to help students discover and develop their values through assignments in the humanities: English, history, civics, ethics, and languages.

- Read a novel or biography about someone who found meaning in his or her work. Identify this person's values. Find passages that show how this person chose behaviors consistent with his or her values, and how this person was willing to struggle.

- When discussing how words and phrases operate in a text, discuss how word choice reflects the values of the author and activates the values of the reader.

- Read television, music, advertisements, and other media. Identify the goals that the author or creator presumes the audience has. Analyze, in a class discussion or essay, whether these goals are consistent with students' own values.

- Compare and contrast two or more texts on a similar topic, analyzing the authors' different values and how proposed actions reflect those values.

- Write an essay about some of the values a book character, historical actor, community member, or classmate represents. Use values-consistent actions as evidence to support a thesis about this person's values.

- Analyze decisions in history, in a book, or in the community as consistent or inconsistent with values.

- Write a narrative that explores how the expression of a value changed over time—for the student him- or herself (memoir), for a character (fictional story), or for a historical figure (biography).

- Analyze historical, literary, political, or cultural conflicts as values conflicts.

- Incorporate the grammar of values (adverbs), behaviors (verbs), and struggles (nouns) into the study of a target language.

- Do EMPOWER activities, or parts of them, in a target language.

These are great ideas for English

Nice chapter—often hard to envision how educational theory looks in practice.

If you follow the Common Core State Standards, you can consult the website www.corestandards.org to ensure that as your students incorporate their values into their work, they're also achieving specific academic standards. For instance, discussing how words and phrases operate in a text fits well with the anchor standard CCRA.R.4 (National Governors Association Center for Best Practices & Council of Chief State School Officers [NGA & CCSSO], 2010a).

EMPOWER Work in Science, Technology, Engineering, and Mathematics

For her seventh-grade mathematics class, Mila teaches a unit on ratios, rates, and proportions. After showing her students how to calculate unit rates, she poses the following problem: "I am trying to decide among three different cars to buy. I live in Manhattan and drive to the Bronx every weekday, and I like to take long road trips during my summers. Local gas prices are going up, and we might experience gas shortages. Which car would be the most cost-effective option for me?" She shows her students how to research car prices and miles per gallon rates, map her yearly highway and city mileage, and set up algebraic equations to calculate her approximate yearly gas expenditures in order to figure out which car she should buy.

Mila wants to teach her students how to use algebra in real life to help with decision making, so she decides to create a project in which her students use mathematics to help make decisions in their own lives. Her car problem serves as a useful example of how *she* used mathematics to help her make an important decision, so she discusses the values she wants to serve, such as living sustainably, using money responsibly, and spending her vacation time adventurously.

From there, Mila guides her students through a values-clarification exercise and a brainstorm of ways they can use unit rates to help them make values-consistent decisions, like which phone plan would be most effective or which kinds of snacks would fit their activity levels. The students give oral reports on how they used rates, proportions, and percentages to help them make decisions, what values they are serving with these decisions, and how they'll use similar mathematics to help make values-guided decisions as they get older.

Here are more suggestions for how students can access their values through assignments in the disciplines of science, technology, engineering, and mathematics (STEM).

- Collect and graph data about how much time or money they spend in a particular domain and how satisfied they feel. Make a scatterplot graph, best-fit line, and equation in slope-intercept form that shows whether there is a functional relationship, a correlation, or no relationship between time or money spent and satisfaction. Explain the findings and commit to behaviors based on the data.

- Use systems of equations and inequalities to model whether solutions to corporate, state, or school problems are viable. Discuss whether mathematically viable actions are values consistent.

- Audit the school's schedule, calendar, operating budget, curriculum, or physical plant. Use ratios and percentages to show how allocations of time, money, learning, space, or energy reflect values.

Practical
applications
to class-

- Use trigonometric functions to model periodic phenomena related to values (for example, studying and taking breaks, sleeping and being awake, or spending time alone and with friends). Compare and contrast real life with these mathematical models, and make commitments.

- Apply geometric methods to redesign school or community spaces to promote particular values, such as using resources efficiently or working collaboratively.

- Use the tools of probability to model the likelihood of doing a valued behavior in various contexts, such as treating another person compassionately during a test, at lunch, and during a game. Determine whether different variables are independently or dependently related to the valued behavior. Discuss how people can base their behaviors on values rather than probabilities. Share commitments.

- Discuss successes and failures of famous scientists, mathematicians, and inventors in terms of their own values and the values of their time periods and cultures.

- When learning lab procedures (safety, measurement, and equipment use), connect the procedures to values and discuss whether and how students live those values in their daily lives.

- At the end of a lab report, write about why the experiment or investigation matters to the student-scientist himself or herself, or in the world.

- Engineer a solution to a problem at home, at school, or in the community. If the problem is too big for the student to solve, examine how he or she could solve a smaller version of the problem or take a small step toward solving the problem using the time and materials that are available.

If you follow the Common Core State Standards, you can consult the website www.corestandards.org to ensure that as your students incorporate their values into their work, they're also achieving specific academic standards. For instance, collecting and graphing data fits well with the eighth-grade statistics and probability standard 8.SP.A.1 (NGA & CCSSO, 2010b) and redesigning learning spaces works with the high school geometry standard HSG.MG.A.3 (NGA & CCSSO, 2010b).

EMPOWER Work in Physical Education

Mike coaches varsity baseball. His strongest players have graduated and the new guys don't have as much natural talent or experience. As a group consisting mostly of sophomores and juniors, the boys also don't have an established team's interdependence and identity. Mike knows that the goal of playing any competitive sport is to win games, but he recognizes that this probably won't be a winning season. He wants his athletes to take a realistic view of their own level of play while at the same time know their coach believes in them. Mike decides to spend the season building up his team not only in terms of their baseball skills, but in terms of their values as players and team members.

Each practice begins with the players sitting in a circle, all on the same level, as a reminder that they're all one team. Mike asks each player to talk about his own role on the team and to notice how each role matters for the team's success. For example, Nick might not yet be good enough to play in games, but he's very organized and is in charge of keeping the equipment neat and accessible so the other players have it when they need it. The superstar second baseman, Bernie, practices with Nick to help him with his throwing accuracy. Bernie's role, besides leading the team's defense during games, is making sure he leaves a strong legacy when he graduates.

In the circle, each player also shares an attainable goal that is in his control. For example, since many factors influence whether a player gets a hit—and since even great players fail to get hits the majority of the time—Mike encourages his players to see the ball, a skill any player can work on and that doesn't depend on someone else. Once they can see the ball, they work on making contact with the ball (but not necessarily getting a hit). Committing to a series of incremental steps helps shape the players' ability to do what's necessary for the team during games, and sharing his commitments allows teammates to support each other in achieving their goals. While not everyone shares his deepest feelings at first, the routine of forming the circle at every practice shows more hesitant players that others will respect and nurture them.

In athletics and in academics, it's easy to fixate on outcomes. Players who focus only on winning might cheat, use performance-enhancing drugs, lose or gain too much weight, or take other actions that harm their bodies and their integrity. If the focus is only on outcomes, players feel satisfied only if and when they get that outcome. Continual reflection, before and after games, allows students to focus on how their process reflects their values. Am I improving my skills? Am I trying new things? Am I the player I want to be? Are we the team we want to be? Is this still fun?

Here are more ideas for bringing student values into physical education classes and programs—athletics, fitness, health, and human development.

- Create a personal rubric for what it means to improve performance in a sport, based on values. Include play skills (dribbling, passing, shooting) and relational skills (playing fair, including others). Create a practice plan for improvement. Partner with a peer to help each other realize specific goals on the rubrics.

- Create practice routines in small groups based on the group members' values.

- Design a values-consistent wellness plan that includes nutrition, exercise, sleep, and relaxation. Lead the class through part of the exercise routine. Explain how the wellness plan aligns with personal values.

- Analyze controversial performance-enhancing practices in terms of students' own values.

- Examine the qualities of action that respected local and national athletes bring to the processes associated with their sports: how they practice, warm up, play games, treat teammates and members of opposing teams, care for their bodies and minds, and so on.

- Add discussions of values development into lessons about growth and change that occur during adolescence. Discuss how values themselves have remained constant and have changed, and how the expression of values can remain constant and change as students become older and more mature.

- Watch media clips with messages related to drugs, alcohol, smoking, or body image. Identify the goals that the author or creator presumes the audience has. Analyze whether these goals are consistent with students' own values.

EMPOWER Work in the Arts

Ron has been a visual arts teacher for eighteen years, and one of his classes is a photography elective for ninth and tenth graders. While some of these students are interested in learning to compose and manipulate a photograph beyond what they can do with their phones, many take the class because they need to fulfill their arts requirement and think this is the easiest way. Over the years, Ron has found that his students experiment increasingly less with focus and lighting; he guesses that they're used to taking photos to be posted on social media and have trouble thinking of them as art. He's also noticed that the students' written statements that accompany their work at the final exhibition seem sort of flat. The young artists have no trouble explaining *how* they created their work, but they don't say *why*.

Ron wonders if his students need more guidance in learning how to choose subjects that mean something to them. He leads a discussion on how organizations articulate their values, for example in school charters, corporate mission statements, and town board resolutions. Then each student chooses an organization that he or she is connected to in some way—whether by buying its products, using its services, contributing to it, or living near it—and takes photos of ways the organization succeeds and fails to live by its values. One student takes photos of his favorite pizzeria, which claims a commitment to sustainability; the photos include bags of organic produce and a compost bin (to show how the pizzeria succeeds in its commitment) and huge piles of paper napkins and pizza boxes (to show how it fails).

In class critiques, and later in their written statements, students analyze everyone's work in terms of technical and artistic qualities and how it conveys the difference between stated and enacted values.

Here are other ways to help students incorporate their values into their artistic endeavors, in music, dance, theater, film, and 2-D and 3-D art classes.

- Create a portfolio of artwork, in a single medium or in a variety of media, where each piece represents a different way to live by a chosen value.

- Choreograph a dance that represents failing to live by a particular value and then progresses toward living by that value.

- When learning a new piece of music or theater, experiment with different ways of playing or singing it using adverb values. For example, try playing it hopefully, honestly, and carefully.

- Draw, paint, or sculpt an abstract representation of struggling to live by an important value.

- Create a functional object that represents or encourages qualities of action that students want to bring to its use (for instance, a serving dish that encourages eating adventurously, inclusively, or prudently; or a vase that represents living simply, appreciatively, or boldly).

- Write an artist's statement to accompany a painting, drawing, sculpture, film, or other piece of art. Describe the values that guided the artistic process and that the artist has expressed in the work.

- Create a values-based personal rubric for what it means to improve performance in a musical, dance, or theater ensemble. Include technical skills (pitch, rhythm, and dynamics) and relational skills (listening and responding to others). Create a practice plan for improvement. Partner with a peer to help each other realize specific goals on the rubrics.

Curriculum That Increases Values Awareness

No matter what subject you teach, your curriculum is already values driven. Teachers and administrators, school boards and departments of education, and professional and parent associations all make choices about which understandings, knowledge, and skills are most important for students to learn. What they call "most important" depends on their values. Why not give the students themselves a role in deciding what and how they learn, and thus an opportunity to learn the content and processes that matter most to them? You can increase options for how students incorporate their values by giving them choices in topics, resources, tasks, processes, groupings, or work products.

However, just because they *can* make values-consistent choices doesn't mean they *will*. Consider a science fair where students can investigate any phenomenon. Some students take the assignment as an opportunity to ask questions that genuinely matter to them. One girl finds photos of the beach near her house that were taken when she was little, retakes photos of the same beach, and studies how the ecosystem has changed over time. Her report conveys her sense of loss and expresses her desire to restore the beach where she used to play. A boy who has friends in the grades above and below him puts out a schoolwide survey to see what factors contribute to developing friendships across grade levels, and he uses his data to develop a set of tips on how and why to make friends with older and younger students. But for every project like those, there are students who reuse the same topics every year, replicate work they found by searching for *science fair* online, pick topics the teacher cares about in the hope of getting a better grade, or turn the assignment into a joke. Given lots of choice, students might pick whatever sounds easy or fun.

As with any skill, students will need your support in clarifying their values with respect to the curriculum and making choices consistent with those values. The rest of this chapter explains various ways you can do that, including getting students to articulate why a chosen topic is important, showing examples of what work looks like when the person who created it cares about the topic, creating open-ended yet

[handwritten note in margin: I already do a lot of this — my final]

well-defined assignments, giving post-assignment reflections that ask about values-consistent behavior, completing the assignments you're asking students to do, sharing the values that guided you in creating the assignment, and allowing students to make their own mistakes.

Get Students to Articulate Why a Topic Matters

If you ask outright, "Why is this topic important to you?" some students will easily identify and communicate their genuine feelings. Others will tell you what they think you want to hear or give sarcastic responses that don't leave them vulnerable. Others simply won't know why they care about a topic, or they'll repeat what they've heard at home or from friends.

Figure 11.1 offers a protocol you can use to structure discussions on why topics matter. The small-group, student-led, timed format encourages greater honesty and makes room for more voices. We designed the questions to get students thinking about the antecedents and consequences of choosing the topic ("What in my life led me to care about this, and what in my life will change if I study it?") and to examine the topic from their past, present, and future perspectives, as well as the perspectives of people who matter to them. Feel free to change the questions, lengths of time, group sizes, and anything else in the protocol to fit your students' needs.

This protocol is for students who are helping each other choose topics to study. Try it after students have thought about what topic they might choose but before committing to one.

1. Form a group of three.

2. One member of the group (the presenter) talks about a topic using the following prompts. The presenter doesn't have to go in any particular order or get to all the prompts. The other group members silently listen and take notes. (Four minutes)

   - What have I experienced that draws me to this topic?

   - Why study this topic at this particular point in my life?

   - What do I most want to get out of studying this?

   - If I study this, what important things will I be able to do next?

   - How does this topic connect to other things that matter to me, to my family, in my community, or in the world?

   - If I don't pick this topic, how might it affect me or someone else?

3. The presenter is silent while the group members say back what they heard. The presenter takes notes. (Two minutes)

4. Repeat steps 1 and 2 so each member of the group becomes the presenter. (Six minutes per group member)

5. Each member of the group commits to a topic—the one he or she talked about, some variation of it, or a new topic altogether—and explains why he or she is making the choice to study it. (Two minutes per group member)

Source: Adapted from Porosoff, 2014.

Figure 11.1: Choosing topics that matter.

*Visit **go.SolutionTree.com/instruction** for a free reproducible version of this figure.*

Show Diverse Exemplars of Personally Meaningful Work

Even when a student cares about a topic, he or she won't necessarily put effort, thought, or a sense of personal investment into schoolwork on that topic. Students need to see what work looks like when its creator cares, so they'll know what *their* work can look like when they care. And since there are many topics worth caring about and many ways to show they care, your students will need to see many different examples.

Use this!

For instance, in Wayne's unit on spoken-word poetry, students do an activity that Sarah Kay (2011) referenced in her TED Talk: make a list of ten things you know to be true. The students list things like, *I know my shoes are blue*, and, *I know I'm in English class*. Wayne gets annoyed and frustrated. Why aren't they choosing topics they actually care about? Then he realizes he hasn't *taught* his students to notice how spoken-word poets care about their topics.

So Wayne shows a bunch of videos, including Benjamin Barker's "Rubik's Cube" (Button Poetry, 2013), Hieu Minh Nguyen's "Traffic Jam" (Button Poetry, 2014a), and "Unforgettable" by Pages Matam, Elizabeth Acevedo, and G Yamazawa (Button Poetry, 2014b). After each video, the students work with a partner to list ten things each of these poets knows to be true. When they repeat the activity of listing ten things, the students mix statements like *I know LeBron is better than Jordan* with statements like *I know women make seventy-eight cents for every dollar men make* and *I know I'm sick of people asking why I don't have a mom*. After sharing, the students write about any topic they either listed or heard that they think is important, and these writings form the basis of their spoken-word performances.

If Wayne had only shown "Traffic Jam," which is about the poet's relationship with his father, he might have gotten a dozen poems about fathers (or traffic) rather than poems about all kinds of topics that matter to the students. Students who see only one model of work might get caught up in the topic itself rather than understand the bigger concept that caring about the topic affects the quality of the work product.

Create Open-Ended Yet Well-Defined Assignments

Well-designed assignments address multiple learning standards simultaneously, serve instructional and assessment functions (since students are learning while doing the project, and its outcome is evidence of their learning), and require higher-order thinking skills such as analysis and evaluation (Krathwohl, 2002). Beyond that, assignments can give students the opportunity to choose topics they care about, create something that matters to them, and develop values-consistent life skills like collaborating effectively or showing resilience after a setback.

An assignment that's too specific probably won't feel meaningful to everyone and sometimes won't feel meaningful to anyone, except maybe the teacher. Imagine an art teacher showing Vincent van Gogh's (1889) *The Starry Night* and then telling her students to paint a night sky. Maybe some young artists will find meaning in this task, like if they happened to see a rainbow at dusk the day before or have fond memories of stargazing with their grandparents, but others won't feel all that connected to the topic. You can picture those students' paintings, can't you? A poor replica of van Gogh's painting here, some black paint slapped on a canvas there.

An assignment that's too broad might make students feel overwhelmed by the infinite possibilities or frustrated by the thought that there's some singular right way. The art teacher says, "Paint anything!" Again, some of her students know exactly what they want to do, but some just paint whatever pops into their heads, and others try to think of subjects that will get their classmates to laugh. Still others stand in front of their canvases feeling stuck, perhaps until they overhear the teacher praising one of their classmates ("Oh, Emily, what a beautiful elephant!") and then try painting something as similar as possible, but not copying, so they can get praise too ("Sheila, is that a rhinoceros?").

Since *The Starry Night* is a fantasy version of what van Gogh saw from his hospital window, perhaps the art students could create their own fantasy versions of what they see from their windows. They could discuss what in van Gogh's painting is real and what's fantasy, identify what they see from their own windows, and brainstorm fantasy versions of those features. They could explore how van Gogh used texture, color, and light to convey what was important to him and then decide how they will convey what's important to them.

As you're creating an assignment, consider its purposes related to instruction (teaching skills and concepts), assessment (seeing the extent to which students have learned skills and concepts), and management (setting them up to do their best work using available time and resources). Try to define the purposes as specifically as you can, and then write an assignment that serves them without imposing extra constraints.

Encourage Values-Based Reflection

After any assignment, lesson, unit, or marking period, you can ask your students to identify their values and then reflect on the extent to which they lived that value in class. Say Malik values treating other people supportively. At the end of the year, he could write about how supportively he behaved toward his classmates. After a group project, he could ask his peers to rate his supportiveness. At the close of a lesson, he could simply take a moment to think about things he did that day to show support. Reflecting on the extent to which they've acted consistently with their values can help students notice, remember, and keep doing their behaviors within and beyond the class.

Do Your Own Assignments

A good way to become aware of how well an assignment provides opportunities to tap into what matters is to do it yourself. You might find you need to add lessons, modify the assignment, or leave it as it is. Doing your own assignment also means you can share your work product with your students, and if they see you digging deep, they'll know they have permission to dig deep too. If your assignment is challenging, intellectually or psychologically, your students will get to see you fail and then recommit to the work.

Share the Values That Guide You in Your Work

What do you most want your students to get out of this learning experience? What do you want them to be able to do next? How does this assignment connect to the students' lives, their other classes, and their community? What messages *don't* you want them to take away? Your students don't have to share your values, but if they see why the assignment matters to you, they might find their way to why it matters to them. They'll also bear witness when you describe work you genuinely care about. Have you ever listened to people who are really passionate about their work describe how they came to it, do it, and feel about it? Listening to you describe your work just might inspire your students to seek out meaning in theirs.

Let Your Students Mess Up

You might find yourself trying to rescue students from their own poor choices. Perhaps you ask a student to pick a different topic, split up an unproductive group, or recommend a different process. These are all the normal inclinations of teachers who care about their students. Still, we recommend letting them experience the consequences of their choices and then helping them notice those consequences. Ask them to describe what they did in as much detail as possible. "What was the result? How satisfied were you with that outcome?" After students have completed a few similar assignments and described their processes for doing each one, you can ask, "How were the processes similar? How were they different? How did they lead to similar or different outcomes? What will you do next time?"

Some students might not notice what did or didn't work, and some might not choose more effective strategies the next time. You always have the option of telling them, but asking questions gives them a chance to discover their own mistakes and choose for themselves what they want to do in the future.

From Curriculum to Inquiry

This chapter offers some ways you can integrate EMPOWER work into the academic curriculum, from humanities and sciences to arts and athletics. If you're willing to be flexible about the form your assignments take, you might find ways they can continue serving their functions within your curriculum while providing students opportunities to clarify and commit to their values. As you incorporate EMPOWER work into your courses, you might be interested in seeing how your efforts make a difference for your students. The next chapter helps you do that.

Chapter 12

• • • • •

EMPOWERING INQUIRY
How to Assess the Impact of Helping Students Pursue Their Values

Most of us teachers think about how to improve our practice, but we don't necessarily collect and analyze our own data to see what's working. Why would we? We have enough to do during our so-called free time without making more work for ourselves.

But as the teacher, you are with your students throughout the week and can see the impact of your work. You're in the position to make adjustments because you understand how they'll work for your students, in the context of your school's schedule, physical layout, and administrative priorities. You have the professional judgment to question your own work and the capacity to innovate and improvise as necessary. Besides, if you don't tell your own story about what's working in your classroom, who will—and what will that story say?

The process of asking questions about your own practice, collecting and analyzing your own data, and using those data to make informed changes is called *action research* (Sagor, 2011). To do action research, you don't need money or special resources. All you need is a willingness to examine and improve your practice. Action research can be tremendously empowering, because you get to choose variables that matter to you and figure out ways to systematically observe and collect your own data, as opposed to being someone else's subject. You also get to watch your students benefit from improvements to your practice. You can see what works in your classroom, for your students, and make adjustments as you see fit. As you make those decisions, orderly data can only help.

In this chapter, you'll learn what data are relevant to collect (and what aren't), how to choose a research design, and how to recommit to empowering students if your data are not what you expected or hoped.

Collecting Relevant Data

What kinds of data should you collect if you want to see whether your attempts to empower students are working? Schools usually collect evidence of academic achievement, and they sometimes send surveys to see how students feel about various aspects of school. However, data on students' achievement and happiness might be misleading if your goal is to discover whether they're making school meaningful through values-consistent action. Before we suggest types of data that can show whether your activities and conversations are having an empowering effect, we'll briefly discuss why data on student achievement and happiness are irrelevant in helping you assess EMPOWER work. After that, we discuss relevant data sources, including students' academic work, preparation and participation records, communications from colleagues and parents, self-evaluations of academic work, and self-reports of values-consistent behavior.

Ordinarily, the goal of school is "to ensure that students graduating from high school are prepared to take credit bearing introductory courses in two- or four-year college programs or enter the workforce" (NGA & CCSSO, n.d.) or the achievement of other knowledge and skill benchmarks. So ordinarily, we collect data to look for evidence of student achievement. Achievement data—grades, test scores, college admissions—are certainly relevant to schools, students, and communities, but they usually aren't relevant in assessing the extent to which students are making school meaningful.

Good grades mean the student knows and is able to do things that the larger education community values. If we're looking for whether students understand and enact their *own* values, academic achievement is only relevant for students who value knowing and doing what the education community teaches and assesses. Schools shape student values, but so do families, friends, neighborhoods, cultural and religious backgrounds, and personal histories. Given the tremendous diversity among students' experiences, it seems unlikely that any student's values would match up exactly with the values that guide the design and grading of their assignments. Academic achievement data are of limited relevance in assessing the EMPOWER work's impact.

What about data on positive emotions? Whether students feel happy also gives us very little insight into whether they're making school meaningful. Perhaps you've watched a student work hard, produce something brilliant, and then say it went horribly. Yui writes beautiful, heartfelt, expertly composed essays, and she turns them in groaning, "This was *agony*. I spent *forever* on it." But when the teacher asks if she regrets the time and effort she put in, she looks away and says, "Well, I'm glad I *wrote* it." Has she shown her essay about her stepdad *to* her stepdad? "Yes." What did he say? "He liked it." No smile. Yui is not enjoying herself. She'd much prefer an easier assignment that she can knock out in twenty minutes and spend the rest of her evening chatting with her boyfriend. But she's writing about topics that matter to her, by her own reluctant admission. If you ask her what her favorite class is, she'll say "math." Her teacher is funny and her friends are in the class. But if you ask which pieces of work are most important to her, which have the greatest impact, which she'd save in a fire, she'll say her essays.

Connecting schoolwork to sources of personal meaning *can* lead to better grades (Chase et al., 2013) and *might* increase happiness, but these would just be pleasant bonuses. Relevant data on the impact of EMPOWER work should measure the extent to which students know what makes their lives meaningful, do what it takes to make school meaningful, and accept some discomfort in the process.

What kinds of data would show these impacts? We suggest using students' academic work, preparation and participation records, colleague and parent communications, self-evaluations of academic work, and self-reports about values-consistent behaviors.

Students' Academic Work

When you assess student work, you look for evidence that students have mastered concepts and procedures that matter in your discipline or across disciplines. If your students are performing original spoken-word poems, you might look for effective imagery, poetic devices, and vocal techniques. If your students are doing a scientific experiment, your rubric might include a testable hypothesis, clearly displayed data, and a thoughtful analysis. But when you look at student work, you can *also* look for evidence of their values. Maybe you hope to see your students writing poems about topics that matter to them, even if those topics are painful. If the students are doing experiments, maybe you hope they'll explain personal and community implications in their conclusions.

You wouldn't necessarily base student grades on the extent to which their values come through in their work. While students often produce better work when they care about the subject matter, it would be coercive to include an item like *Writes about deepest hopes and fears* or *Bares soul* on the grading rubric. Students might feel like you require or expect them to share private or painful information, or they might make up experiences if they don't think their real ones are deep enough. School assessment tasks gauge academic knowledge and skills, not willingness to self-disclose. Even if students are comfortable sharing their experiences, if they're working for a grade, they're not necessarily finding satisfaction in the work itself. Making students' grades contingent on incorporating their values isn't empowering. But you can still actively teach them how to put their values into their work and look for evidence that they're doing it, not to assess them, but to assess yourself.

You can even make yourself a rubric for each assignment, separate from the student rubric, to measure the extent to which student values show up in their work. Figure 12.1 (page 188) illustrates two examples of double rubrics, pairing a student rubric showing performance criteria on the assignment with a teacher rubric that includes criteria on whether students are expressing their values through their work. What will your students' work look like if they're aware of and committed to their values? Try making your own double rubric.

Assignment: Spoken-Word Poetry Performance			
Student Rubric: Using the spoken-word poetry performances we've watched in class as models, write and perform your own spoken-word poem about a topic that matters to you.			
Elements	**Developing**	**Proficient**	**Exemplary**
Concrete and specific imagery brings the subject of the poem fully to life.			
Use of poetic devices such as metaphor, juxtaposition, onomatopoeia, and repetition is purposeful and effective.			
Use of vocal techniques including tone, volume, pitch, and pacing helps convey the meaning of the poem.			
Teacher Rubric: Elicit student work that reflects values awareness.			
Elements	**Number of Students Developing**	**Number of Students Proficient**	**Number of Students Exemplary**
Poems contain strong messages about personally important struggles or issues.			
Students seek feedback from peers or other teachers so they can revise their performances for maximum impact.			

Assignment: "Using Water Quality Indicators" Lab Report	
Student Rubric: Based upon the water quality indicators lab we did in class, write a lab report that includes the following sections: purpose, hypothesis, materials, procedure, observations, and discussion.	
Expectation	**Points**
Give a clear, specific explanation of the purpose of testing water quality.	____/10
Explain a hypothesis for how clean our water is, based on knowledge from the course.	____/20
Accurately list materials used to conduct the experiment.	____/10
Clearly describe the procedure used to test water quality.	____/10
Organize observations and data in clear, accurate charts and tables.	____/20
Write a discussion using data to support conclusions about the water quality.	____/30
Teacher Rubric: Elicit student work that reflects values awareness.	
Expectation	**Number of Students**
Explain the importance of water quality in personal terms.	____/72
Give a deeper or more thorough explanation of results than in the previous lab report.	____/72
Reference sharing the analysis with a family member, community member, community leader, or news outlet.	____/72

Figure 12.1: Two examples of double rubrics.

Visit **go.SolutionTree.com/instruction** *for a free reproducible version of this figure.*

Records of Student Preparation and Participation

Most teachers set expectations for student preparation and participation. For example, an orchestra teacher might expect middle school students to bring their sheet music to class, properly care for their instruments, and practice at home. A high school French teacher might expect students to arrive at class with their books, speak only in French, and turn in their homework on time.

Students' accountability to classroom expectations is often under aversive control. They have to comply with our wishes or we'll penalize them in some way: a lower grade, lost free time, a phone call home, an exasperated sigh, or a mildly humiliating comment. When they don't meet expectations, they apologize ("Can I borrow a pencil? I'm sorry") as if the problem is that *we're* inconvenienced. If you punish students who don't prepare or participate, you might get them to bring their stuff and talk in class, but you'll also get them to focus on your happiness instead of their own learning. Instead of using aversive control, you can help students link their preparation and participation to their own values. What do they need to do to create an environment in which they and their peers can learn meaningfully in your class?

As you're assessing the impact of EMPOWER work, you can have your students use a rubric like the one in figure 12.2 to track their own preparation and participation and to make values-based commitments.

My Responsibilities in Mathematics 7	Rarely	Sometimes	Often	Almost Always
I come to every class with my textbook, notebook, pencil, and calculator.				
During demonstrations, I listen actively, take notes, ask questions, and offer ideas.				
I make productive use of class time by solving problems, conferencing, checking my work, and revising.				
I seek additional explanation of the material, feedback on my work, and strategies for improvement.				

What about your work in mathematics 7 is important or meaningful to you?

What one small, specific behavior do you intend to try that will contribute to making mathematics 7 more meaningful for yourself? Begin your sentence with the words *I will*.

Figure 12.2: Sample student responsibilities rubric.
continued ⇨

What one small, specific behavior do you intend to try that will contribute to making mathematics 7 more meaningful for your classmates? Begin your sentence with the words *I will*.

You could also collect student preparation and participation data yourself. Data points such as the number of pages read, problems attempted, or revisions made can suggest a student's engagement level. If the point of collecting these data is to see trends in values-based action, not to hold all students accountable to classroom expectations, then you won't need to check every student every day. You can take data on a random sample of days, for the whole class or even for a few students, to see if your EMPOWER work is making a difference.

Communications From Colleagues and Parents

If you help your students become aware of and commit to their values, other people might observe differences in their behavior that you don't see. A colleague mentioning that a student has become more engaged in class, or a parent emailing to ask your opinion about her son because "you seem to get him," can suggest the effects of EMPOWER work.

Another indicator of student empowerment is when parents show interest in your course content. If parents start asking for book recommendations or sharing articles with you about issues you teach, that's a good sign that your students are talking about the material at home and finding meaning in it.

Student Self-Evaluations of Academic Work

Many teachers give students some sort of self-evaluation task at the end of a lesson, assignment, or term. The way students describe their process of doing their work might reveal a greater sense of meaning and vitality.

For example, some teachers use exit slips at the end of class to see what students took away from the lesson and to help them consolidate their understanding. A popular format is 3–2–1: three things they learned, two questions they have, and one way the lesson connects to prior learning or outside interests. Regularly using exit slips can reveal, for example, whether students begin to ask more creative questions, or whether their questions and connections reveal increasing personal investment in the material. Because you're the one determining what it means for a question to be creative or for a statement to sound like the student is personally invested, your biases will figure in. If you want more objective data, you can see if the students start to write more on their exit slips after they've done some EMPOWER work.

Other kinds of exit slips prompt students to observe their work process, give feedback on the lesson itself, or share any thoughts and feelings they have (Marzano, 2012). Again, giving the same questions regularly can reveal the impact of EMPOWER work. Are students more honest in their self-observations? Do they give more feedback on lessons? Are they sharing more thoughts and feelings, and are they becoming less guarded in what they share?

You might also ask students to reflect after they complete larger assignments, or at the end of an entire term. Opportunities to observe and describe their work process and its results help students repeat behaviors that worked and replace behaviors that didn't (Johnston, 2012). Give prompts such as these: "Describe, in as much detail as possible, your process for doing this piece of work. How was your process similar to and different from processes you've used in the past? Describe the product that resulted. What about it are you satisfied with? What about it do you wish you could change? The next time you get a similar assignment, what strategies do you want to keep using? What new strategies do you want to try?"

If you give the same reflection prompts at the end of every assignment or term, you can see if the quantity or content of students' statements change after they've done EMPOWER work. Look for statements that indicate awareness of or commitment to values, like, "It wasn't my best piece of writing but it really made me think about my experience differently," "I've never really shared what was in that essay," or, "Next time I can try to experiment a little bit more." Such statements not only demonstrate growth but show that students can articulate *how* they're growing in ways that matter to them.

Student Self-Reports About Values-Consistent Behaviors

A more direct way to find out if EMPOWER work is impacting students is to ask them. Some students will easily be able to tell you whether they approach school in a values-consistent way. Others will tell you whatever they think will please you or keep them out of trouble. All kinds of factors will influence their answers, from how you word the question to how they feel about themselves and about school on that particular day to how keen they are on self-reflection; they also might not notice, remember, or be able to describe their behaviors, or they'll describe them in a way that you won't be able to interpret (Schwarz & Oyserman, 2001).

Imagine a student who writes *I always prioritize my schoolwork. My dad constantly tells me how important schoolwork is, so I always put in 100 percent of my energy. I never see friends outside of school because I'm too busy studying.* You might read this and think this student is overly concerned with pleasing a tyrannical father and ignores her values with respect to her social life. And you might be right. But it's also possible that this student values her learning and her close relationship with a loving father, and that the peer interactions she experiences at school are perfectly satisfying. Based on her self-report, you can't know. You could ask more questions, but you might not have time for thorough, one-on-one conversations with every student, and any answers the student does give will be affected by all the same limitations as the original self-report—not to mention your own biases as you interpret them.

All of that said, asking students about their experiences can be worthwhile for the students and for you. They get to notice how they behave, what circumstances prompt them to behave in values-consistent ways, and how their behaviors affect them. They also get to see that you care. You get to hear directly from them about their experiences with your teaching, and some of their responses will undoubtedly be illuminating. One way to ask about their experiences is to distribute a questionnaire like the one in figure 12.3. The questionnaire can help students think about the extent to which they're enacting their values at school.

These questions are about how you approach school. Each question describes two opposite ends of a range of behaviors. For each question, write a number between 1 and 10 to rate your behavior for this past week.			
Exploration	Do others decide what's important at school . . .	1 ←——→ 10	. . . or am I curious about how I can live by my values at school?
Motivation	Am I doing my work to get a reward (like a good grade, someone's approval, or the relief of being done) . . .	1 ←——→ 10	. . . or am I doing my work because it helps me learn and grow in ways that matter to me?
Participation	Do I put my energy toward whatever comes up at school . . .	1 ←——→ 10	. . . or do I create my own opportunities to do meaningful work?
Openness	Do I hold back my genuine self, stories, strengths, and weaknesses . . .	1 ←——→ 10	. . . or do I share them with my classmates and teachers?
Willingness	Do I do what feels familiar, comfortable, easy, or fun . . .	1 ←——→ 10	. . . or am I choosing to do what matters even if it's hard or painful?
Empathy	Do I get stuck in my own judgments of what other people should do or be . . .	1 ←——→ 10	. . . or do I show kindness and understanding toward others when they struggle?
Resilience	Do I get stuck in my own judgments of what I should do or be . . .	1 ←——→ 10	. . . or do I show kindness and understanding toward myself when I struggle?

Figure 12.3: Do I empower myself to make school meaningful? (student version)

Visit **go.SolutionTree.com/instruction** *for a free reproducible version of this figure.*

A particular student's results can help you encourage more values-consistent behavior. For high scores, you can ask about successful action: "How do you share your vulnerabilities? When is it hard? What do you do when it's hard?" For middling scores, you can ask students to compare successes to failures: "What were some times when you chose to do something meaningful knowing it would be hard? What was that like? What were some times when you chose what was easy or fun? What did you miss out on? What could you try next time?" For low scores, you can explore new possibilities: "How come you're at a 2 and not a 1 or a 0? What would it take to move you from a 2 to a 3?" If you give the questionnaire multiple times, you can ask about changes: "How did you move from a 5 to a 7? What have you been doing to make your work meaningful? How do you feel about yourself when you make your work meaningful? Do you plan to keep yourself at a 7 next month? What will you do to keep the 7?" When students talk about how and why they act in accordance with their values, they become more aware of contextual influences on their behavior so they can choose what works in the future.

You can also select one item from the questionnaire to use as an open-ended writing prompt. If you're particularly interested in willingness, you could ask, "During our last unit, what were some times when you chose to serve your values even if was hard or painful? What were some times when you did what felt familiar, comfortable, or fun?" Or to focus on resilience, you could ask after a challenging assignment, "While you were working on this, when did you show kindness and understanding toward yourself? When did you get stuck in your own judgments of what you think you should do or be?" Giving one pair of questions allows students to respond in greater depth without getting overwhelmed. If you ask the same pair of questions after each unit or assignment, you can track changes in what and how much students write.

Choosing A Design to Study Your Practice

Even when we see the kinds of outcomes we want to see—students expressing curiosity about their values, making their work meaningful, treating each other kindly, and so on—we can't say for sure that our classroom activities *caused* the outcomes. Increased values awareness, committed action, and willingness to struggle could be the result of some other factor, such as maturation or events outside the classroom. Also, we're all likely to notice and emphasize evidence that confirms our expectations while ignoring or downplaying that which refutes our expectations. If this uncertainty bothers you, you can use a research design that allows you to conclude that your work is causing the outcomes. Such research designs include single-case studies and multiple-baseline studies.

Seeing Data Trends: Single-Case Designs

In a single-case research design, the teacher graphs data for one student before and after a lesson, activity, assignment, or conversation to see if the student's behavior changes. What could a single-case research design look like and what does the resulting chart reveal?

Imagine that Tina teaches a high school girls' fitness class for students who aren't on athletic teams. Some take the class because it seems like the easiest physical education option; sometimes these girls don't show up for class at all. Others talk about how exercising will make them fit into skinny jeans or look good for prom. Tina can certainly understand why the girls think that way; they're constantly inundated with sexist messages about how they should look and act. But what about their values? How do they want to treat their bodies?

Tina decides to show a brief excerpt of the documentary *Miss Representation* (Newsom, Acquaro, Scully, & Johnson, 2011) to expose the influence of media messaging. The girls list messages they're getting about their bodies, and then Tina asks, "When you think about those messages, whose voices are telling them to you? What do those voices sound like?" The girls start saying things like "tiny waist" and "size zero" in deep, booming voices. From there, Tina leads her girls in using the deep voices to sing messages they get about their bodies to the tune of songs on their workout playlist. The girls laugh throughout their workout and leave class still singing. The next day, Tina passes out the "Examples of Values" handout (page 214) and wet-erase markers, and her students write adverbs that express how they want to treat their bodies on the windows and equipment in the fitness room.

Throughout the semester, all of Tina's students keep journals where they monitor their nutrition, exercise, sleep, and other self-care practices. Tina wonders whether she'll see an increase in statements expressing kindness to themselves. She selects one journal at random and graphs the data.

Figure 12.4 displays what Tina's graph might look like. The horizontal *x*-axis shows the days when the student wrote in her journal. The vertical *y*-axis shows the number of statements in which she expressed kindness toward herself. The chart includes baseline data, showing what the student did before the EMPOWER activity. Having at least three points of baseline data shows Tina how many statements of self-kindness the student was already making, how consistently she was expressing self-kindness, and whether she was starting to change her behavior before the activity. The dashed line shows when the class did the singing activity. Tina's chart shows that her student's behavior did change shortly afterward. She's making more statements of self-kindness.

If you want to see whether the behavior of one of your students changed after doing EMPOWER work, you can make your own graph. Visit **go.SolutionTree.com/instruction** to access a blank, customizable chart. The *x*-axis represents different points in time when you collect data. The *y*-axis represents a behavior that indicates values awareness, commitment to values, or willingness to struggle.

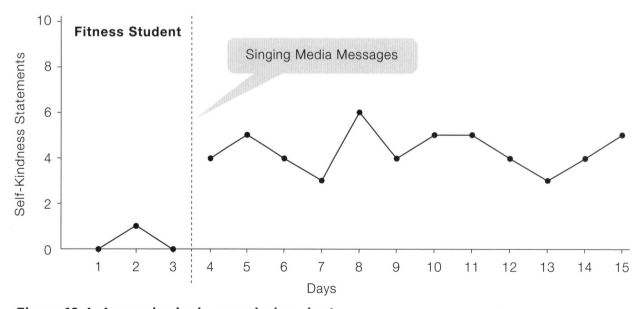

Figure 12.4: A sample single-case design chart.

Inferring Causality: Multiple-Baseline Designs

One student's chart will show *whether* the student's behavior changed, but it won't show *why*. Did Tina's student start expressing more kindness toward herself *because* the singing activity got her to distance herself from media messages about how her body should look and focus more on being kind to herself, or did something else prompt her increased self-kindness? In any case, something interesting is going on for this student that might not have been apparent had Tina not chosen to collect these data and chart the results.

If Tina wanted to go a step further, she could do what's called a multiple-baseline design, which is when different students experience the same lesson, activity, assignment, or conversation but at different points in time (Hayes, Barlow, & Nelson-Gray, 1999). Imagine that Tina teaches another section of physical education, a mixed-gender class on basketball. Initially, she doesn't do any willingness or values exploration work there because she doesn't think it's necessary. The students in her basketball class show up, play hard, and don't talk about losing weight in time for prom. But they're exposed to the same media culture. Maybe she could try the singing media messages activity with them too? And with the soccer team she coaches?

Figure 12.5 (page 196) shows what Tina's chart for this multiple-baseline design might look like. It uses the same process as a single-case design—take baseline data, do the EMPOWER work, and take more data—with the same activity repeated in three different settings at different points in time.

Tina's charts reveal three promising outcomes. The fitness student went from making very few statements of self-kindness to making more, the basketball player became more consistent in expressing self-kindness, and the soccer player's expressions of self-kindness had been trending downward but then started trending upward. Since these different students did the singing activity at different times, Tina can't attribute the changes in their behaviors to some outside event. Something about Tina's activity is making a difference.

If you take data, you can look for changes in the level, consistency, or trend of a values-consistent behavior. Even a change in just one student is encouraging, but if you use a multiple-baseline design—doing the same activity in different classes at different times—you can conclude that your EMPOWER work caused the changes. Visit **go.SolutionTree.com/instruction** for a blank multiple-baseline chart.

Recommitting to Your Values

In assessing the impact of the work you've done to empower your students, you might find that the activities and conversations have failed miserably. Students don't keep their commitments, they set ridiculously low-stakes goals, or they make fake goals to do things they would have done anyway. Maybe they get so stuck in their own people-pleasing or rule-following agendas that they stick with what's easy and comfortable, or they think you don't *really* care whether they make school meaningful.

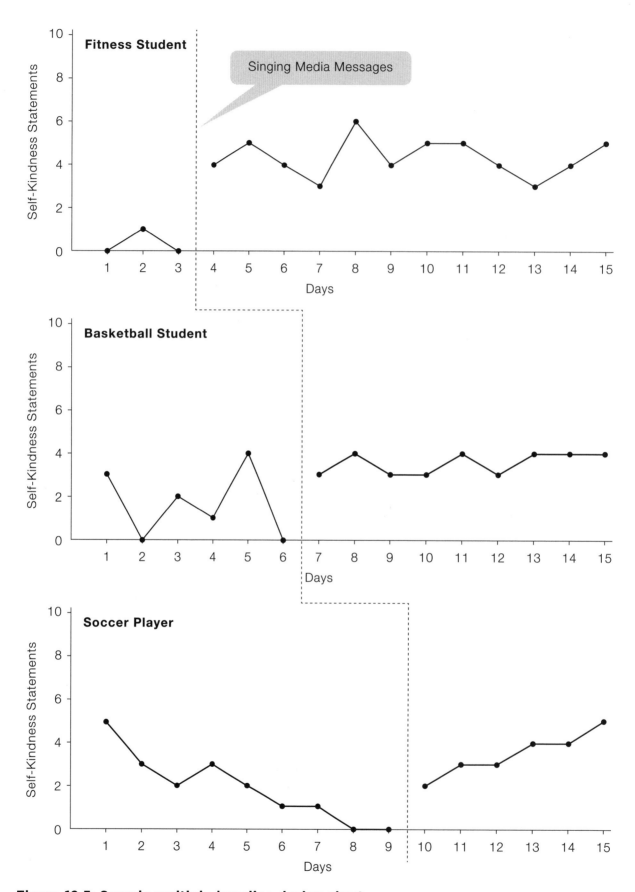

Figure 12.5: Sample multiple-baseline design chart.

The point isn't for the activities and conversations to go perfectly or to shatter students' worlds; it's to build behavioral momentum—to get the students used to values-consistent action by starting small and easy, thus increasing the likelihood that they'll commit to their values more often and in bigger, more challenging ways (Nevin, 1992). Hayes (2005) offers the following suggestions for building patterns of values-consistent action.

- Encourage students to define the specifics: what they will do, when, where, how, and with whom. They'll be much more likely to keep their commitments if they know exactly what to do.

- Focus on the short term: this week, today, or right now. Starting now means students are already building a behavioral pattern of committing. Waiting means they're building a pattern of waiting.

- Celebrate tiny successes. Reinforcing values-consistent behaviors increases students' likelihood of engaging in more values-consistent behaviors.

- Help students notice behavioral patterns as they form. That awareness allows them to build the lives and school experiences they want for themselves.

- If they express guilt about not keeping commitments, hopelessness over their ability to keep commitments at all, a belief that they're not the kind of person who does this, or another psychological barrier, you can normalize that experience and teach them how to accept those thoughts and feelings without letting them get in the way of committing to their values.

- If they describe external or structural barriers, you can help them find creative workarounds, supportive allies, and additional resources. If their goals are still unattainable, you can offer emotional support, help them come up with other ways to enact their values, and (if you're inclined) take action against any injustices that hold them back.

When students break their commitments—and they will—you can remind them that they always have the power to recommit to their values. Kelly Wilson and Troy DuFrene (2010) put it this way:

> In that moment, the moment in which we notice that we're out of alignment
> with one of our values, can we pause, notice our dislocation, and gently return?
> It's difficult to imagine a value of any magnitude that will not involve a lifetime
> of gentle returns. This turning back makes all the difference. (p. 133)

When you study the impact of this work, look for those gentle returns in your students. Look for them in yourself.

From Your Practice to Yourself

Assessing the impact of your work *is* work. Determining what kinds of observable evidence will indicate values awareness, commitment to values, and willingness to struggle—that's work. Designing a single-case or multiple-baseline study to assess your work? That's more work. But even if you see all of this as extra work, we hope you'll *also* see the ability to assess the impact of your practice as empowering. In the next chapter, you'll find more ways you can empower yourself—by becoming aware of your own values, committing to them, and developing greater willingness to struggle in their service.

Chapter 13

· · · · ·

EMPOWERING YOURSELF
How to Bring Your Own Values to Your Work

In *Teaching to Transgress*, author and activist bell hooks (1994) explains that before she started college, she thought professors were intellectuals searching for enlightenment in themselves and in their students. But once in college and on the path to becoming a professor herself, she quickly made a discovery that might sound painfully familiar:

> The only important aspect of our identity was whether or not our minds functioned, whether we were able to do our jobs in the classroom. The self was presumably emptied out the moment the threshold was crossed, leaving in place only an objective mind—free of experiences and biases. There was fear that the conditions of that self would interfere with the teaching process. (pp. 16–17)

[handwritten margin note: Don't really view it this way. Feel like I have prof. autonomy.]

We can fear that bringing our whole selves to school will somehow interfere with our teaching, or we can celebrate the ways our experiences inform and expand our work in the classroom. In this chapter, we consider some of the ways values awareness can help us bring our whole selves to our teaching and become the empowered teachers that hooks imagines. We'll see how our empowerment involves overcoming our avoidance, modeling values-consistent behaviors, building our professional capacities, doing our own values work, and committing to values-consistent actions.

Overcoming Your Own Avoidance

When you were little, did you ever play teacher? Lauren (who not coincidentally has the same name as one of the authors of this book) used to pretend her stuffed animals were students and she was the teacher. Even after spending most of her adult life in the classroom, Lauren still sometimes feels like she's playing teacher, with her teacher moves and teacher phrases and teacher voice. A student comes to class with nothing to write on. Lauren self-righteously eyes his desk and asks in her teacher voice, "Where's your notebook?"

Sure, her annoyed feelings are justified. How can her sixth graders become better writers when they don't bring their notebooks, or when they don't write in class or read at home? But when Lauren uses that teacher posture and tone, or when she shoots a teacher look at students who whisper during a writing activity or don't do the reading, what happens next? Do the students suddenly start bringing their materials, participating more actively, and doing the reading? Do they work harder at improving their writing and ask for help they need? Do they write more creative essays? Do they treat each other more kindly? Or do Lauren's teacher behaviors just make the students feel embarrassed and shut down?

When Lauren uses her teacher voice and teacher moves, she's all caught up in some image of *teacher*—the very same one she was acting out as a six-year-old playing school. Caught up in that teacher image, she loses contact with her values as an *actual* teacher. But she doesn't want to hold herself up to some predefined form of what a teacher is supposed to say and do. She wants to make important learning happen. She wants to *teach*.

Playing teacher is only one example of how avoiding unwanted feelings can get in the way of effective teaching. How many of these behaviors do you use in class as ways to avoid feeling annoyed, frustrated, afraid, anxious, embarrassed, or sad?

- Using a teacher voice
- Overpreparing for lessons
- Calling attention to your status, such as by using technical terms or referring to your advanced degrees or years of teaching experience
- Doing all or most of the talking
- One-upping your students; showing them you're the smartest person in the room
- Using costumes and props—classroom keys, a badge, a whistle, a coffee mug, a briefcase, or anything students don't wear or carry but you do—to show you're the one in charge
- Assigning busywork because you're afraid of what might happen if students don't have enough to do
- Staying away from certain topics because you're afraid students might ask a question you don't know the answer to
- Trying to convince students that they need to do things your way
- Withholding feedback that might upset your students or their parents
- Using euphemisms

- Giving easy tasks because you don't want your students to feel unhappy
- Entertaining students, for example through stand-up comedy, storytelling, or fun activities that lead to little if any significant learning
- Staying quiet while your students tell jokes or stories that derail the lesson
- Counting minutes left in class, hours left in the day, or days left before vacation

Like most behaviors, these can have multiple functions. We might wear badges because our schools require all staff to do so *and* to display our authority to students. We might stay quiet when a student tells a long story because we want to model respectful listening *and* because we'd feel bad interrupting. The questions to ask yourself about these behaviors are the same ones you'd ask your students to help them assess whether a behavior serves their values: What are you doing? How is it working? What is it costing you and your students (Strosahl et al., 2012)?

If we discover that our behaviors are getting in the way of teaching and learning, what can we do about them? Well, we can vow never to do them again, but the act of stopping avoidance behaviors to keep from feeling like we're bad teachers—that itself is an avoidance behavior!

Stopping avoidance behaviors also doesn't work particularly well, since—as you might have noticed when you read the list of examples—there's a wide variety of ways to avoid our own thoughts and feelings. If we stop an avoidance behavior, a new one will often bloom in its place (Friman, Hayes, & Wilson, 1998). Say a teacher spends hours preparing detailed lesson plans because he wants to avoid feeling *Used to do this.* anxious or embarrassed if he were to make a mistake. He realizes that all his planning prevents him from responding authentically to his students' ideas and questions, so he decides to stop overpreparing and go *YES.* with the flow. However, he's no more willing to feel anxious and embarrassed, so every time he forgets or misstates a point, he apologizes excessively. He can't connect authentically with his students when he's busy apologizing all the time. *SO TRUE. Let that go.*

Like our students, we get attached to images of what we think we should be (smart, knowledgeable, likeable, fun) and what we think we're not allowed to do (lose control of our classrooms, upset students, not know an answer, mishandle a situation). But we too can learn to *have* uncomfortable thoughts and feelings *and* continue to act in accordance with our values, both so we can make teaching more meaningful for ourselves and so we can model values-consistent behavior for our students.

Modeling Values-Consistent Behavior

You model behaviors for your students all the time. They watch you use the quadratic formula, correct comma errors, or center clay on a wheel, and then they give it a try. You probably also model relational skills like listening and sharing. EMPOWER work is no different: your students will understand how to discover and commit to their values if they watch you discover and commit to yours first.

We're not suggesting that you merely participate in this work; we're suggesting that you go *first*. The point isn't to make yourself the center of attention or to disclose inappropriately personal information that would make your students uncomfortable. They're not empowered if they're freaked out or overly focused on you. If you're not sure whether sharing something would help or hurt, you might talk to a supportive colleague, and you can err on the side of caution. But if you, the teacher, share your values and vulnerabilities first, you create an atmosphere of trust and compassion—a sense that you're all in this together.

This sense of togetherness is very different from how teachers usually relate to students. A teacher traditionally gives directions for students to follow, serves as the expert in the room, and acts as a detached professional. In EMPOWER work, everyone in the room is an equal, vulnerable, sharing participant. A teacher traditionally assesses, evaluates, and disciplines students. In EMPOWER work, everyone in the room takes a nonjudgmental posture. This doesn't mean you *never* use authority in your classroom; it means you can move between using authority and acting as a co-participant, depending on the context. If these different and conflicting ways of being are important to you, you'll need the flexibility to choose behaviors that work in a particular moment. You can cultivate that flexibility by clarifying your values as a teacher, committing to those values, and developing the willingness to take on different roles.

Building Your Professional Capacities

Beyond helping us support students and accept unpleasant feelings that our difficult jobs evoke, values awareness also has the potential to make us better teachers, colleagues, and learners. Values-consistent curriculum design can improve our teaching; values-conscious collaboration can improve our work with colleagues; and values-relevant professional development can improve our learning.

Values-Consistent Curriculum Design

How do teachers know what belongs in a unit and what doesn't? One way is to follow traditional or current exemplars of best practice. Imagine a ninth-grade English teacher who has his students read Lorraine Hansberry's 1959 *A Raisin in the Sun* because it's considered a classic and that's what ninth graders have always read. His students then act out scenes in groups because when he was a student, one of his favorite assignments involved acting out scenes from Jerome Lawrence and Robert Edwin Lee's 1955 *Inherit the Wind*, and at a workshop on the 21st century classroom, he saw a video where students worked in acting troupes to produce one-act plays.

Instead of holding our teaching up to a predefined form, we can focus on how it *works*—how well we're getting students to understand important concepts and master important skills. Which concepts and skills we deem important depends on our values. A ninth-grade English teacher who understands his values might have his students act out scenes from *A Raisin in the Sun* because the project gives students opportunities to make decisions collaboratively, practice communication skills they'll need in the real world, and experience literature more deeply using their bodies. If for some reason the ninth grade stops reading *A Raisin in the Sun*, the teacher can design a new project that serves these same functions.

In designing learning experiences, we might ask ourselves questions like, "Why does this matter? What do I most want my students to get out of this? What do I want my students to be able to do next? How does this connect to the students' daily lives, their other classes, or the real world?" Guided by our values, we can decide what to emphasize, what to leave out, how to structure lessons so they build to a larger understanding, and how to assess that understanding.

Values-Conscious Collaboration

Being aware of our values can also help us collaborate more effectively. Suppose Martin and Eva are discussing how they should teach their upcoming unit on *A Raisin in the Sun*. Martin wants the major assignment to be an acting project, and Eva wants her students to write their own plays. If all they talk about is the assignment itself and not the values it serves, then here's what could happen:

- The teachers agree to disagree. Martin's class does acting and Eva's does playwriting. The students benefit from each teacher's individual strengths but not from their collective strengths.

- The teachers argue over which approach is better. They arm themselves with research and expert opinions to support their positions but undermine their relationship and their program.

- Both teachers do smaller versions of both approaches. Their students spend a week acting and a week writing one-act plays. The projects lack depth and serve neither teacher's values.

- One teacher goes along with the other's approach for the sake of avoiding conflict. Eva assigns the acting project without really understanding how or why to do it, and she ends up disappointed in her students and resentful of her colleague.

Now imagine that instead of focusing on the *form* their assignment takes, both teachers listen for each other's values. They realize that both want their students to express their creativity, develop skills that endure beyond the task itself, and make literature personally relevant. Understanding common values helps teachers defuse tension and proceed from a place of mutual respect. Even if they give different assignments, they can ask each other for feedback without feeling judged, and they've kept open the possibility of future collaborations. Instead of limiting ourselves to one set of so-called best practices, our teams and departments can expand our repertoire to include a wider variety of practices that all help our students learn.

Values-Relevant Professional Development

Understanding our values also allows us to expand what we consider relevant professional development, helping us see beyond the limits of our goals, scope, and sequence. Imagine that Eva finds out about an upcoming engineering workshop for K–6 teachers. Most high school English teachers would ignore it. But because she understands her values, she might sign up to see how engineering programs encourage students to take risks and show resilience. While she attends, she might learn something about the engineering design process that she can apply to the writing process in her English class. She might also meet people who share her values and build relationships with teachers she wouldn't have met otherwise. Pursuing values-relevant professional development helps us find meaningful learning, creative ideas, and new interactions.

In addition, being clear on our values might make us more likely to notice them from day to day. If we pay close attention during these moments, we might get ideas for enhancing our curricula or classroom practices. For example, if Martin knows he values 100 percent participation, then in his daily life—at family dinners, at town environmental board meetings, on television shows—he's more likely to notice participatory events as such and, from them, learn things he might be able to apply in his classroom. Being aware of our values not only makes more professional development count as relevant, but it makes every life experience a potential source of professional development.

Doing Your Own EMPOWER Work

How can you discover what qualities of action are important in your life, particularly your teaching life? One way is to do it alongside your students. As you lead the activities from part I of this book, you can do them yourself. You can also consider how your own values affect the processes outlined in part II: one-on-one conversations with students and parents, discussions with colleagues, curriculum design, and self-assessment.

If doing EMPOWER work alongside your students and thinking about how your values inform your practice don't feel like enough, we invite you to try some of the following EMPOWER exercises designed just for teachers. Try them on your own or with trusted colleagues, at home or in a private space at school, at any point when they feel relevant.

Exploration: Magic Moment

What was a time at school when something wonderful—almost magical—happened? Tell the story of that magical moment in your classroom or teaching practice. Include as much detail as possible. What time of year was it? What time of day? What were you doing? What was going on? Then what happened? How did you feel? How did everyone else feel?

Even if you've told the story before, tell it again to someone or write it out for yourself. What qualities of action were you bringing to that magic moment? How can you bring those qualities of action to more moments of your work, even if they don't turn out to be as magical?

Activities to explore our values—all creative. Highly symbolic, reflective

Motivation: Thank-You Note

Imagine it's the last day of the school year. Students are saying goodbye and expressing their appreciation. There's one note in particular that strikes you. Maybe it's from a student who's meant a lot to you or one who's been especially challenging. Maybe the note is from a parent—perhaps even one you don't always get along with, but who finally recognizes the contribution you made to his or her child's life. What does this note say? Try writing it.

Imagining the end of the year helps you clear away the moment-to-moment challenges of your school life and pay attention to what you truly want to stand for as a teacher. If the thank-you note shows what you want your students to end the year thinking, what will you do right now?

Participation: Buzzword Yoga

Pick an education buzzword that you keep hearing. It might relate to a worthwhile practice or it might be a passing fad, but either way, it's suddenly coming out of every mouth at your school (including, perhaps, your own). Now imagine that this word or phrase is the name of a yoga pose. Invent the pose. Do it if you're physically able. Every time you hear yourself or someone else using the buzzword, imagine a yoga instructor's gentle voice telling you to get into this pose, and imagine yourself doing it.

Differentiation! Neuroplasticity! The Common Core! EMPOWER! However you regard these or any other concepts, new programs and practices constantly beset teachers. Even when the new thing matches your values, and even if you're someone who loves to learn and grow as a professional, buzzwords and jargon can be exhausting. People can overuse buzzwords to the point that they lose their meaning or co-opt them to serve a particular agenda, and the concepts these buzzwords refer to can become new ways for us to judge ourselves as not capable or knowledgeable enough. Turning these words into yoga poses is a playful reminder that they're just words. The actions are what matter. How do you want to enact this concept?

Openness: Colleagues You Admire → We need more collaboration at work...

Who are a few colleagues you look up to? Write about some of the inspiring things these colleagues do. Share some pieces of your writing with some of these colleagues.

If you're lucky enough to have colleagues whose work moves you or fills you with admiration, their actions might tell you something about the teacher you hope to be. That doesn't mean you have to do exactly what these colleagues do or live up to some standard you think they set. However, if you start to think about qualities of action they bring to their work, you might get a clearer sense of qualities you want to bring to yours. Sharing what you wrote is a generous way to show your appreciation. It also gives you an opportunity to seek your colleagues' support and guidance as you become the teacher you want to be.

Willingness: Struggle Keys

This exercise is adapted from Take Your Keys With You (Hayes, Strosahl et al., 1999), which uses keys as reminders of values.

Think of an aspect of your job that you hate doing. Get a key. Either go to your local hardware store or find an old key you no longer use. Paint, bejewel, or decorate the key so it stands out. Then write the struggle on one side, as in figure 13.1. What can you do because you engage in this struggle? What value is this struggle connected to? Write the value on the other side of the key. Put the key on your keyring so you have a reminder of the valued outcomes you can access with it.

Figure 13.1: A struggle key (front and back).

What do the keys you carry every day allow you to open? Your home? Your classroom? Your car? Places where loved ones live? A locker, cabinet, or drawer? Whatever your keys access must be important to you, or you wouldn't bother locking them. Keys are also a bit burdensome. We have to remember where they are and keep them with us, or else we can't get into our homes or cars or cabinets. Similarly, values have all kinds of struggles associated with them. Placed on your keychain, which you probably touch several times a day, your struggle key will remind you of the values you're serving when you do the part of your job that you dread.

Empathy: Judgment Factory

Imagine your mind as a factory that efficiently produces judgments (Harris, 2009). Try to picture this judgment factory: the shapes of the machinery, the conveyor belts, the colors of the lights. Make up a sound that the machinery makes when it pops out a new judgment. Whenever you judge someone else in a way that goes against your values, hear that sound.

Victor came without his notebook again? Seriously, what is *up* with that kid? Bzzzhhh-puh! Out comes a shiny new judgment from the judgment factory. Vividly imagining our minds as factories churning out judgments (and making silly noises in the process) can make the judgment a little less powerful, which leaves more power for you to decide how you want to act in that moment. Who is this person your factory is making judgments about? How does this person feel? What does this person need?

Resilience: Bad Essay Introduction

Think of the last time you told yourself you were weak, stupid, sloppy, ineffective, or bad in some other way. Write a statement about what you were doing, as if you are an inexperienced writer introducing an essay: *In this essay, I will discuss why I am so stupid. I will provide three examples of my stupidity and use evidence to support my claims.*

Do your students write essays? Do any of them begin their essays this way? While well-written formal essays don't usually contain statements about what the writer is doing, a statement about your thinking process can help you notice that your thoughts are products of your mind and don't have to determine your actions.

Committing to Values-Consistent Action

Annoyance, frustration, anger, disappointment, guilt, sadness, despair—they're all part of our range of human emotions. As teachers who care, we open ourselves to these feelings when our students break their commitments to us, to each other, and to themselves. In these painful moments, we can give ourselves the compassion we're so good at giving our students. We can remind ourselves that our hard work has been worthwhile, allow ourselves to grieve over our losses, and assess how we've acted consistently and inconsistently with our own values.

Figure 13.2 (page 208) is a tool you can use to check in with yourself about how you're living by your values at school. It is very similar to the student version in figure 12.3 (page 192). We do not intend this as yet another way to find yourself inadequate. If you use it with self-compassion, it's a way to help yourself make values-conscious decisions about what to do next.

Since most values-consistent living carries some pain (or at least the threat of pain), another helpful strategy for keeping commitments is to practice mindfulness. This isn't the kind of mindfulness where you're sitting serenely on a cushion for forty-five minutes to de-stress. Rather, this is mindfulness that trains you to open yourself up to difficult sensations, thoughts, and feelings so you'll be better at it in moments when it's hard to stay committed to your values. Try holding a piece of ice for a full minute and really noticing how uncomfortable it is without distracting yourself with other thoughts, or stand with your arms in the air for three minutes and really pay attention to the ache. Although activities like these sound masochistic, they're ways to practice the skill of willingly experiencing the pain that tags along with committing to values.

While a few of the activities in this book will only work for students, most can apply to you. Again, you can do them along with your students, since hearing you articulate your values, make commitments, and struggle to keep them can be a powerful learning experience for them. You can also try doing them with your colleagues; working together to make commitments is a great way to strengthen the relationships within your department, team, or whole faculty. Even one supportive colleague can make all the difference. You can cheer each other on when you succeed, help each other find creative workarounds when you encounter barriers, and have values conversations when your *shoulds* and *can'ts* inevitably show up.

Values are big and broad and lifelong, but commitments are small, specific, and time bound. What exactly will you do? When? Where? How? Who else is involved? What resources do you need? If you succeed, what will you do next? If for some reason it becomes impossible to do what you planned, what's a different way to act on the same value? What small step can you take today?

These questions are about how you approach school. Each question describes two opposite ends of a range of behaviors. For each question, write a number to rate your behavior for this past week.			
Exploration	Do others decide what's important at school . . .	1 ◄——► 10	. . . or am I curious about how I can live by my values at school?
Motivation	Am I doing my work to get a reward (like good test scores, administrative approval, or the relief of being done) . . .	1 ◄——► 10	. . . or am I doing my work because it helps my students learn and grow in ways that matter?
Participation	Do I put my energy toward whatever comes up in my job . . .	1 ◄——► 10	. . . or do I create my own opportunities to do meaningful work?
Openness	Do I remain detached, professional, and the expert in the room . . .	1 ◄——► 10	. . . or do I share my genuine self, stories, strengths, and weaknesses with my students and colleagues?
Willingness	Do I do what feels familiar, comfortable, easy, or fun . . .	1 ◄——► 10	. . . or am I choosing to serve my teaching values even if it's hard or painful?
Empathy	Do I get stuck in my own judgments of what my students and colleagues should do or be . . .	1 ◄——► 10	. . . or do I show kindness and understanding toward them when they struggle?
Resilience	Do I get stuck in my own judgments of what I should do or be . . .	1 ◄——► 10	. . . or do I show kindness and understanding toward myself when I struggle?

Figure 13.2: Do I empower myself to make school meaningful? (teacher version)

Visit **go.SolutionTree.com/instruction** *for a free reproducible version of this figure.*

From Yourself to Yourself

You can make school more meaningful for yourself, whether you're doing that work alongside your students or on your own. Clarifying and committing to your values might enable you to be more present with your students, and it might equip you to model values awareness, values-committed action, and willingness to struggle. It might even improve your overall effectiveness as a teacher and colleague. The potential benefits to your students are compelling, but we think your own empowerment is a good enough reason to do this work.

Conclusion

• • • • •

PATHS TO EMPOWERMENT

We hope you've found something in this book that inspires you to help your students transform what school means. We began with ways to empower students directly by helping them discover and commit to their values, and then we moved into ways to empower them indirectly by using student values to inform teaching practice. But if you're feeling hesitant about implementing some of the activities, try going backward. Start with part II, making some small shifts in your own practice to incorporate your students' values. Then you might feel more confident leading the activities from part I, or you might be more willing to lead them without feeling confident.

We also hope *you* feel empowered. In contextual behavioral science, from which we drew many of the concepts in this book, the way we define what's "good" depends on the function we're trying to serve in a particular context. What if you define *good teaching* as teaching that helps students explore what matters to them, find motivation to do their work, participate in crafting their school experiences, open up to each other, willingly struggle, empathize, and show resilience? What if you define *best practices* as those that empower students to act on their values?

In schools, change sometimes feels like it's going way too slowly, or way too quickly but in the wrong direction. You might find yourself wishing you could do more, frustratedly waiting for those with authority to recognize problems and take constructive action. In the meantime, we offer you some activities and practices to try on your own, some topics to bring up in conversations, and some ideas for larger-scale innovations. When the time for change does come, you will be a model of best practice. You will have developed a vision and cultivated relationships with allies who share your vision. We hope to position teachers who think about student empowerment to become leaders in their schools and in the teaching profession.

The first activity in this book uses paper airplanes as a metaphor for choosing the qualities of our actions. Making a paper airplane involves changing the functional properties of the paper. You change what the paper means. A paper airplane is something *you* make. Something a little irreverent. Something full of possibilities. Something that can fly.

Appendix

• • • •

EXAMPLES OF VALUES

Examples of Values

How do you want to live your life? How do you choose to work, relate to others, play sports, make art, relax, or do other things that matter to you?

Values are qualities of action that make life meaningful. Here are some qualities of action that make some people's lives meaningful. Does behaving in any of these ways make your life meaningful?

Actively	Dutifully	Independently	Prudently
Adventurously	Efficiently	Industriously	Purposefully
Appreciatively	Enthusiastically	Inspiringly	Resiliently
Assertively	Excellently	Inventively	Resourcefully
Attentively	Fairly	Kindly	Respectfully
Authentically	Faithfully	Knowledgably	Responsibly
Beautifully	Flexibly	Lovingly	Reverently
Boldly	Forgivingly	Loyally	Simply
Cautiously	Freely	Mindfully	Skillfully
Compassionately	Generously	Modestly	Spiritually
Consciously	Gracefully	Open-mindedly	Supportively
Cooperatively	Helpfully	Passionately	Sustainably
Courageously	Honestly	Patiently	Tactfully
Creatively	Hopefully	Peacefully	Thankfully
Curiously	Humbly	Playfully	Thoroughly
Deliberately	Imaginatively	Powerfully	Trustworthily
Determinedly	Inclusively	Productively	Wisely

References & Resources

• • • • •

Allport, G. W. (1954). *The nature of prejudice*. Cambridge, MA: Addison-Wesley.

Aversive stimulus. (2011). In S. Goldstein & J. A. Naglieri (Eds), *Encyclopedia of child behavior and development* (p. 190). New York: Springer.

Berkowitz, M. W., & Bier, M. C. (2005). *What works in character education: A research-driven guide for educators*. Washington, DC: Character Education Partnership.

Biglan, A. (2015). *The nurture effect: How the science of human behavior can improve our lives and our world*. Oakland, CA: New Harbinger.

Biglan, A., & Hayes, S. C. (1996). Should the behavioral sciences become more pragmatic?: The case for functional contextualism in research on human behavior. *Applied and Preventive Psychology, 5*(1), 47–57.

Blackledge, J. T. (2003). An introduction to relational frame theory: Basics and applications. *Behavior Analyst Today, 3*(4), 421–433.

Blackledge, J. T. (2015). *Cognitive defusion in practice: A clinician's guide to assessing, observing, and supporting change in your client*. Oakland, CA: New Harbinger.

Bradbury, R. (1950). There will come soft rains. In *The martian chronicles*. New York: Doubleday.

Brown, B. (2010). *The gifts of imperfection: Let go of who you think you're supposed to be and embrace who you are*. Center City, MN: Hazelden.

Button Poetry. (2013, August 22). *Benjamin Barker—"Rubik's cube" (NPS 2013)* [Video file]. Accessed at www.youtube.com/watch?v=68K6KeQloDg on August 17, 2016.

Button Poetry. (2014a, May 21). *Hieu Minh Nguyen—"Traffic jam"* [Video file]. Accessed at www.youtube.com/watch?v=Q7RHM1xQMiw on August 17, 2016.

Button Poetry. (2014b, September 4). *Pages Matam, Elizabeth Acevedo and G. Yamazawa—"Unforgettable"* [Video file]. Accessed at www.youtube.com/watch?v=Xvah3E1fP20 on August 17, 2016.

Chance, P. (1998). *First course in applied behavior analysis*. Pacific Grove, CA: Brooks/Cole.

Chase, J. A., Houmanfar, R., Hayes, S. C., Ward, T. A., Vilardaga, J. P., & Follette, V. (2013). Values are not just goals: Online ACT-based values training adds to goal setting in improving undergraduate college student performance. *Journal of Contextual Behavioral Science, 2*(3), 79–84.

Cisneros, S. (1991). *The house on Mango Street.* New York: Vintage Books.

Clayton, T. M. (1995). *Changing organizational culture through relational framing* (Unpublished master's thesis). University of Nevada, Reno.

Dahl, J. C., Plumb, J. C., Stewart, I., & Lundgren, T. (2009). *The art and science of valuing in psychotherapy: Helping clients discover, explore, and commit to valued action using acceptance and commitment therapy.* Oakland, CA: New Harbinger.

Elbow, P., & Belanoff, P. (2000). *Sharing and responding* (3rd ed.). Boston: McGraw-Hill.

Fitzpatrick, M., Henson, A., Grumet, R., Poolokasingham, G., Foa, C., Comeau, T., et al. (2016). Challenge, focus, inspiration and support: Processes of values clarification and congruence. *Journal of Contextual Behavioral Science, 5*(1), 7–15.

Flores, K. S. (2008). *Youth participatory evaluation: Strategies for engaging young people.* San Francisco: Jossey-Bass.

Fox, E. J. (2006). Constructing a pragmatic science of learning and instruction with functional contextualism. *Educational Technology Research and Development, 54*(1), 5–36.

Friman, P. C., Hayes, S. C., & Wilson, K. G. (1998). Why behavior analysts should study emotion: The example of anxiety. *Journal of Applied Behavior Analysis, 31*(1), 137–156.

Geiger, K. B., Carr, J. E., & LeBlanc, L. A. (2010). Function-based treatments for escape-maintained problem behavior: A treatment-selection model for practicing behavior analysts. *Behavior Analysis in Practice, 3*(1), 22–32.

Gilbert, P. (2010). *The compassionate mind: A new approach to life's challenges.* Oakland, CA: New Harbinger.

Gilbert, P. (2014). The origins and nature of compassion focused therapy. *British Journal of Clinical Psychology, 53*(1), 6–41.

Guskey, T. R. (2015). *On your mark: Challenging the conventions of grading and reporting.* Bloomington, IN: Solution Tree Press.

Haas, J. R., & Hayes, S. C. (2006). When knowing you are doing well hinders performance: Exploring the interaction between rules and feedback. *Journal of Organizational Behavior Management, 26*(1–2), 91–111.

hack. (n.d.). In *Dictionary.com.* Accessed at www.dictionary.com/browse/hack on February 24, 2017.

Hansberry, L. (1959). *A raisin in the sun: A drama in three acts.* New York: Random House.

Harris, R. (2009). *ACT made simple: An easy-to-read primer on acceptance and commitment therapy.* Oakland, CA: New Harbinger.

Hayes, S. C. (2005). *Get out of your mind and into your life: The new Acceptance and Commitment Therapy.* Oakland, CA: New Harbinger.

Hayes, S. C., Barlow, D. H., & Nelson-Gray, R. O. (1999). *The scientist practitioner: Research and accountability in the age of managed care* (2nd ed.). Boston: Allyn & Bacon.

Hayes, S. C., Barnes-Holmes, D., & Roche, B. (Eds.). (2001). *Relational frame theory: A post-Skinnerian account of human language and cognition.* New York: Kluwer Academic.

Hayes, S. C., & Brownstein, A. J. (1986). Mentalism, behavior-behavior relations, and a behavior-analytic view of the purposes of science. *The Behavior Analyst, 9*(2), 175–190.

Hayes, S. C., Brownstein, A. J., Haas, J. R., & Greenway, D. E. (1986). Instructions, multiple schedules, and extinction: Distinguishing rule-governed from schedule-controlled behavior. *Journal of the Experimental Analysis of Behavior, 46*(2), 137–147.

Hayes, S. C., Brownstein, A. J., Zettle, R. D., Rosenfarb, I., & Korn, Z. (1986). Rule-governed behavior and sensitivity to changing consequences of responding. *Journal of the Experimental Analysis of Behavior, 45*(3), 237–256.

Hayes, S. C., Hayes, L. J., & Reese, H. W. (1988). Finding the philosophical core: A review of Stephen C. Pepper's *World Hypotheses—A Study in Evidence. Journal of the Experimental Analysis of Behavior, 50*(1), 97–111.

Hayes, S. C., Strosahl, K. D., & Wilson, K. G. (1999). *Acceptance and commitment therapy: An experiential approach to behavior change.* New York: Guilford Press.

Hayes, S. C., Strosahl, K. D., & Wilson, K. G. (2012). *Acceptance and commitment therapy: The process and practice of mindful change* (2nd ed.). New York: Guilford Press.

hooks, b. (1994). *Teaching to transgress: Education as the practice of freedom.* New York: Routledge.

Hooper, N., Saunders, J., & McHugh, L. (2010). The derived generalization of thought suppression. *Learning and Behavior, 38*(2), 160–168.

Johnston, P. H. (2012). *Opening minds: Using language to change lives.* Portland, ME: Stenhouse.

Karabenick, S. A. (Ed.). (1998). *Strategic help seeking: Implications for learning and teaching.* Mahwah, NJ: Erlbaum.

Karabenick, S. A., & Newman, R. S. (Eds.). (2011). *Help seeking in academic settings: Goals, groups, and contexts.* New York: Routledge.

Kay, S. (2011, March). *If I should have a daughter . . .* [Video file]. Accessed at www.ted.com/talks/sarah _kay_if_i_should_have_a_daughter on August 17, 2016.

Kemmis, S., McTaggart, R., & Nixon, R. (2014). *The action research planner: Doing critical participatory action research.* Singapore: Springer Science + Business Media.

Kishi. (n.d.). *Super Mario Bros.: Peach edition*. Accessed at www.romhacking.net/hacks/1229 on August 17, 2016.

Kolts, R. L. (2016). *CFT made simple: A clinician's guide to practicing compassion-focused therapy*. Oakland, CA: New Harbringer.

Kolts, R., & Chodron, T. (2015). *An open-hearted life: Transformative methods for compassionate living from a clinical psychologist and a Buddhist nun*. Boston: Shambhala.

Krathwohl, D. R. (2002). A revision of Bloom's taxonomy: An overview. *Theory into practice, 41*(4), 212–218.

Lawrence, J., & Lee, R. E. (1955). *Inherit the wind*. New York: Random House.

Lee, B. (n.d.). *100 life hacks that make life easier*. Accessed at www.lifehack.org/articles/lifestyle/100-life-hacks-that-make-life-easier.html on August 17, 2016.

Levin, M. E., Luoma, J. B., Vilardaga, R., Lillis, J., Nobles, R., & Hayes, S. C. (2016). *Examining the role of psychological inflexibility, perspective taking and empathic concern in generalized prejudice* (Paper 1093). Accessed at http://digitalcommons.usu.edu/psych_facpub/1093 on March 6, 2017.

Lillis, J., & Hayes, S. C. (2007). Applying acceptance, mindfulness, and values to the reduction of prejudice: A pilot study. *Behavior Modification, 31*(4), 389–411.

Luciano, M. C., Salas, S. V., Martinez, O. G., Ruiz, F. J., & Blarrina, M. P. (2009). Brief acceptance-based protocols applied to the work with adolescents. *International Journal of Psychology and Psychological Therapy, 9*(2), 237–257.

Luoma, J. B., Hayes, S. C., & Walser, R. D. (2007). *Learning ACT: An Acceptance and Commitment Therapy skills-training manual for therapists*. Oakland, CA: New Harbinger.

Luoma, J. B., & Platt, M. G. (2015). Shame, self-criticism, self-stigma, and compassion in acceptance and commitment therapy. *Current Opinion in Psychology, 2*, 97–101.

Manson, M. (2014, September 18). *7 strange questions that help you find your life purpose*. Accessed at http://markmanson.net/life-purpose on August 17, 2016.

Marshall, S. L., Parker, P. D., Ciarrochi, J., Sahdra, B., Jackson, C. J., & Heaven, P. C. L. (2015). Self-compassion protects against the negative effects of low self-esteem: A longitudinal study in a large adolescent sample. *Personality and Individual Differences, 74*, 116–121.

Marzano, R. J. (2012). Art and science of teaching: The many uses of exit slips. *Educational Leadership, 70*(2), 80–81.

McDonald, J. P., Mohr, N., Dichter, A., & McDonald, E. C. (2013). *The power of protocols: An educator's guide to better practice* (3rd ed.). New York: Teachers College Press.

McHugh, L., & Stewart, I. (Eds.). (2012). *The self and perspective taking: Contributions and applications from modern behavioral science*. Oakland, CA: New Harbinger.

Miller, W. R., & Rollnick, S. (2013). *Motivational interviewing: Helping people change* (3rd ed.). New York: Guilford Press.

Najmi, S., & Wegner, D. M. (2008). The gravity of unwanted thoughts: Asymmetric priming effects in thought suppression. *Consciousness and Cognition, 17*(1), 114–124.

National Governors Association Center for Best Practices & Council of Chief State School Officers. (n.d.). *Frequently asked questions.* Accessed at www.corestandards.org/resources/frequently-asked -questions on August 17, 2016.

National Governors Association Center for Best Practices & Council of Chief State School Officers. (2010a). *Common Core State Standards for English language arts and literacy in history/social studies, science, and technical subjects.* Washington, DC: Authors. Accessed at www.corestandards.org/assets /CCSSI_ELA%20Standards.pdf on December 19, 2016.

National Governors Association Center for Best Practices & Council of Chief State School Officers. (2010b). *Common Core State Standards for mathematics.* Washington, DC: Authors. Accessed at www .corestandards.org/assets/CCSSI_Mathematics%20Standards.pdf on December 19, 2016.

National School Reform Faculty. (n.d.). *Framing consultancy dilemmas and consultancy questions.* Accessed at www.nsrfharmony.org/system/files/protocols/framing-dilemmas.pdf on June 28, 2017.

Neff, K. D. (2011). *Self-compassion: The proven power of being kind to yourself.* New York: Morrow.

Neff, K. D., Hsieh, Y.-P., & Dejitterat, K. (2005). Self-compassion, achievement goals, and coping with academic failure. *Self and Identity, 4*(3), 263–287.

Neff, K. D., & McGehee, P. (2010). Self-compassion and psychological resilience among adolescents and young adults. *Self and Identity, 9*(3), 225–240.

Nevin, J. A. (1992). An integrative model for the study of behavioral momentum. *Journal of the Experimental Analysis of Behavior, 57*(3), 301–316.

Newsom, J. S. (Director), Acquaro, K. (Director), Scully, R. K. (Executive Producer), & Johnson, S. E. (Executive Producer). (2011). *Miss representation* [Motion picture]. United States; Girls' Club Entertainment.

Oliver, J. [Joe Oliver]. (2013, February 12). *Passengers on a bus—An acceptance and commitment therapy (ACT) metaphor* [Video file]. Accessed at www.youtube.com/watch?v=Z29ptSuoWRc on August 17, 2016.

Poe, E. A. (1846, November). The cask of amontillado. *Godey's Lady's Book, 33,* 216–218.

Porosoff, L. (2014). *Curriculum at your core: Meaningful teaching in the age of standards.* Lanham, MD: Rowman & Littlefield.

Porosoff, L. (2016, September 27). *Flight plan* [Blog post]. Accessed at www.tolerance.org/blog/flight -plan on April 12, 2017.

Rowling, J. K. (2008, June). *The fringe benefits of failure* [Video file]. Accessed at www.ted.com/talks/jk_rowling_the_fringe_benefits_of_failure on August 17, 2016.

Ryan, A. M., Hicks, L., & Midgley, C. (1997). Social goals, academic goals, and avoiding seeking help in the classroom. *Journal of Early Adolescence, 17*(2), 152–171.

Sagor, R. (2011). *The action research guidebook: A four-stage process for educators and school teams* (2nd ed.). Thousand Oaks, CA: Corwin Press.

Salinger, J. D. (1951). *The catcher in the rye.* Boston: Little, Brown.

School Reform Initiative. (n.d.). *Tuning protocol: Examining adult work.* Denver: Author. Accessed at http://schoolreforminitiative.org/doc/tuning_adult_work.pdf on August 17, 2016.

Schwarz, N., & Oyserman, D. (2001). Asking questions about behavior: Cognition, communication, and questionnaire construction. *American Journal of Evaluation, 22*(2), 127–160.

Sidman, M. (1989). *Coercion and its fallout.* Boston: Authors Cooperative.

Skinner, B. F. (1981). Selection by consequences. *Science, 213*(4507), 501–504.

Steege, M. W., & Watson, T. S. (2009). *Conducting school-based functional behavioral assessments: A practitioner's guide* (2nd ed.). New York: Guilford Press.

Strosahl, K. D., Gustavsson, T., & Robinson, P. (2012). *Brief interventions for radical change: Principles and practice of focused acceptance and commitment therapy.* Oakland, CA: New Harbinger.

Sue, D. W. (2010). *Microaggressions in everyday life: Race, gender, and sexual orientation.* Hoboken, NJ: Wiley.

Sugai, G., Horner, R. H., Dunlap, G., Hieneman, M., Lewis, T. J., Nelson, C. M., et al. (2000). Applying positive behavior support and functional behavioral assessment in schools. *Journal of Positive Behavior Interventions, 2*(3), 131–143.

Turrell, S. L., & Bell, M. (2016). *ACT for adolescents: Treating teens and adolescents in individual and group therapy.* Oakland, CA: Context Press.

Ushakaron. (2011). *Instructions for a traditional paper plane.* Accessed at https://upload.wikimedia.org/wikipedia/commons/c/c4/Paper_Airplane.png on February 3, 2017.

van Gogh, V. (1889). *The starry night* [Painting]. New York: Museum of Modern Art.

Verplanken, B., & Holland, R. W. (2002). Motivated decision making: Effects of activation and self-centrality of values on choices and behavior. *Journal of Personality and Social Psychology, 82*(3), 434–447.

Villatte, M., Villatte, J. L., & Hayes, S. C. (2015). *Mastering the clinical conversation: Language as intervention.* New York: Guilford Press.

Vonnegut, K. (1961, October). Harrison Bergeron. *The Magazine of Fantasy and Science Fiction, 21*(4), 5–10.

Wegner, D. M., & Erber, R. (1992). The hyperaccessibility of suppressed thoughts. *Journal of Personality and Social Psychology, 63*(6), 903–912.

Wegner, D. M., Schneider, D. J., Carter, S. R., & White, T. L. (1987). Paradoxical effects of thought suppression. *Journal of Personality and Social Psychology, 53*(1), 5–13.

Wilson, K. G. (2009). *Mindfulness for two: An acceptance and commitment therapy approach to mindfulness in psychotherapy.* Oakland, CA: New Harbinger.

Wilson, K. G., & DuFrene, T. (2010). *Things might go terribly, horribly wrong: A guide to life liberated from anxiety.* Oakland, CA: New Harbinger.

Wilson, K. G., & Murrell, A. R. (2004). Values work in acceptance and commitment therapy: Setting a course for behavioral treatment. In S. C. Hayes, V. M. Follette, & M. M. Linehan (Eds.), *Mindfulness and acceptance: Expanding the cognitive-behavioral tradition* (pp. 120–151). New York: Guilford Press.

Wilson, K. G., Sandoz, E. K., Flynn, M. K., Slater, R. M., & DuFrene, T. (2010). Understanding, assessing, and treating values processes in mindfulness- and acceptance-based therapies. In R. A. Baer (Ed.), *Assessing mindfulness and acceptance processes in clients: Illuminating the theory and practice of change* (pp. 77–106). Oakland, CA: New Harbinger.

Index

• • • • •

Solutions for Modern Learning series
Bryan Alexander, Gayle Allen, Bruce Dixon, Will Richardson,
Roger C. Schank, Audrey Watters
Prepare students for 21st century success. This thought-provoking collection—authored by leading experts from around the globe—engages educators in a powerful conversation about learning and schooling in the connected world. In short, reader-friendly formats, these books challenge traditional thinking about education and help to develop the modern contexts teachers and leaders need to effectively support digital learners.
BKF692, BKF685, BKF687, BKF693, BKF688, BKF686

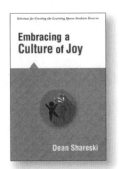

Embracing a Culture of Joy
Dean Shareski
Although fun is sometimes seen as a barrier to real learning, joy is a vital part of effective education. Learn how to have meaningful conversations about where joy gets left out in schools, and discover how to equip students with the skills and qualities they'll need to achieve academic success—as well as to live fulfilling lives—by bringing joy to classrooms each day.
BKF730

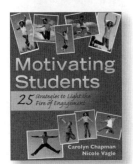

Motivating Students
Carolyn Chapman and Nicole Dimich Vagle
Learn why students disengage and how to motivate them to achieve success with a five-step framework. Research-based strategies and fun activities show how to instill a lasting love of learning in students of any age. Classroom tips and troubleshooting advice for common motivation problems prepare readers for the real-world ups and downs of motivating students.
BKF371

You've Got to Reach Them to Teach Them
Mary Kim Schreck
Navigate the hot topic of student engagement with a true expert. The author explores the many factors involved in bringing out the best in students, such as relationships, emotions, environments, and expectations. Become empowered to demand an authentic joy for learning in your classroom. Real-life notes from the field, detailed discussions, practical strategies, and space for reflection complete this essential guide to student engagement.
BKF404

Classroom Habitudes
Angela Maiers
You know students need to acquire 21st century skills. But how do you work those skills into the curriculum? Learn how to use the content you already teach to challenge students to think critically, collaborate with others, solve new problems, and adapt to change across new learning contexts. Help students build the seven habitudes—habits of disciplined decisions and specific attitudes—they need to succeed.
BKF542

a division of

Solution Tree

Visit SolutionTree.com or call 800.733.6786 to order.

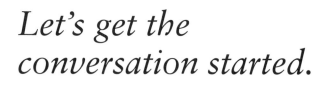